WORLD WAR II FROM ORIGINAL SOURCES

THE U-BOAT WAR IN THE ATLANTIC
Volume III : 1944-1945

EDITED BY BOB CARRUTHERS

Pen & Sword
MARITIME

This edition published in 2013 by
Pen & Sword Maritime
An imprint of
Pen & Sword Books Ltd
47 Church Street
Barnsley
South Yorkshire
S70 2AS

First published in Great Britain in 2011 in digital format by
Coda Books Ltd.

ISBN 978 1 78159 161 1

A CIP catalogue record for this book is
available from the British Library

Printed and bound by CPI Group (UK) Ltd, Croydon, CR0 4YY

Pen & Sword Books Ltd incorporates the Imprints of Pen & Sword Aviation, Pen &
Sword Family History, Pen & Sword Maritime, Pen & Sword Military, Pen & Sword
Discovery, Pen & Sword Politics, Pen & Sword Atlas, Pen & Sword Archaeology,
Wharncliffe Local History, Wharncliffe True Crime, Wharncliffe Transport, Pen &
Sword Select, Pen & Sword Military Classics, Leo Cooper, The Praetorian Press,
Claymore Press, Remember When, Seaforth Publishing and Frontline Publishing

For a complete list of Pen & Sword titles please contact
PEN & SWORD BOOKS LIMITED
47 Church Street, Barnsley, South Yorkshire, S70 2AS, England
E-mail: enquiries@pen-and-sword.co.uk
Website: www.pen-and-sword.co.uk

CONTENTS

CHAPTER 7
MAY - AUGUST 1943

CHAPTER 8
NORTH ATLANTIC
SEPTEMBER 1943 - FEBRUARY 1944

CHAPTER 9
MAY - AUGUST 1943

CHAPTER 10
JUNE - SEPTEMBER 1944

CHAPTER 11
OCTOBER 1944 - MAY 1945

APPENDICES

- C H A P T E R   7   -

MAY-AUGUST, 1943

BASIS OF POLICY BETWEEN FEBRUARY AND AUGUST 1943 - DÖNITZ'S FIRST MEASURES

334. Requirements of Naval Policy

Historians of the Second World War will no doubt refer to May 1943 as marking the turning-point after which the German U-boat campaign began to collapse under the weight of the combined Allied effort. Yet, in the two years that followed, the U-boat remained unchallenged in its role as Germany's principal naval weapon. Why was this? Did the German authorities really believe that, by means of an all-out effort with the old and new types of U-boat, it was possible to repeat past successes? Did they not realise by May 1943 that the U-boat campaign was ultimately bound to collapse? To answer these questions it is necessary to look beyond the Atlantic - the scene of most of the events described in the preceding volumes - and to consider the general war situation as it then appeared to the responsible German leaders.

It must be admitted that until the beginning of 1943 there had been frequent differences of opinion between the Flag-Officer U-boats and the German Naval Staff; but when Admiral Dönitz became Commander-in-Chief of the Navy these were largely eliminated, for the advice given by the operational staff of the U-boat Command now carried much greater weight than before. Right from the outbreak of war, Dönitz had been consistent in regarding the U-boat as the principal means of waging war against Great Britain and the United States and, once the war had commenced, it was certainly no longer possible to build up a surface fleet in time to challenge the vast superiority of these great maritime powers. Now, in February

1943, when the enemy had begun his air offensive against Germany, when radar had radically altered the basis of surface-ship operations, and when the provision of adequate light forces for the protection of our sea communications also presented difficulties, it was out of the question to think in terms of a balanced German fleet. For Germany the only practical course was, therefore, to continue to apply those means of naval warfare that, despite the enemy's control of the sea, could still threaten, or at least do considerable damage to, his sea communications. Chief amongst these means was the U-boat, which alone could penetrate into waters controlled by the enemy. Next in importance came motor torpedo-boats, mines and aircraft and, lastly, the few remaining heavy ships available for operations in those areas where they could be given air cover or support from coastal batteries.

Persistent shipping losses had already caused the Western Allies great embarrassment, forcing them to apply vast resources to the defence of their shipping and to provide the replacements essential for freedom of military movement. Attack on their shipping was quite the most unpleasant feature of our naval operations, besides being the only means we had of inflicting serious damage, and hence it had to continue with all vigour.

335. Dönitz's plans as Head of the Navy
When Dönitz became Commander-in-Chief of the Navy on 30th January 1943, not only were there anxieties over the future of U-boat operations, but he found himself faced with the problems of a general war situation which was already unfavourable, if not desperate. The continued achievements of the Allies in the Mediterranean, the increasing pressure of their air and naval attacks on our coast and sea communications, the air offensive against Germany and its effect on our war industries, shortages in manpower, materials and fuel, and the *Luftwaffe's* failure to support our naval operations - none of these factors was fully appreciated by large sections of the German people or the *Wehrmacht*, who had complete confidence in Dönitz and hoped that he would now be able to achieve greater success with the Navy.

From the first day in his new office, Dönitz aimed at securing priority for new and better equipment, for the faster development of U-boats and for an improvement in the capacity of the dockyards. As for the new types of U-boat, it was already evident to him that, apart from the Walter propulsion unit, plans for the Type XXI would have to be hurried on. He also envisaged a considerable expansion of the next most important offensive weapon - the motor torpedo-boat. In the summer of 1940 Germany had found herself in possession of advanced bases on the Channel coast - an acquisition never dreamed of in peacetime - and so within easy striking distance of the regular daily convoys that plied the English coast in both directions, carrying goods essential to the British economy. During the next two and a half years, however, E-boat action against these convoys had been on a relatively small scale, never more than 15 boats being employed at any one time, but Dönitz had in mind a considerable expansion of this form of attack to the use of massed flotillas on suitable nights. As regards other German surface forces, only the Arctic still presented some opportunities for offensive operations against the Murmansk convoys.

None of these offensive possibilities could be fully exploited unless supported by air reconnaissance and, despite the failure of previous attempts to secure the support of the *Luftwaffe*, Dönitz was now determined to obtain Göring's consent, not only to co-operation with the navy, but also to intensive independent air operations against Allied shipping through bombing, mining and aerial torpedo attacks.

For the operations of all naval forces it was essential to keep open the operational ports, at a time when the ever-increasing threat of the enemy's sea and air forces already underlined the inadequacy of our local defence flotillas for sweeping and protecting the approach channels to the bases and the routes along the extensive coastline from North Cape to the Spanish frontier. Moreover, it was highly important to keep the Baltic clear of mines for the uninterrupted training of the U-boats. Any dislocation of these sea communications would not only interfere with our offensive operations, but could even affect our ability to hold Norway and Finland, with dire consequences to the war economy. Hence, as compared with 1942, it was essential to introduce a greatly increased building programme for destroyers, torpedo-boats, minesweepers, motor-minesweepers, sperrbrechers and small patrol vessels.

336. The question of the big ships

Within a week of becoming Commander-in-Chief of the Navy, Dönitz had to submit to Hitler a programme for the decommissioning of the big ships. This had been ordered by Hitler early in January and had been the immediate cause of Admiral Raeder's resignation. Dönitz first heard of this Führer order when he assumed his new office and at once examined its implications. Viewed from the standpoint of his new and wider responsibilities he very soon realised the strategic value of keeping the big ships in commission in Norway, where they could still be used for offensive and defensive operations, and thus in his second talk with Hitler on 26th February 1943, which was more stormy than the official record suggests, he pressed strongly for the retention of the battleships *Tirpitz* and *Scharnhorst*, and the cruiser *Lützozv*, for operations against the Allied convoys to Russia.

It has been maintained by some that Dönitz was only interested in submarine warfare and that he never stood up to Hitler; yet this is belied by his attitude towards the question of the big ships, as confirmed by his own staff officers, who were well aware of the nature and details of these meetings. If in the further course of this narrative the author draws on his personal experience and on the recollection of other staff officers concerning the activities of Admiral Dönitz, it is done solely in the interest of historical accuracy, for official documents, alone, cannot be expected to convey a true perspective in such personal matters.

337. Labour requirements for repair of U-boats

On examining the current building programme for all types of warship, as handed over by Admiral Raeder, Dönitz came to the conclusion that it could not be carried out, for neither steel nor labour allocations were sufficient. Furthermore, considerable tension had built up between Raeder and Speer - the Director of Armaments - and between their respective staffs, and the first need, before attempting any expansion of building, was to remove this tension and the resulting bottlenecks.

We were not getting the fullest value from our existing U-boats because, during 1942, the time occupied by routine refits had steadily increased owing to labour shortages - at the end of 1941 the ratio of sea time to dockyard time was 6 to 4, while by the end of 1942 it had fallen to 4 to 6. Similarly, the final adjustment trials of new boats had taken only three weeks in 1941 as compared with six weeks in 1942. This shortage of labour was mainly due to the recruitment of skilled and other workers for the army, and their replacement by unskilled labour; at his meeting with Hitler on 8th February 1943, Dönitz therefore secured an order putting all workers engaged on the construction or repair of U-boats into a reserved category. At the same time he obtained Speer's promise of more labour for the repair of U-boats.

338. Greater steel and labour allocations for the 1943 building programme

The navy's monthly steel allocation had been 160,000 tons in 1939 and had averaged 177,000 tons during 1941; but despite increasing steel production in 1942, only 119,000 tons were allocated in the second quarter of that year (335)[1]. These allocations had been and still were inadequate, with the result that U-boat building, although bearing priority, failed to achieve its target. The building of other types of naval vessel was even more adversely affected, with only up to 50 per cent of the planned tonnage of many types being completed. The monthly steel quota for the first quarter of 1943 was 121,000 tons, which fell 60,000 tons short of the amount required to complete

1 Numbers in brackets refer to the author's notes and sources, which will be found at the end of this volume.

the outstanding items of the 1942 programme; and on 6th March 1943 Dönitz besought Hitler for an additional 60,000 tons a month, arguing that this increase would still only raise the navy's quota to 6-4 per cent of the total steel production, as compared with allocations of 10-3, 22-5, 14-7 and 22-5 per cent, respectively, to the air force, the army, the Armaments Ministry and for civilian purposes (336). Hitler approved only an extra 45,000 tons, which was, however, sufficient for our most urgent immediate requirements.

The expanded naval building programme, later known as the 1943 programme, was submitted to Hitler on 11th April 1943. It provided for the building of 27 operational U-boats a month in the latter half of 1943 and for the maintenance of this building rate in 1944, when there was to be a gradual transition to the production of the 200-ton-heavier Type VIIC/42 U-boat. In addition, three large transport U-boats were to be built monthly. The plan also envisaged the annual construction of 18 destroyers and torpedo-boats, 72 E-boats (instead of 24 as hitherto), 74 minesweepers, 72 motor-minesweepers, 300 patrol and escort vessels, 35 sperrbrechers and 900 shallow-draft craft (gun-barges, flak-barges, ferry-barges and the like).

To carry out this programme the navy needed the immediate allocation of a further 30,000 tons of steel and progressively greater quantities as time went on, together with a further 55,000 armament workers and additional production facilities. Hitler approved the programme, but declared that it was impossible to release the requisite labour and material resources from industry, suggesting instead that the work should be undertaken by the existing industrial organisation. It therefore now remained to devise a satisfactory method of implementing the programme.

339. Efforts to obtain increased air support at sea
From his experience as FO U-boats, Dönitz was already well aware of Göring's intransigent attitude towards air participation in the war at sea, and with steadily increasing demands on the *Luftwaffe* for both support of military operations and the defence of Germany, Göring had little difficulty in finding plausible objections to the

navy's requests. From his first conference with Hitler on 26th February 1943, Dönitz constantly sought to convince him of the need for the provision of adequate air support for the navy, and finally persuaded him to tackle Göring on the subject. Dönitz had in fact begun direct negotiations with Göring on 25th February, when stress had been laid on the need for the earliest possible provision of sufficient durable long-range reconnaissance aircraft to carry out a six-sortie Atlantic surveillance twice daily. Göring had promised his full support to this aim, maintaining that one Geschwader would be adequate for the purpose (337). Hitler agreed to examine the possibility of making available three six-engined BV 222 flying-boats, which were then being used for transport duties on the Eastern Front, while consideration was also given to providing four-engined Ju 290s, which were due to come into service at the end of the year, and the projected Me 264 - the so-called American Bomber - at a later stage. The He 177s, which had been promised in the summer of 1942, were still not available.

Other questions of air co-operation, thrashed out towards the end of April between the Chiefs of the Naval and Air Staffs (*Vizeadmiral* Meisel and *Generaloberst* Jeschonnek), included the provision of air cover for U-boats in the Bay of Biscay and the mounting of air attacks on Coastal Command bases in southern England. *Fliegerführer* Atlantic had already planned to employ long-range fighter aircraft (FW 190s with extra tanks and Me 201s) against Coastal Command aircraft as they were leaving the English coast and, since we knew the exact times at which these aircraft took off, the plan had every promise of success. However, it could not be put into full operation owing to lack of aircraft. Meisel therefore reiterated his demand for more fighter aircraft for this purpose. Additionally he demanded air attacks on the coastal traffic around Britain, air co-operation with surface forces against the Murmansk convoys, air support for E-boat operations in the Channel and, finally, increased fighter protection for our shipping between the Hook of Holland and the Elbe. Göring and Jeschonnek agreed to co-operate, but made no definite promises.

In the past, the few U-boat operations given air support had suffered because of bad aerial navigation, identification errors and difficulties in communication between U-boat and aircraft; consequently Dönitz, in discussing the May crisis with Hitler on the 31st of that month, stressed the need for a naval flying school at Gotenhafen on the Baltic, where the naval airmen could be trained for operations over the sea and exercise with U-boats undergoing their convoy attack training (338).

MAY 1943
REVIEW OF THE MAY CRISIS

340. The crisis due to tardy application of new technical ideas
With the adoption of the measures described in the three previous sections, long-term preparations were made for the revival of the U-boat campaign, and at the beginning of May we were looking forward to the delivery within the next few months of larger numbers of operational U-boats, while greater air co-operation could be expected in perhaps a year.

Another requirement of equal importance was the speeding up of improvements to the U-boats' armament, which had been in hand since the summer of 1942, so as to master the ever-increasing enemy threat in the Atlantic. Immediately on becoming C-in-C Navy, Ddnitz had apprised himself, by personal visits to the production centres and experimental establishments, of the state of progress in the production of armaments and *electro*nic equipment and, through his intervention, many bottle-necks in production were eliminated. He also put the naval radar research authorities in touch with the Government research office. At a meeting with the leading scientific and industrial authorities, both Dönitz and the Director of the Naval Communications Division stressed the urgency of catching up with the enemy's advances in radar, and from these discussions it soon emerged that neither science nor industry had been adequately briefed as to the nature of the U-boats' radar problems. Now, however, they saw considerable, as yet unexplored, possibilities in the camouflaging of U-boats against radar detection, which promised to solve the enemy radar problem.

In the midst of this intense activity, and beset by worry over the deterioration of the situation in the Atlantic, we were confronted by the May crisis. The magnitude of this crisis and the rapidity with which it followed our outstanding successes of March, came as a shock to Dönitz and his staff; however, its causes were obvious. The U-boat had not been defeated by some new, highly lethal weapon such as a homing bomb or torpedo, but by the sheer weight of the enemy opposition, above all by aircraft, whose effectiveness had been greatly increased by the fitting of a radar which the U-boats had been unable to detect. On the other hand, none of the new U-boat weapons - AA guns, anti-destroyer torpedoes and radar, which had been put into production in the summer of 1942 - had yet become available for use and for this reason we regarded the crisis as temporary.

341. Heavier flak armament expected within three months
Since the end of 1942, increasing demands from all branches of the armed forces had heavily taxed the armament industry, with the result that the equipping of the boats with 2-cm quadruple AA mountings had been delayed (Section 296). These mountings were now becoming available and the first two were fitted at the end of May, a further 72 were expected in July and August and, from August onwards, all boats leaving the Biscay bases would be so equipped (339). Trials with the quick-firing 2-cm twin had been most satisfactory and delivery of fourteen of these mountings had been promised by mid-July, with subsequent deliveries at a rate which would ensure the equipping of most of the boats by September. By 1st June a new 2-cm HE shell would also be available, the so-called *Minengeschoss* (mine shell) with a Hexogen filling three times the size of the old and possessing great destructive power against unarmoured surfaces (from 1st July this ammunition was used in combination with an improved armour-piercing shell fitted with

tracer). The new automatic 3-7-cm AA gun had been perfected, was being produced and was to be available in the autumn. It fired an HE shell far more destructive than the 2-cm and was expected finally to eliminate the disadvantage under which the boats had suffered hitherto, because of their inferior AA armament.

342. Radar, radar search receivers and decoys

At the end of May 1943, our scientists were still in doubt as to the enemy method of location and, although the use of centimetric radar was suspected, such was not to be confirmed until January 1944.[2] The reasons for their uncertainty and their belated appreciation of this fact were that, although well over a thousand of the *Metox* and *Grandin*[3] observations recorded by the U-boats between March and May 1943 had Iain between 120 and 250 centimetres, the number of cases in which U-boats had been approached by undetected aircraft was very small. Thus the non-detection could be attributed either to the dead sectors of the radar search receivers or to intermittent radiations which were difficult and often impossible to register owing to the method of operating the receivers, or to impulse frequencies on or beyond the range of the receivers, which could not be registered at all (Section 235). Moreover, despite the capture of the *Rotterdam-Gerdt* at the beginning of 1943, our scientists still doubted the feasibility of introducing centimetric radar for general operational use because of the great technical difficulties involved. For these reasons we pinned our hope to a new radar search receiver known as the *Hagenuk-Wellenanzeiger* or *Wanze*, large numbers of which were to become available in August. This instrument covered a wider wave-band, which it swept automatically, and, being fitted with an optical indicator, was capable of registering intermittent radiations and wavelengths which were undetectable by the existing receivers. With *Wanze*, therefore, the U-boats would run less risk of being surprised from the air.

---

2 This evidently refers to ASV radar Mk III (3,297 MHz or 9.1 cm) which was first fitted operationally to the Leigh-light Wellingtons in the Bay of Biscay in March 1943.
3 A radar search receiver with the same frequency as the *Metox*.

An instrument for detecting carrier frequencies beyond the range of the *Metox* and *Wanze* had long been under development, but had not yet reached the production stage. However, a crystal detector for the interception of centimetric radar, later known as *Naxos*, was expected to be ready before the end of the year.

Unfortunately, little progress had been made in the development of active radar. The comparatively few sets (*Gemageräf*) already in use at sea could be used for both air and surface search, but owing to its narrow beam this equipment was slow in operation and useless in a seaway; however, work on the improvement of this and the development of lighter and more efficient instruments was pressed on vigorously.

Aphrodite, a radar decoy, was to be introduced in July. This was a hydrogen-filled indiarubber balloon, to which was attached aluminium foil producing a radar echo similar to that of a U-boat conning tower, and its mass employment by U-boats approaching or attacking a convoy at night was expected to afford considerable protection against air and surface radar. Radar protection for U-boats in the Bay of Biscay was to be provided by *Thetis*, a buoy fitted with a long spar to which metal foil was secured.

343. Prospects of improvement through new weapons
With *Wanze* and the new AA armament, the U-boats had greater prospects of triumph in the Atlantic battle, for it was hoped that *Wanze* would provide timely warning of the approach of enemy aircraft, while the heavier AA guns would enable the U-boat to beat off air attack should she be unable to dive in time to avoid it.

But this protection was of limited value if aircraft were co-operating with surface A/S forces, for the U-boat would then also need a weapon with which to defend herself against the latter; this weapon, the acoustic homing G7es torpedo, or *Zaunkönig*, was to be ready by October. The forerunner of *Zaunkönig*, the Falke, which had a speed of 20 knots and was fitted with a contact pistol, had already been in limited use since the beginning of the year (Section 245), and the first hit was obtained by U.221 against HX 229 and

SC 122 on 18th March.[4] The *Zaunkönig*, which had a speed of 24-5 knots and a range of 5,700 metres, could be fired from all positions at vessels steaming at 10 to 18 knots. It had a combined contact and magnetic pistol and could therefore also be used against destroyers, corvettes, sloops, trawlers and other shallow-draught vessels. It was the long-awaited "destroyer-buster". Since the probability of hitting was greatest when the enemy inclination was 180 degrees, pursuing A/S vessels were expected to become the first victims of this torpedo, which would doubtless inspire more cautious behaviour on the part of the captains of independently operating escort vessels and so preclude the recurrence of incidents such as occurred during the attack on SC 129 on 12th May 1943, when single corvettes were able to drive off as many as six U-boats simultaneously.

344. Final conclusions regarding the May crisis

Dönitz had no doubt that the planned simultaneous introduction of these new weapons and *electro*nic devices would, for a time, give to the U-boat an advantage over the enemy defences and so restore the balance obtaining before the set-back of May 1943. Nevertheless, it was appreciated that in war the technical advances of one side are as a rule subsequently neutralised or even surpassed by the other. Thus no effort was spared in exploiting every possibility of maintaining the effectiveness of the conventional U-boat until such time as fundamentally new types[5] were ready for operations.

345. Armament Minister becomes responsible for naval construction

Events in May presaged heavier U-boat losses, and it then appeared probable that the building of 30 U-boats a month, approved on 11th April, would be inadequate. This figure therefore had to be increased, but it was hardly likely that the navy would be given the requisite facilities for this purpose, since the situation in the whole armaments industry was already strained. The only solution was to place naval

---

4 U.221 was not the first to use Falke with success. It had been used effectively on 16th March by U.603 (2200 GMT) and U.758 (2322 GMT) against convoy HX 229.
5 Presumably a reference to work being carried out on Types XXI and XXIII U-boats.

construction and repairs in the hands of the Armament Minister, as suggested by Hitler on 11th April (Section 338).

So Dönitz, after further consultation with Speer, was determined to take this step, which, he believed, was the only way of ensuring that the navy's demands would receive equal treatment with those of the other branches of the armed forces. The directive authorising the transfer of naval construction to the Armaments Minister was submitted to Hitler at a conference on the 31st May 1943, at which Dönitz reported on the crisis.[6] In his report, Dönitz stated that U-boat operations were being frustrated by enemy location gear, the nature of which had not yet been clearly established, but that counter-measures would be found. He could not foresee to what extent operations could be revived, since enemy opposition was increasing, but it was nevertheless essential to continue the campaign if only to tie down enemy forces. The U-boat building drive had therefore to be maintained and the rate of construction raised from 30 to 40 boats a month. Hitler approved this new programme and signed the above-mentioned directive.

JUNE-AUGUST 1943
DEVELOPMENT OF NEW-TYPE U-BOATS

346. The large *Electro* boat (Type XXI)

The *Electro* boat, later known as the Type XXI, was a fundamentally new type with streamlined hull and very powerful batteries designed for a high submerged speed. She possessed outstanding fighting qualities. The design was first suggested by the U-boat constructors Schürer and Bracking at a Paris conference in November 1942 between FO U-boats, Professor Walter, and officials of the Naval Construction Office, the constructors emphasising that a boat of 1,600 tons would be required to house the batteries. At that time Dönitz favoured a smaller boat of less than 1,000 tons, which would be

---

6 This conference is reported verbatim in "Führer Conferences on German Naval Affairs, 1939-1945", which appear in *Brassey's Naval Annual*, 1948, page 331.

easier to handle, both surfaced and submerged, and more resistant to depth-charge attack than a larger, more complicated boat. Moreover, a much greater number of smaller boats could be produced from our limited steel and non-ferrous metal allocations, which, in view of the need to solve the problem of interception in the Atlantic without air reconnaissance, was itself a decisive factor. However, Dönitz later declared himself prepared to accept a larger boat, provided that she attained a high submerged speed.

Theoretical calculations were begun in January 1943 and by June the preliminary design was completed. The projected submerged speed was 18 knots (full) for one hour and a half, or 12 to 14 knots for 10 hours, which represented an immense advance on the existing types of U-boat, whose full submerged speed did not exceed six knots for 45 minutes. We estimated that the new boat had sufficient speed and battery capacity to close and attack a merchant ship or convoy, submerged, once it had been sighted or located by other means, while her echo-ranging gear and improved hydrophone, together with high speed, would enable her to press home her attack in the face of strong opposition from air and sea. She would be capable of firing 18 out of a total of 20 torpedoes in less than 20 minutes, and, by virtue of her deep-diving capacity, manoeuvrability and long endurance at a high silent-running speed (60 hours at five knots as compared with the existing boats' 20 to 30 hours at 1-5 knots), her chances of eluding pursuit or withstanding a protracted counter-attack would be greater. When being pursued the U-boat would no longer be "blind", since her echo-ranging gear would enable her to establish the position and, to some extent, the intentions of her pursuers and to take appropriate avoiding action. Her heavy displacement had an advantage, in that it permitted a much greater fuel capacity which would extend her radius of action to the whole of the North and South Atlantic.

347. Approval given for building of Type XXI U-boats
Though the *Electro* boat's designed speed was much inferior to that of the Walter boat, the Naval Staff considered that precedence should be given to the building of the former, for her propulsion

followed traditional lines and she could therefore be built more quickly. However, the development of the Walter boat, which since the beginning of 1943 had been pursued with the utmost speed, was to proceed concurrently, and work on four prototypes was to continue. Additionally, 24 Type XVIIB and two Type XVIII were to be laid down before the end of the year (Section 465).

Before the building of the Type XXI U-boat could proceed it was first necessary to obtain Hitler's approval, for only he could decide whether the additional demands on industrial capacity could be reconciled with the priorities of the other two Services. At a conference with Hitler on 8th July 1943, Dönitz reported the completion of the Type XXI design and urged that building should be given the highest priority. He pointed out that the new boat would be able to operate mainly submerged and thereby minimise the enemy's advantage in the field of radar location; it was therefore vital to build these boats as soon as possible. Hitler agreed and approved the adoption of the Type XXI U-boat.

348. Continued attack on enemy shipping

The original period fixed for the construction of the first boat, from the drawing-board to her final completion was 17 months, which for Dönitz was far too long. He accordingly consulted Speer, who thought it possible to shorten this period and to commence mass production in the summer of 1944, provided that priority was accorded over other naval and civil building commitments. Dönitz and the Naval Staff were thereby confronted with a decision of the greatest import. Here was a project which would at once impose heavy demands on our armaments-production capacity, to the detriment of other building commitments, but which would have no effect on the war at sea until the autumn of 1944 at the earliest. The question was, in view of the immensity of the Allied shipbuilding and A/S drive, would the Type XXI U-boat still be powerful enough in 1944 and 1945 to operate successfully in the Atlantic? As far as Dönitz and the Naval Staff were concerned, the answer was in the affirmative. According to our shipbuilding authorities the Allies were unable, in the foreseeable future, to increase the average convoy speed to beyond 10 knots, so that the advantage of speed would remain with the U-boat for some years. If the situation in the Atlantic again deteriorated, the schnorkel would permit operations to be conducted entirely underwater (Section 420). Considering the slow pace at which methods of combating a submerged U-boat had improved since the beginning of the war and the difficulties involved in introducing a fundamentally new A/S technique, the *Electro* boat's prospects vis-a-vis the enemy A/S forces should therefore still be a good two years hence.

Yet another question had to be examined. Had not the enemy so increased his merchant shipping tonnage by the autumn of 1943 that it was no longer possible for us to reduce it to a dangerous level? But Naval Intelligence Division estimated that by 30th May 1943 the Allies had replaced only 15-5 million tons out of a total of 30 million tons lost (340), requiring them to make up considerable leeway before reaching even the tonnage available to them at the outbreak of war. Thus the war against shipping had to be intensified by every available means - the new pressure and acoustic mines, E-boats, and both German and Japanese aircraft and U-boats. As regards our own U-boats, we had reason to hope that, from the autumn of 1943, operations by the old types would again be made effective. Even if Allied new construction exceeded losses we could still not give up; on the contrary, we should have to redouble our efforts in order to deny the enemy shipping space for large-scale landings in Europe - a consideration of ever-increasing importance. As early as August 1943, the Army Staff estimated that, although the enemy had adequate military forces for several simultaneous medium-scale landings, such as operation "Torch" (341), he still had insufficient shipping space available for this purpose; but once he overcame this last obstacle, the threat of a landing would apply equally to Norway, the Channel coast, Southern France, Italy and the Balkans. In these circumstances the Supreme Command would find it difficult, indeed almost impossible, to arrange any disposition for the available military anti-invasion forces. A successful invasion of Europe would put victory within the enemy's grasp; thus it was essential that sinkings be maintained in order to withhold from him that global military operational freedom for which he was striving.

349. The small Electro boat (Type XXHI)

It was originally intended that the Type XXI U-boat should replace the Type IX; but after the May crisis, Dönitz decided that she should also take the place of the Type VII for convoy attack duties. Her size, however, rendered her unsuitable for work in the North Sea and shallow-water areas, for which purpose, but principally for operations in the Mediterranean, a small *Electro* boat was designed - the Type XXIII, which had a displacement of 300 tons, a full submerged speed of 12 knots and was extremely easy to control. Some of these boats were to be built in the Mediterranean, while others could, if necessary, be transported in sections by land or inland waterway.

350. Transition to building of Types XXI and XXIII

Transition to the building of the Types XXI and XXIII was ordered on 13th August 1943, with the stipulation that the change-over must in no way interrupt the continuity of U-boat production. At the same time the building of the Type VIIC/42, of which only a few of the 180 ordered had been laid down, was cancelled, while the building programme of the Types VII and IX was allowed to lapse. It was estimated that if our losses continued on the same scale as in July and August 1943, the current building programme would provide, up to the summer of 1944, sufficient reinforcements of old-type boats to enable us to maintain pressure on the enemy.

351. Personnel requirements

The estimated manning requirement for the whole of the 1943 building programme, in the period June 1943 to September 1944, was about 335,000 officers and men (342). Of these, 60,000 were needed by the U-boat arm for the manning of more than 600 projected U-boats, for the expansion of U-boat bases and training flotillas and for the new escort vessels and target ships; 172,000 were required for the manning of the remaining naval vessels; 86,000 for the coastal defences; and about 28,000 for the naval radar service. After detailed discussion between the C-in-C Navy and the Manning Department, the total figure was reduced to 262,000 and finally submitted to Hitler at the conference of 8th July 1943. Keitel, the Chief of Staff of the Supreme Command of the Armed Forces, considered the provision of such large numbers to be impracticable; in the end, however, it was agreed that the requisite personnel should be made available as and when the new ships and establishments became ready for manning. In actual fact, by the autumn of 1944 our personnel requirements were still not fully met.

MAY-AUGUST 1943
OPERATIONAL PLANS

352. Question of the entire abandonment of the Atlantic

Let us return to 24th May 1943, the date on which operations against North Atlantic convoys were suspended (Section 333). While those boats with adequate fuel were heading to the south-west of the Azores, Dönitz had time to consider what further steps should be taken. The question arose as, to whether, in order to avoid further heavy losses, the Atlantic should not be entirely abandoned until the new weapons became available; but the idea was rejected since, with only 110 protected U-boat berths available in the Atlantic bases, a large number of boats would consequently have remained exposed to Allied air attack. Moreover, such inactivity would have been harmful to the morale of the crews and would have lost them that contact with the enemy, by which means alone we could remain conversant with the latest developments in A/S techniques. It was therefore decided that those boats low in fuel, which, it will be remembered, were still on the North Atlantic convoy routes, should remain there, being replaced, as necessary, in order to conceal our withdrawal from the enemy. The boats proceeding to the south-west of the Azores were immediately to be formed into a group for attacking UGS convoys; but whether these boats would need reinforcement could not be foreseen. Most of the Type VIIC and Type IX U-boats, which were shortly due to sail, were to operate with the support of U-tankers in remote areas, where the danger from the air was comparatively small; any further boats available - depending chiefly upon the extent of losses in transit - were to carry out a group attack against a USA-UK convoy, in which the radar decoy *Aphrodite* was to be used. However, this attack was not carried out. for we were very soon to learn that such an operation would have ended in disaster.

NORTH ATLANTIC AND BAY OF BISCAY

353. Deception in the North Atlantic

When those boats low in fuel had assumed their allotted positions, a radio deception scheme was put into operation, by which it was hoped to persuade the enemy that many U-boats were still operating in the North Atlantic. Some U-boats were therefore detached to the south-west of Ireland and some to the south of Iceland to transmit messages simulating the routine reports of boats entering the Atlantic from Western Europe or Norway, while others were sent to the Greenland coast or to the Azores, transmitting signals designed to lead the enemy into deducing the presence of U-boats refuelling, or of an operational group shifting position. We were not too optimistic as to the efficacy of the scheme, since we believed the enemy's knowledge of U-boat positions to be obtained mostly by aircraft radar rather than by direction-finding. Moreover, sooner or later he was bound to realise from the mere absence of attacks that we had few boats in the area. Yet for three weeks he appears to have been unaware of the real situation. On 4th June, for instance, the British "U-boat Situation Report" stated that up to 20 boats were presumed to be operating between Newfoundland and Greenland and, on the 5th, a considerable number was presumed to be located north of the Azores, whereas the actual number patrolling on those dates had dropped to three owing to further losses and to boats having to return to base.

Two U-boats had been lost since 24th May. These losses were worrying and difficult to explain. The Commanding Officers had been warned to take no risks, to proceed with the utmost caution and, because of the danger of being D/F'd, to move well away after transmitting a radio message. Now, for the first time, suspicion fell upon American submarines, whose presence and patrol areas had been established by Radio Intelligence and promulgated to the boats. For, although U-boats transiting the Bay of Biscay had been ordered, on 22nd May, to proceed at night on electric motors so as to facilitate the audible detection of approaching aircraft, in practice the rush of water through the flooding slots in the casing always served to drown any such noises, and Commanding Officers therefore chose to proceed on their diesels at a speed compatible with good maneuverability, so laying themselves open to submarine attack.

We had intended to keep the small number of boats on the North Atlantic convoy routes more or less constant by sending reliefs from Germany. But this could not be done. Of 13 which had sailed for this purpose from bases in Germany and Norway up to 10th June, two were lost while passing through the Iceland passage and two after a brief spell in the operational area. Two more were so severely damaged by bombs *en route* that they had to proceed direct to western France. Furthermore, owing to the precarious refuelling situation south of the Azores, three Type IXC boats had to be despatched at high speed to act as tankers in that area and thus, in June 1943, the average number of U-boats in the operational area never exceeded six.

No replacements were sent from western France, for, by the middle of June, we no longer doubted that the enemy had tumbled to the original deception; although this could not be proved, owing to the introduction, on 10th June, of new British enciphering methods, which had put an end to the decryption of the "U-boat Situation Reports" and other radio messages. But confirmation was seen in enemy press announcements stating that the U-boats had been driven from the North Atlantic convoy routes.

At the end of June two more U-boats - as yet unequipped with additional anti-aircraft guns - were lost south of Iceland and, now that deception was no longer viable, FO U-boats considered himself justified in prohibiting the sailing of further boats from Germany until equipped with quadruple mountings. Four already in transit west of Norway were therefore diverted to the north and placed at the disposal of SO U-boats Norway for minelaying in the Kara Sea. As a result of these measures there were no U-boats in the Atlantic area between Newfoundland and the British Isles for nearly two months.

354. Vain search for convoys south-west of the Azores

Convoys between the USA and the Mediterranean had now been running at regular intervals for almost six months. We were well acquainted with the times of their departure and arrival on each side of the Atlantic, but still knew very little about their routes; and as our operations between January and April 1943 had resulted in failure, FO U-boats now regarded the prospects of interception as very slender. However, on 24th May there was no other North Atlantic area in which the boats at sea, and still fit for action, could be employed with even a faint prospect of success.

According to the plot, a UGS convoy - UGS 9 - was due in 43 degrees West about 1st June, and another - GUS 7 A - on the 2nd, the latter being reported by an agent as having passed the Gibraltar Strait on 23rd May. On the night of 31st May, group *Trutz*, consisting of 16 boats, formed patrol line on the aforesaid meridian between 32 and 38 degrees North, and on the afternoon of 4th June three boats at the southern end of the line were attacked by carrier-borne aircraft, of which one was shot down. These aircraft could have formed part of the advance cover of the UGS convoy, in which case the convoy could not have been more than 200 miles to the westward and may even have lain just ahead of the patrol line; so, to prevent the enemy slipping unnoticed through the wide gaps left between boats, the line was closed in and moved to the southeast. When no contact had been made by the following evening, it was presumed that the convoy had already circumvented the line to the north or south and the formation was therefore dissolved to allow the boats to refuel from U.488. This action proved premature, for three days later - on the 8th - after the boats had already reached the tanker 600 miles to the northward, two east-bound ships escorted by carrier-borne aircraft and destroyers[7] were sighted by the outward-bound U.758, a good 100 miles south of group *Trutz's* patrol area of 5th June. Had these ships belonged to the awaited UGS convoy - which was indeed assumed - the convoy must have been considerably further west on 4th June than estimated, and the aircraft sighted that day must either have come from a detached carrier, or have had a far greater range than 200 miles.

A few days later we received confirmation that, in addition to the aircraft carriers accompanying UG and GU convoys, others patrolled independently in the whole convoy area, and also that the range of their aircraft was greater than we had hitherto supposed.

355. First action with quadruple mountings

During her contact with the enemy on 8th June, U.758 had fought a bitter engagement with carrier-borne aircraft. As she was the first boat with quadruple mountings to go into action, her experiences were of particular interest to us. The following is quoted from her log:

"… 1850, 8th June 1943. Smoke and mastheads of the destroyer again in sight. Two aircraft circling over the convoy.

1918. Attack from starboard by low-flying Lysander type aircraft. I open fire and score a considerable number of hits as she approaches. Before finishing her attack she turns off sharply and jettisons four 250-lb bombs about 200 metres on the starboard beam. She then drops a smoke-float and returns to the convoy. I withdraw to the south-west at high speed. The damaged plane is relieved by another Lysander and a Martlet, which circle me, without attacking, at a

---

7 In fact, an American support group consisting of the aircraft carrier *Bogue* and the destroyers *Clemson*, *Greene* and *Osmond Ingram*, whose aircraft had attacked the three U-boats of group *Trutz* on 4th June, without loss.

range of 4,000 to 5,000 metres and at a height of 9,000 feet. I open fire occasionally without hitting.

1945. Another Martlet, coming in low from starboard, attacks with gunfire. She receives numerous hits, and as she reaches my stern turns sharply left dropping four bombs which fall about 25 metres away in my wake. The aircraft leaving a broad trail of black smoke then crashes into the sea. Our AA armament will keep bomber aircraft off to 3,000 or 4,000 metres. Several broke off their approach flights when 2,000 to 3,000 metres away.

At about 2000, two low-flying Mustangs attack with gunfire. We score several hits on each. One is damaged and returns to the convoy. She is relieved by another. Two of my 2-cm automatic guns have been shot out of action. Eleven members of the guns' crews and lookouts have been slightly wounded. I decide to dive..."

U.758 inflicted damage on several other aircraft in the course of the action, but she herself was also damaged through diving too late. Nevertheless, we considered that the results on the whole augured well for the boats equipped with quadruple mountings.[8]

356. Last attempt to locate Mediterranean-bound convoys

The refuelling of group *Trutz* by U.488 went off quickly and smoothly. Incidentally, this was the last refuelling operation that did. The 16th June found the boats on the 50th meridian awaiting two convoys - an east-bound expected on the 17th and a west-bound expected on the 20th. The group was drawn up in three parallel patrol lines of 4, 7 and 4 boats respectively, disposed on a south-easterly line of bearing, the boats being 100 miles apart in the outer lines and 50 miles apart in the inner. This disposition gave a virtual distance between boats of 25 miles, while the depth of deployment in line of bearing was intended to ensure that, if one boat was located from the air, adjacent boats would not be detected at the same time and betray the whole disposition. The large gaps between boats were accepted. The formation had waited in position for six days

---

8 These attacks were carried out by Avenger and Wildcat aircraft from the Bogue. One Avenger was damaged.

without the least sign of enemy activity and had just been ordered eastward to meet the next west-bound convoy, when, on 22nd June, the awaited UG was sighted - again fortuitously - by a boat on her way to the Caribbean. This convoy had taken unexpectedly bold avoiding action and passed a good 300 miles to the southward of the group. Pursuit was out of the question, for at best it would have taken three or four days to locate the convoy, by which time it would have been enjoying continuous air cover from African bases. So the boats continued eastwards to a position 200 miles south-west of the Azores, where they remained in three patrol lines - the inner line being extended northwards by four fresh boats - from 27th to 29th June. As the next convoy also failed to appear, further attempts to locate UG convoys were abandoned.

"… We assume that in each case the patrol line was circumvented after being located ahead of the convoy by high-flying carrier-borne aircraft (this theory has been substantiated by the Commanding Officer of U.558, an experienced officer). In this part of the Atlantic

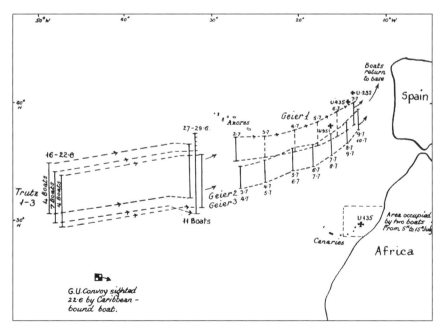

Plan 61. Groups Trutz and Geier, 16th June-10th July 1943.
Operations against UGS and GUS convoys.

the widest possible avoiding action can be carried out without substantially lengthening the convoy route and, as we are unable at present to intercept enemy aircraft radar, there is no point in sending any more U-boats into mid-Atlantic for the purpose of intercepting UG and GU convoys. Apart from the difficulties of location, operational conditions have become so bad as a result of continued fine weather and the presence of enemy aircraft carriers, that it would be unprofitable to continue the operations..." (343).

The search for convoys south and west of the Azores was never resumed.

The boats of group *Trutz* now headed towards the Spanish coast, proceeding in three patrol lines - *Geier* 1 to 3 - at intervals of a day's run. If fuel permitted they were to form a stationary disposition in an area west of Cape Finisterre, where they would be least accessible to aircraft from England and Gibraltar. The boats were barely 500 miles from the Spanish coast when air attacks began and, as they continued eastward, enemy air activity became so intense that, on 8th July, the Commanding Officers were given permission to return to base if they found the opposition too strong. Despite every precaution, U.232, U.951 and U.435 fell victims to these attacks. Similar conditions were experienced by U.135 and U.193 between the Canaries and the African coast, where they had been sent after the dispersal of group *Trutz*. U.135 never returned. Group *Trutz's* operation had been a dismal failure; despite the loss of five U-boats not a single convoy ship had been sunk.

357. Measures for the protection of U-boats in the Bay of Biscay
Since March 1943, our losses in the Bay of Biscay had steadily increased. Nine U-boats were lost there in May, representing a quarter of the total losses in the Atlantic area, and seven other boats were so heavily damaged by aircraft bombs and cannon-fire that they were unable to dive, reaching harbour only with great difficulty. It was distressing for the men that, because of enemy air activity, their home waters should have become the most dangerous part of the whole Atlantic, with the *Luftwaffe* powerless to intervene. As a result

of pressure from C-in-C Navy, additional Ju 88 CVIs had indeed been made available, but these aircraft were now much inferior to the enemy's and could only operate in groups of a minimum of six against lone flying-boats and four-engined bombers. Consequently only two or three air patrols were flown daily, which, while barely allowing of air escort for U-boats returning damaged, did not suffice to drive off enemy aircraft. What could be achieved with adequate air forces was illustrated on 1st June 1943, when all available aircraft - 23 Ju 88s - were despatched to 11 degrees West as air escort for U.563, which was unable to dive. They failed to locate the U-boat, but succeeded in shooting down four British aircraft, including two Wellingtons and a Dakota. Reinforcements of Ju 88s, or Me 410s, which were more suited to our purpose, were still not forthcoming, but we did not give up hope.

Some improvement was expected from the introduction of the flak U-boats, the first of which - U.441 - became operational on 22nd May 1943. This type was originally planned in September 1942, but completion was delayed by the shortage of weapons. She carried two quadruple 2-cm, one 3-7-cm and two single 2-cm guns. Four days after sailing, U.441 fought her first action, in which she shot down a Sunderland aircraft, but she herself was severely damaged by bombs and cannon-fire and had to break off her patrol. We regarded this incident as indicative of the effectiveness of the heavier AA armament, for one could assume that the enemy pilot had made this suicidal attack unaware of what he was up against. On 20th May 1943 an order was made for the conversion of ten Type VIIs into flak U-boats for use in the inner Bay. Weeks would, however, elapse before this and the general equipping with heavier flak was completed, so other and more immediate steps had to be taken to reduce losses.

Occasionally in 1942 a few U-boats in company - e.g. a disabled U-boat and another as escort - had fought their way back through the Bay of Biscay against repeated air attacks, and it was then found that by combining their fire-power and adjusting their courses to give an all-round distribution of fire, attacking aircraft could be beaten off, or at least put off their bomb aim. This procedure seemed to offer even greater possibilities for a larger group of boats and, moreover, was regarded by experienced U-boat commanders as being practicable. It was therefore decided, on 29th May 1943, that the boats should in future proceed through the Bay of Biscay in company.

358. Initial promise of group procedure in the Bay

One particularly strong argument in favour of this group procedure was that, despite instructions to the contrary, U-boats were still diving on being surprised by aircraft. This was evident both from the logs of damaged U-boats and from the observations of our patrolling aircraft, which frequently passed over U-boats in the act of diving, with their sterns still above water. There was no doubt that most of the U-boat casualties were due to belated diving. In company, however, the increased fire-power should give commanders more confidence to remain surfaced in an air attack. That they should be so encouraged was of such decisive importance to the future of the campaign that initially Dönitz ordered that from 29th May, in suitable weather, all groups should proceed surfaced by day and remain so in the event of air attack.

The potential group defensive power could only be fully exploited if each commander knew exactly what he had to do and acted in concert with the others. With several boats in company, lookouts could be double-banked and the radar search watch shared. Furthermore, as each boat would have only a small sector of the wave-band to scan, a much more thorough radar search could be made, with greater likelihood of detecting intermittent radar emissions. On 5th June it was ordered that those boats equipped with active radar should use this to augment the sky search. Outgoing groups were issued with their orders before sailing, while general instructions for group procedure were radioed to the boats then at sea, the organisation of individual groups being left to the senior officers of the returning boats, from whom the remainder received their instructions at the rendezvous in 15 degrees West (344).

While the boats returned two or three at a time, they left in groups of as many as five, since it was thus possible to provide them with air cover in the swept channels and sometimes beyond. First reports on the new procedure, which reached us by 10th June, proved to be more favourable than anticipated. One commander reported that "one could see and hear more" and another that the division of the radar search among the group had enabled eleven intermittent radar emissions to be detected. A few groups came through the Bay unmolested, while others reported having repulsed repeated attacks. Three weeks later, however, the enemy began to adjust his tactics accordingly. On sighting a group, an enemy aircraft would now remain out of gun range, yet so close that the U-boats could not risk diving, and continue to shadow until further aircraft arrived, when a concerted attack would be carried out. Patrolling interceptor fighters - Mosquitoes and Beaufighters - were also occasionally brought into attacks. On 13th June Dönitz commented in his war diary:

"… This new development puts the groups at a disadvantage, since their combined fire-power cannot be expected to provide adequate defence against a simultaneous attack by several aircraft. Experience in the next few days will show whether the group procedure is right or not…"

But next day the procedure had to be modified; a group of five boats, after repelling several attacks by a single aircraft, was subjected to a simultaneous attack by four heavy fighters, which inflicted severe casualties among the crews of U.68 and U.155, forcing these two boats to return to base. It was thus evident that the new group tactics were too hazardous and we had, therefore, to revert to the old practice of traversing the Bay submerged, only surfacing during the day to recharge batteries, but if enemy air activity were too strong during the day, recharging had to be carried out at night. The group tactics could nevertheless be regarded as having been successful for, although nearly as many boats passed through the Bay as in May 1943, only three were lost and two forced to return.

The sinking of U.564 illustrated the tenacity with which the enemy air force sought to destroy a damaged U-boat. U.564 was one of an outgoing group of five which was attacked by a Sunderland, 250 miles north-west of Cape Finisterre. The aircraft was shot down, but not before damaging U.564 to such an extent that she had to return to base. The damaged U-boat and her escort - U.185 - were later located, north of the Spanish coast, by an enemy aircraft which maintained contact until further aircraft could be summoned. In the ensuing attack on 14th June U.564 was sunk, her survivors being picked up by U.185 and transferred that evening to two destroyers - Z.24 and Z.25 - which had put out from le Verdon.

359. Enemy blockade of the Bay

Now that his transatlantic convoys were no longer threatened, the enemy apparently reduced his protective escort forces and, with the hunter groups thus made available, instituted a blockade of the Bay of Biscay. Sightings and direction-finding indicated that the bulk of these forces were operating north and north-west of Cape Finisterre, where enemy land-based planes could only remain for a limited time. Incidentally, the loss in June of U.449 and U.119 was attributed to these surface forces.[9]

"… This systematic blockade can become a very serious menace. Having to run continuously submerged because of intensive British aircraft activity, the boats exhaust their batteries, and are then compelled to surface for recharging. Thus the presence of these enemy surface forces will result in considerably increased U-boat losses, since experience has shown that they can be summoned up by the aircraft in an extremely short time…" (345).

The only forces available for combating the blockade were destroyers and torpedo-boats, of which there were no more than five on the Biscay coast. Had they put to sea, the enemy would have been warned by agents within a few hours and could have engaged them in force; furthermore, losses amongst these destroyers and torpedo-boats would have made it impossible to provide escort to

---

9 Correctly.

returning blockade-runners and disabled U-boats. A destroyer raid on the blockading forces was considered from time to time, but it was always agreed that such a risk could only be taken under the most favourable possible circumstances - i.e. with the maximum serviceable forces, adequate air cover and in the absence of enemy supporting cruisers and aircraft carriers - but these conditions were never fulfilled.

Owing to their vulnerability, the available FW 200 aircraft were restricted to high-altitude attacks, which were of little avail against fast-moving surface craft. There was, however, another possibility, namely the *Kehlgerät*, radio-controlled glider bomb, which was steered to its target by a parent aircraft which had not so far been used operationally. Certain of *Fliegerführer* Atlantic's units were already undergoing instruction in the use of this weapon and authority was sought, at the highest level, for its employment against the blockading naval forces. This was granted, but, as usual, weeks elapsed before the order was implemented, and meanwhile the enemy operated undisturbed.

Every possible measure was applied in support of the U-boats and, by straining our resources to the limit, the fighter-bomber patrols were augmented by Ju 88 CVI aircraft, though this restricted the activity of our anti-submarine aircraft to the eastward of 8 degrees West. Unfortunately, the promised Me 410s, which alone were probably a match for the Beaufighters, were withdrawn after one sortie on 15th July, for the defence of Germany. The situation was also eased to some extent by intensifying air reconnaissance of the blockade area, as a result of which, together with an analysis of direction-finding observations, we were able to deduce the current positions and movements of the blockading surface forces, as well as the location and periods of enemy air activity over the Bay of Biscay. These few passive measures were of course inadequate, and consequently, in the first three weeks of July alone, seven U-boats were lost and three severely damaged, including the tanker U.462 for the second time and the flak U-boat U.441, whose bridge personnel and guns' crew were decimated by the fire of three simultaneously attacking Beaufighters. In this latter incident, 10 were killed and 13 wounded, including the commander and watch-keeping officers, and the doctor just managed to bring her back to harbour .

On 18th July 1943, group procedure was criticised for the first time by a U-boat commander from sea, who advised against groups of more than two boats. Though there were now many objections to the procedure, FO U-boats had to be guided by its overall effectiveness and could not therefore concede to this view. Results between 1st and 20th July spoke clearly in favour of retaining the procedure, only three boats being lost from groups, which comprised 75 per cent of the Bay transits, against four from the remaining 25 per cent, which sailed independently.

360. Abandonment of group procedure

The deterioration in the situation towards the end of July transcended our worst fears. Enemy efforts to block the U-boats' outward routes increased in fury. In order to convey an impression of the U-boats' bitter struggle against enemy aircraft, it would be well here to dwell upon a few of the dramatic day-to-day incidents which occurred at this period, including the loss of the U-tankers, which had a detrimental effect on operations in remote areas.

Among the boats approaching readiness for sea were four U-tankers, which were urgently needed in the Atlantic. In order that they should have adequate protection, and also to shorten their time in transit, a destroyer escort was provided. The first group, comprising U.459 and the minelayer U.117, was escorted from Bordeaux to a position 180 miles north of Cape Ortegal, whence, from 24th July, the boats proceeded independently. The second group, consisting of the supply boats U.461, U.462 and the 740-ton U.504, was also escorted without incident as far as 8 degrees West, whence they continued in company. On 30th July, one day after dropping the escort, U.461 reported that, following repeated attacks by single aircraft, the group was being attacked by five aircraft simultaneously, 150 miles north of Cape Ortegal, and requested fighter protection. This was approved, but the nine Ju 88s already on patrol had insufficient fuel to reach the scene of action. The enemy's sighting of the group having evoked considerable W/T traffic on the part of his air and surface forces, the group was immediately dissolved and ordered to proceed independently. It is doubtful, however, if this message was ever received, for no further reports came from the group.[10]

Incidents now followed in rapid succession. On 1st August U.383 was attacked several times and disabled, 240 miles south-west of Brest. U.218, which should have been with her, and U.706 and U.54[11], which were estimated to be in the vicinity, were ordered to render assistance; at the same time three large torpedo-boats were sailed. Next morning, U.218 and U .706[12] reported that they themselves were under attack by aircraft and that enemy surface forces were also in the vicinity, an observation confirmed by our aircraft reconnoitering ahead of the three torpedo-boats. On arrival at U.383's reported position, the aircraft sighted a large oil patch and several British ships heading away to the westward, but when the torpedo-boats reached the spot at about 1600 on 2nd August they found no survivors.[13] The formation had now reached 11 degrees West and, although continually reported by shadowing aircraft, continued in a south-westerly direction to the assistance of another disabled U-boat, U.106, which had been attacked by a Mosquito aircraft at about 0930 on 2nd August and badly damaged. Repairs had, however, been effected, and a limited diving capacity restored, so the torpedo-boats were instructed to pick her up in 12 degrees West at 2000 on 2nd August and escort her back. The U-boat, proceeding submerged, reached the given position at about 1900 and was able to establish, by hydrophone, the approach of torpedo-boats from the eastward. At 1951, however, the hydrophone bearing started to draw away to the northward, whereupon the U-boat surfaced and followed

10 All three U-boats were destroyed on 30th July 1943, two by British shore-based aircraft and the third by ships of the British 2nd Escort Group patrolling the Bay.
11 U.454 had already sunk earlier that day by an RAF Sunderland aircraft.
12 U.706 was sunk on 2nd August by a Liberator of the USAAF.
13 U.383 had foundered the previous night owing to damage received from a British Sunderland aircraft.

up at high speed. We will let the commander of U.106 continue the narrative:

"... 1952: Sunderland approaching from ahead, range 800 metres, medium height. I open fire on her at once and she sheers off to starboard, circling us outside gun range. In order to deny her the opportunity of attacking, I am forced to keep her ahead, so that I gain little on the torpedo-boats. Two minutes later a second Sunderland dives out of the clouds and commences to circle us. On reaching favourable positions, they attack from each bow, blazing with their guns. The one to the starboard is engaged by the quadruple 2-cm; the one to port by the single 2-cm and machine guns. The former turns off a little and drops at least six bombs, which detonate about 50 metres astern and cause severe concussion in the boat. The latter, whose fire had knocked out the layer, trainer and two loading number of the quadruple, dropped her bombs almost simultaneously on the port quarter. The port engine-room switchboard is torn from its securings and catches fire. The starboard diesel stops. Thick smoke fills the boat, which lists to port with a bad leak. Five minutes later the aircraft return to the attack. We engage them as before. The single 2-cm is shot out of action. The bombs fall very close and cause further damage. The port diesel also stops. Both electric motors are out of action. The boat is out of control and settles appreciably by the stern because of the inrush of water. Chlorine gas is coming from the batteries. At 2008 a third attack is made and, since casualties among the guns' crews have been replaced by non-gunnery ratings, our fire is less accurate. The aircraft, engaging with all her guns, drops four bombs which detonate about 10 metres away. The boat continues to settle and the Senior Engineer reports that she can no longer be kept afloat.

"'Abandon ship!' Rafts are manned and inflated. The crew spring overboard with them, except five men manning the AA armament.

"2015: Fourth attack. Aircraft repeatedly attacks with gunfire, wounding several men in the water and shooting up a number of rafts. My guns have run out of ammunition, and I jump overboard with the last five men. Shortly afterwards there is a heavy explosion in the boat and she sinks rapidly, stern first, to the cheers of the swimming crew.

"The aircraft flies over us several times without shooting and then drops two smoke-floats. I and 36 of the crew, clinging to lifebuoys and a rubber dinghy, are picked up at dusk by the three torpedo-boats…"

On 2nd August the departure of U-boats from the Atlantic bases was stopped, while those which had sailed on the previous day were recalled. Groups in transit were disbanded and returning commanders were recommended to keep close to the Spanish coast, if necessary disregarding territorial waters. Losses in the Bay since 20th July had not then been established, but a few days later the absence of boats' routine reports revealed the melancholy truth - of the 17 which had sailed, 10, including three valuable U-tankers, had been lost and one severely damaged. Once again the ratio of losses in groups compared to that among boats proceeding independently pointed in favour of the group procedure, but it would have been wrong to continue with it, since the groups, despite their higher fire-power, were unequal to the enemy's combined attacks and, above all, were an inducement to the enemy to concentrate strong air and surface forces against them. Hence it followed that, even with the addition of the twin 2-cm guns, the boats would be unable to fight their way through the Bay against the enemy air patrols and would have, in future, to sneak through on widely dispersed routes with the aid of a good radar search receiver. Sailings had therefore to be suspended until the *Wanze* radar search receiver became available at the end of August. Returning U-boats kept close to the Spanish coast. The enemy, soon realising this, instituted a close watch here and to the westward, and it was only due to the protection afforded against radar by a steep coastline and numerous fishing vessels that all the boats passed here without loss.

REMOTE OPERATIONS
AND REFUELLING AREAS

361. Better prospects in remote areas

From January to May 1943 there were only five to ten U-boats in the coastal areas of the Central Atlantic, including the Caribbean - just sufficient to maintain pressure on the enemy. Apart from the fact that we had been unable to reinforce them, there had been little cause to do so, since, up to April 1943, sinkings per boat per day were higher in the North Atlantic. But when, in May, sinkings in the latter area fell sharply, it was logical to direct attention to the now more profitable remote areas. Generally, traffic in these areas also proceeded in convoy, but it was more easily found since the routes were perforce denser than in the North Atlantic, and unprofitable group search techniques were thus unnecessary. Herein lay the decisive advantage, for in these circumstances the enemy would be given no chance of detecting from the air the formation of a group ahead of a convoy, and he would thus be unable to concentrate his air and surface forces in time to frustrate an attack. There was also another factor. Convoys in the Caribbean and on the Brazilian and African coasts were not only less strongly escorted, but the escort vessels themselves were regarded by the U-boat crews as being "harmless" in comparison with those in the North Atlantic. Whether this inferiority was due to lack of training or experience or to poor equipment we did not know, but to us it was a recognised fact, and at that time a single U-boat had a better chance of firing torpedoes at a convoy sighted in these areas than had a whole group of boats against a US-UK convoy. But, in view of the rapidity with which enemy A/S defences had developed in 1943, it was impossible to tell whether all these assumptions were still wholly applicable. Even in the most favourable conditions .the boats might be able to fire off all their torpedoes, and those boats which were equipped for mine-laying were therefore ordered to carry mines in addition to torpedoes.

362. Operational plans for the Indian Ocean (group *Monsun*)

The basing of German U-boats on Penang or Sabang for operations in the northern part of the Indian Ocean had already been proposed by the Japanese in December 1942, but this was out of the question until the necessary stocks of fuel, lubricating oil, consumable stores, spare parts and, above all, suitable provisions were available there (346). In the spring of 1943 the Japanese again raised the question of sending German U-boats to the Indian Ocean and requested, moreover, that two U-boats should be turned over to them in order that they might be copied. Dönitz saw no point in conceding this latter request, since he considered the Japanese incapable of building these boats on a scale sufficient to aid the general war on shipping; however, Hitler decided that the Japanese should be given a Type IXC boat in return for supplies of rubber (347).

Whilst there were adequate targets to be found in the Atlantic, Dönitz declined to send U-boats to the Far East. Such an undertaking would have been unprofitable because of the vast distance involved. Moreover, had boats been sailed in April and May 1943, they would have reached the Indian Ocean during the monsoon period and their chances of immediate success would have been small. Nevertheless, on 5th April it was decided that one of the U-cruisers already operating south of Madagascar should return to Penang on completion of her patrol in order to acquire some experience of the base.

In the light of the May crisis and the resulting need to seek less strongly defended areas, the Indian Ocean assumed a different aspect. Here was the only region within reach of our boats, in which, according to available intelligence, shipping proceeded almost as in peace-time and where the defences lagged far behind those in the Atlantic. Thus the moment seemed propitious for extending operations further afield.

Since the northern part of the Indian Ocean was new ground for the German U-boats, their best results were surely to be attained by a heavy surprise attack at a favourable time of the year. So we discarded the original idea of using the six U-cruisers already operating to the south-east of Africa, which besides having only about half their torpedoes remaining would also have arrived in the Arabian Sea in the monsoon period, and Dönitz adhered to his March decision - of which the Japanese had already been informed - to replenish these U-cruisers from a German tanker and then to dispose them to the east and west of Madagascar (348).

The attack in the Arabian Sea was fixed for the end of September, after the monsoon period. It was intended to use six to nine Type IXC boats, later reinforced by the U-cruisers U.200 and U.847, and their preparation was put in hand at once in order that they should be ready to sail in June at the latest.

363. High losses and refuelling difficulties south of the Azores

The prime essential in achieving our planned U-boat concentrations south of the Azores was the availability of refuelling facilities at sea. Previous experience showed that the boats had usually to spend from three to six weeks in the operational area before a single convoy was encountered in a favourable position and this meant that Type IXC U-boats had to refuel once and Type VIIC twice - once on the way out and again on the way back. It was anticipated that difficulties would arise in the refuelling of so many boats, but we were convinced that the task could be accomplished with the large number of U-tankers available. Even if we had been aware of the introduction in June of permanent American aircraft-carrier patrols between the US and African coasts, the operational plan would have remained unchanged, for we could not foresee what grave consequences these new Allied measures, together with the Biscay blockade, were to have for us.

Since May 1942 there had been several U-tankers continually in the Atlantic, of which two only, U.464 and U.116 (a minelayer), had been lost. The tanker situation on 24th May 1943 was therefore most favourable: U.460 was carrying out refuelling tasks to the west of the Cape Verde Islands, U.463, U.488 and U.118 were all outward-bound and U.459 on her way home, while U.462 and U.487 would be ready to sail within two weeks and U.461 in six. But very shortly afterwards the situation altered markedly for the worse. U.463 failed to report clear of the transit area and had to be presumed lost in the Bay at some date prior to 4th June. U.460, after completing her task west of the Cape Verde Islands, had barely enough fuel remaining to replenish three Type VII U-boats and, in order to have her back in the Atlantic as soon as possible with her full establishment of fuel, she was ordered to transfer what remained to U.118 and return to base. The transfer took place 35 degrees West, and U.118 then proceeded to her first refuelling position, 400 miles west-north-west of the Canaries, where, according to a report by U.172, U.118 was destroyed on 12th June by carrier-borne aircraft. Thus, of the four tankers, only U.488 remained.[14]

As the Headquarters plot showed no convoy within 300 to 400 miles of U.118's position at the time of her sinking, we assumed that the enemy, besides using aircraft carriers for the close protection of his convoys, was employing independent carrier groups for general reconnaissance and A/S purposes. This meant that the area between the Azores and the Canaries, extending to 35 degrees West, was now under heavy enemy surveillance. The U-boat commanders were therefore warned accordingly and special instructions were issued to regulate the use of radio and homing signals in future refuelling operations.

The refuelling of group *Trutz*, between 7th and 12th June, had left U.488 with insufficient fuel to meet the requirements of the first contingent of U-boats proceeding to the Caribbean, Guiana coast and the Freetown area: our plan to occupy remote areas with Type VIIC U-boats threatened to break down at the very beginning. Therefore, on 14th June, four outgoing Type IXC U-boats, which by virtue of their small anti-aircraft armament of one or two C.38 machine-guns would have been more vulnerable in the operational area than the Type VII, were ordered forthwith to act as tankers. Of these, U.530 replenished three outgoing and one returning U-boat south-west of the Canaries, while U.536, U.170 and U.535, in conjunction with

---

14 U.463 was sunk on 15th May by a Halifax aircraft NW of Cape Ortegal and U.118 on 12th June by aircraft from USS *Bogue* SW of the Azores.

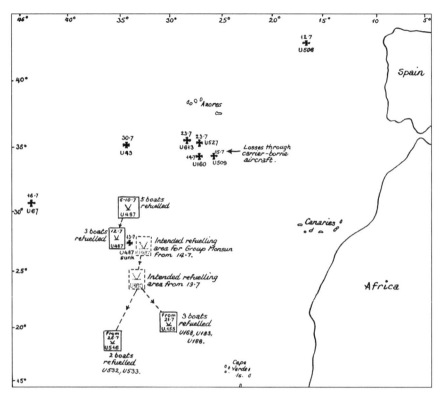

Plan 62. The Atlantic refuelling area, July 1943.
Replenishment of group Monsun

the tanker U.488, refuelled the next 10 Type VIICs close westward
of the Azores. The evolution went off without a hitch, and on 9th
July U.488 headed for base. At the same time U.487 from Germany
was passing westward of the Azores, and this tanker commenced
replenishing the second contingent of U-boats a few days later, 600
miles south-west of the islands.

Nine Type IXC U-boats of group *Monsun*[15] sailed for their long
voyage to the Indian Ocean at the end of June. The tanker, U.462,
was to have proceeded in company to refuel the group 300 miles
east of St Paul's Rocks, while a second replenishment was to have

15 U.188, U.532, U.168, U.509, U.183, U.514, U.506, U.533 and U.516. Two Type IXD
boats - U.200 and U.847 - were also included in the group, but the former was sunk SW of
Iceland, while on the outward passage, and the latter was sunk SW of the Azores, having
been diverted there on emergency refuelling duties.

taken place from a surface tanker south of Mauritius (349). But the plan miscarried when U.462 failed in two attempts to break through the Biscay blockade, being so badly damaged by bombs during the second attempt that several weeks were needed to effect repairs. Group *Monsun*, already at sea, could not wait for her, so U.487 had to take her place and was accordingly ordered to be in position 700 miles south of the Azores by 14th July, to supply each *Monsun* boat, as it arrived, with 40 tons of oil. With this extra quantity they could just make Penang, if for any reason they were unable to refuel again as intended. U.487, which had replenished eight Type VII boats since 6th July, had adequate stores and provisions, but was 150 tons of fuel short of requirements and an outward-bound Type IXC U-boat - U.160 - was therefore directed to transfer all her fuel to the tanker, with the exception of that needed for the return passage. Five boats searched the refuelling area between 14th and 17th July, but there was no sign of U.487. Her loss, which we had to presume, was a heavy blow. Meanwhile it was evident from the absence of reports from two *Monsun* boats - U.506 and U.514 - that they too had been destroyed while proceeding independently through the Bay of Biscay.

It was still possible to replenish the remaining seven *Monsun* boats by employing another outgoing Type IXC - U.155 - as a tanker, in addition to U.160, but now the latter, which had been ordered to a position 200 miles further south, also failed to arrive, so that unless we abandoned the operation entirely there seemed nothing for it but to resort to one of the *Monsun* boats. This we were loath to do, for two U-cruisers, which had meanwhile arrived north and south of Madagascar, were achieving particularly good results, and we therefore expected that the Arabian Sea would offer better prospects.

The replenishment was eventually carried out by U.155 and the *Monsun* boat U.516, 600 miles west-north-west of the Cape Verde Islands, between 21st and 27th July, the latter subsequently returning to Lorient. U.509, however, failed to make the rendezvous, and was presumed lost. Thus, of the nine boats of group *Monsun* only five remained to continue their passage to the Indian Ocean.[16]

In June and July 1943, we lost a total of eight boats south and south-west of the Azores, but the cause of these losses was no longer in doubt, for in addition to several U-boat reports of unsuccessful attacks by carrier-borne aircraft our agents reported that patrolling aircraft carriers had been seen by neutral ships to the west of the Azores. Therefore, on 21st July, all outgoing and returning U-boats were instructed to avoid the area between the Azores and the Canaries.

This surprise Allied action resulted in the loss of two U-tankers and six operational boats within the space of two months, while seven operational boats, which had had to be used as tankers, could no longer be employed in remote areas. Moreover, six type VII boats destined for remote areas had been unable to refuel and had had to be diverted to the Freetown area contrary to our intentions. The enemy had thus achieved a major success and would no doubt employ greater numbers of aircraft carriers in this manner in the future.

364. Operations in remote areas

Those U-boats which in June had been successfully refuelled west of the Azores (Section 354) were disposed off the American coast between Florida and a position to the south of Rio de Janeiro and off Africa between Dakar and the Guinea coast, each boat being assigned a large area and a specific traffic centre. We purposely avoided concentrating the boats, since this would have caused the concentration of the enemy defence. It was left to the discretion of Commanding Officers, having regard to the moon and the strength of the defences, as to whether they should operate close to, or further away from, the traffic centres.

U-boat numbers in these areas reached their peak on 20th July with 30, of which seven were in the Caribbean, seven between Trinidad and the mouth of the Amazon, five patrolling from the north-east

---

16 U.487 was sunk on 13th July by aircraft from USS *Gore* W of Tenerife, U.506 on 12th July by a US Liberator W of Cape Finisterre, U.514 on 8th July by a British Liberator W of Cape Ortegal and U.509 on 15th July by aircraft from USS *Santee* S of the Azores.

coast of Brazil to below Rio, nine off the African coast from Dakar to the Niger estuary and two between the Bahamas and the latitude of Cape Hatteras, where they had been operating since May.

On the whole, initial results were gratifying. During the first few days of July the boats claimed the destruction of 10 ships in convoy and seven independents in the Caribbean and off the Brazilian coast. British records show that seven were sunk and one damaged in convoy and six sunk and one damaged out of convoy. Three more were sunk off Freetown and Lagos. These results were apparently due to the element of surprise, for sinkings began to fall off at once; enemy air activity increased appreciably, and it was soon clear from the Commanding Officers' signals that, faced by air opposition, they had difficulty in maintaining their patrols. Attempts by individual commanders to find traffic off Kingston, Aruba, Curacao, Port of Spain, Pernambuco, Bahia and Rio, and in the Florida Strait, Windward Passage and Anegada Channel had to be abandoned for the same reason.

Aircraft patrols off the African coast were substantially fewer, so that the boats were able to move about more freely, but this did not help much as traffic was scarce. Eventually we formed a reconnaissance line of six boats and had them patrol slowly backwards and forwards in an east-west direction, close to the Ivory Coast, from 23rd July till 2nd August, but nothing was sighted, and we therefore concluded that the enemy was intercepting the U-boats' position reports and diverting his traffic accordingly. He had certainly gained much knowledge in this respect since the summer of 1942.

365. U-tanker losses curtail operations in remote areas

Our assumption that enemy aircraft patrols in remote areas were less effective than those in the Atlantic proved to be false. Indeed, it turned out that most of the aircraft based on the Caribbean and Brazilian coasts were equipped with new long-range radar and that they co-operated well with one another and with the A/S surface forces. Moreover, additional coastal and island air bases appeared to have been established, and consequently the U-boats, though comparatively numerous, were insufficient to split the defences. It was certain that the enemy was well informed of the boats' positions from radio location and also from direction-finding, for which he had frequent opportunities. The U-boat commanders had been warned of this latter danger, but radio silence had often to be broken in order to transmit a situation report, to request a doctor, or when ammunition or equipment had to be transferred from one boat to another. It made no difference whether a boat was located by radar or direction-finding, once located she was relentlessly pursued. Even 300 to 400 miles from the coast the enemy air watch was often so strong that the boats had difficulty in finding time to recharge batteries. One commander reported enemy air patrols as being as strong as in the Bay of Biscay, with radar activity both day and night. It was clear from their radio messages that the boats were successfully repelling many air attacks, yet, although experience had shown that a certain proportion of those subjected to a surprise attack had no time to transmit, the absence of reports from about ten boats caused increasing anxiety towards the end of July.

Owing to the refuelling difficulties already described, the boats in the operational area at this time had only received small quantities of fuel on the outward passage, and we had arranged to provide them with extra supplies on the way home, those from the Caribbean being refuelled by U.459, 600 miles east of Bermuda, and those from the Brazilian coast by U.462, with U.461 in reserve, 400 miles west of Cape Verde Islands. These three U-tankers were, however, lost in transit in the Bay of Biscay in the latter half of July (Section 360)[17] and, as the two remaining U-tankers, U.117 and U.489, could not have met their demands, many of the operational boats had to be recalled, while the rest were instructed to time their return so that they could reach Western France without replenishment. Though refuelling difficulties ostensibly caused us to abandon these areas, it is probable that this step would have been necessary anyhow because of our excessive losses. By 8th August all but five boats

---

17 U.459 was sunk by a Wellington aircraft on 24th July and U.461 and U.462 by Sunderland and Halifax aircraft, respectively, on 30th July, all to the NW of Cape Ortegal.

operating between Dakar and Freetown were heading for home and the last large-scale operations on the fringes of the Central Atlantic had come to an end. Only when our losses were verified did the severity of the U-boats' battle become apparent.

Analysis of U-boat Operations
On the Fringes of the Central Atlantic
20th June to 20th August 1943 (dated 23rd August 1943)

Area	U-Boats		Shipping Casulaties Inflicted By The U-Boats (S - Sunk; D-Damaged)	
	No. Operating	No. Lost	As Claimed by the Boats	Confirmed by Allied Records
US Coast	4 (including 2 with mines)	None	3 totalling 21,000 tons(S), 1 destroyer (S)	3 totalling 21,000 tons (S), 1 destroyer (S)
Caribbean	9	4	3 totalling 21,000 tons (S), 1 destroyer (S)	3 totalling 21,000 tons (S), 1 destroyer (S)
Trinidad to the Amazon	8	3	3 totalling 21,000 tons (S), 1 destroyer (S)	3 totalling 21,000 tons (S), 1 destroyer (S)
Brazilian coast as far as Rio	7	5	3 totalling 21,000 tons (S), 1 destroyer (S)	3 totalling 21,000 tons (S), 1 destroyer (S)
West African coast. Dakar to Gulf of Guinea	15	2	3 totalling 21,000 tons (S), 1 destroyer (S)	3 totalling 21,000 tons (S), 1 destroyer (S)
TOTALS	43	14	3 totalling 21,000 tons (S), 1 destroyer (S)	3 totalling 21,000 tons (S), 1 destroyer (S)

One-third of the U-boats operating in these remote areas had been lost, presumably through air attack, the most dangerous area proving to be the Brazilian coast, from which only one boat - U.172 - returned. Whether the extraordinary effectiveness of the enemy air patrols in this region was due to the employment of particularly fast bomber aircraft or to the efficiency of the pilots, the commander of U.172, *Kapitänleutnant* Emmerman, had been unable to judge. As regards the efficiency of their pursuit of a boat, once sighted, and the offensive spirit of the pilots there was, however, no doubt, as is shown by the following typical incident. U.604, while 150 miles south-east of Pernambuco on 3rd August, was so badly damaged by depth-charges that she was unable to make the return passage home. It was therefore arranged that U.185 should rendezvous with her 500 miles east of Pernambuco on 8th August to embark the crew and scuttle the boat. U.604, the first to arrive, finding lively air activity at the rendezvous arranged a new position 400 miles to the north-eastward, for which U.172 as well as U.185 headed. The boats met on 11th August and, while the two larger boats were taking over fuel and stores from U.604, a Liberator appeared, carried out a determined attack in face of the boats' AA fire and then crashed in flames. U.604 again suffered damage and, as further air attacks were to be expected, she was immediately scuttled and her crew split up between the two returning boats.

366. Refuelling difficulties on return passage

Those boats which still had sufficient fuel to take them to Western France were lucky, for they thereby escaped the danger to which their less fortunate comrades were exposed in the refuelling areas.

Refuelling of the remainder was to be carried out by U.117, 500 miles west of the Azores and commencing on 3rd August with U.66, which was returning from the US coast. Shortly before arrival at the refuelling position, U.66 was attacked by two carrier-borne aircraft, which inflicted bomb damage and numerous machine-gun casualties, including the commander who was wounded in the abdomen. The rendezvous was shifted further northward, but neither boat made it, and it was not until the 6th that they met at a new position proposed by U.66. Air attacks, which again took place during refuelling, caused no damage, but the boats lost contact with each other and a new rendezvous was therefore arranged 200 miles further north, where on the 9th U.66 was forced to dive by carrier-borne aircraft and destroyers. She waited for several days, until finally on 13th August she reported that U.117 had failed to arrive and must be presumed lost. This news was all the more appalling since the tanker, U.489, which should have reported her arrival in the Atlantic at that time, had failed to do so and had therefore certainly been lost in the northern transit area.[18]

Of the 14 boats to be refuelled some were already in urgent need, so that outgoing operational boats had again to be used as tankers and arrangements were made for the refuelling to be carried out between 15th and 18th August, at widely scattered positions.

U.66 finally received fuel and medical assistance from the U-cruiser U.847, which was bound for the Indian Ocean. U.84 returning from the Caribbean was to have replenished from U.760 at the most westerly of the refuelling positions, 700 miles south-west of the Azores, but the latter on arrival there on the 18th encountered two enemy destroyers, which launched a heavy attack on her. U.333, U.571, U.600 and U.618 should have been refuelled by U.525, two of them 700 to 800 miles south of the Azores and the other two the same distance south-west of the Azores, but U.525 did not turn up (she had already been lost)[19] and U.129 had to take her place.

There were still seven boats awaiting replenishment, of which some were now in difficulties and, as a last resort, U.847 *en route* for the Indian Ocean had to be used as a tanker. Refuelling was to take place 800 miles south-west of the Azores, while at the same time some of the survivors of U.604 were to be transferred from U.172 and U.185 to other U-boats. U.185 did not appear, however. The remaining six boats were refuelled by U.847 using fire hoses,

18 U.117 was sunk on 7th August, by aircraft from USS *Card* in mid-Atlantic and U.489 on 4th August by an RCAF Sunderland SE of Iceland.
19 U.525 was sunk on 11th August, also by an aircraft from USS *Card*.

between 23rd and 27th August. Immediately afterwards, the tanker was sunk by carrier-borne aircraft. Thereby our losses in U-tankers and large boats employed as tankers from 24th July to the end of August was raised to seven.

367. Effect of enemy air activity on U-boat minelaying and passage to the Mediterranean

The table overleaf serves to illustrate the adverse effect of enemy air activity on our U-boat minelaying operations.

Of the 11 boats involved in these operations, six were either sunk or damaged on outward passage. Further minelaying operations were planned, but their execution was delayed by the suspension of U-boat sailings already mentioned and by the tardy delivery of both the *Hagenuk* radar search receiver and the quadruple anti-aircraft guns.

The only information we received concerning the effect of the five minefields laid was a radio intelligence report that a British steamship had been sunk off Halifax early in June. We were aware that the enemy took great pains to prevent such information reaching Germany, but the fact that there were no reports at all from neutral sources gave rise to the suspicion that the U-boat mines were not functioning properly. Although no results of consequence could be achieved with such small numbers of mines, they were still expected to compel the enemy to dissipate his resources in maintaining permanent minesweeping and mine-watching organisations at widely separated points on the Atlantic coasts, and if they failed to achieve this there was no point in further minelaying operations. So, despite the fact that there was little hope of really effective operations with the torpedo, few further minelays were planned because of the above-mentioned doubt as to the correct functioning of the U-boat mine.

The enemy air blockade of the Bay of Biscay had a most adverse effect on the passage of U-boats to the Mediterranean. The five boats which had made the passage since April had been insufficient to cover wastage in the area and, in view of the difficulty of forcing the Gibraltar Strait, the next batch of three, which sailed at the end of July, was composed of boats with experienced Atlantic commanders, but all fell victim to the RAF in the Bay of Biscay on their way out .

U-boat	Proposed Minefield	Type Of Mine	No. Of Mines	Date Of Laying	Remarks
U.119	Halifax	SMA	66	1/6/43	-
U.214	Dakar	SMA	15	4/6/43	-
U.117	Gibraltar	SMA	66	-	Sunk by aircraft in the Azores area 7/8/43
U.218	Trinidad	SMA	12	-	Damaged by aircraft in the Bay of Biscay 1/8/43 and forced to return
U.373	Port Lyautey	TMB	12	-	Damaged by aircraft in the Azores area 24/7/43 and forced to return
U.566	Norfolk, USA	TMB	12	29/7/43	-
U.230	Norfolk, USA	TMC	8	21/7/43	-
U.607	Kingston	TMC	8	-	Sunk by aircraft in the Bay of Biscay 13/7/43
U.613	Jacksonville	TMC	8	-	Sunk by surface forces in the Azores area 23/7/43
U.43	Lagos	TMB	12	-	Sunk by aircraft in the Azores area 30/7/43
U.107	Charleston	TMB	12	4/9/43	-

368. Operations off Madagascar

The six U-cruisers, which since the beginning of May had been patrolling off south-east Africa, had met with moderate success. In mid-June they moved eastwards to a position 600 miles south of Mauritius, where on the 23rd they replenished with fuel and provisions from the tanker *Charlotte Schliemann*, sent from Japan. In order that this and future replenishment operations in the same area should not be compromised, the boats were ordered to maintain wireless silence and to refrain from offensive action eastward of 50 degrees East, i.e. within about 600 miles of the replenishment area. Subsequently, U.178 and U.196 occupied the Mozambique Channel, U.181 the Mauritius area, and U.197 and U.198 an area between Lourenco Marques and Durban. U.177 was allocated to the region south of Madagascar, where little enemy air activity was expected and she could use her *Bachstelze*.[20] With its aid the Greek ship *Eithalia Mari* was sighted on 6th August and subsequently sunk. As far as the author is aware this was the only sinking in the war resulting from a *Bachstelze* observation.

This slight movement northward and eastward into a hitherto unoccupied area produced surprisingly good results, 22 ships being sunk by 20th August, mostly in the vicinity of Madagascar. On the 20th, as the last U-cruiser commenced her return passage and just as the first of the *Monsun* boats were rounding the Cape, the enemy air force claimed its first victim, U.197 being damaged by a Liberator and sunk before she could be reached by U.196 and U.181, which were hurrying to her assistance. No survivors were found.

U.196 and U.181 returned to Bordeaux in mid-October 1943, the former after 31 weeks three days and the latter after 29 weeks three days at sea. That U-boat crews should be required to endure an operational cruise of such length would have been inconceivable before the war, notwithstanding the fact that the magnitude of the air threat could not then be foreseen. The physical and mental state of the crew of U.181 on their return bore testimony to the outstanding leadership of their commander, *Kapitänleutnant* Lüth, who, incidentally, was the only U-boat commander to be awarded the *Ritterkreuz* with diamonds (the highest award that could be bestowed upon a German naval officer). Lüth's methods of keeping up the spirit of his crew were many and varied. For instance, "leave on board" was granted to the men in turn, which excused them all duties except action stations, chess and other tournaments were arranged, a

---

20 A kite, fitted with helicopter-type propeller blades, towed by the U-boat and carrying an observer.

newspaper was produced on board and so on, all of which helped to pass the time, particularly during the wearisome outward and return passages.

U.178 entered Penang on 24th August 1943. She was preceded four weeks earlier by U.511, the first German U-boat to enter the base and be turned over as previously arranged to the Japanese. U.51 l's crew remained at the base as spare crew for the boats which were later to operate in the northern part of the Indian Ocean.

METOX PROBLEMS

369. U-boat losses in the Atlantic in July and August heavier than in May

The following is an extract from the war diary of FO U-boats for 23rd August 1943:

"… U-boat operations in the southern Atlantic areas have not met with the success anticipated, but have resulted in unexpectedly high U-boat losses. However, we had no alternative but to occupy these areas, since our heavy losses in the North Atlantic in May had shown that it was not possible to carry on the battle there. If the U-boat campaign was to be continued at all, until such time as the new weapons and equipment were introduced, then all outgoing Type VIIC and IXC U-boats could be sent only to the areas in question…"

The chief object of these operations - to reduce U-boat losses - was not achieved, as is evident from the following table for the period mid-1943.

	April	May	June	July	August
Actual monthly U-boat losses	13	38	16	33	21
Percentage losses of U-boats at sea during the month	11.7	22.2	18.6	39.3	35.6

The table shows that, although fewer boats were actually lost, the percentage losses of the boats at sea were higher in July and August than in May. Of the actual losses, eight per cent occurred in the northern transit area, 35 per cent in the Bay of Biscay, 21 per cent in the area south of the Azores, and 36 per cent in the operational areas. Sixty-four per cent of the boats were therefore lost on their way to or from the operational area. Indeed, just as many were lost on their short passage through the Bay as were lost in several weeks in the operational area, a fact that clearly demonstrated the remarkable effectiveness of the enemy's Biscay blockade.

370. The question of *Metox* radiations

As in May 1943, this sudden and extraordinary jump in U-boat losses (22 were lost between 22nd July and 3rd August) occasioned an intensive and almost desperate attempt to establish how enemy aircraft contrived to locate the U-boats without themselves being detected. So far there had been no conclusive proof of any completely new location system and we were disposed to attribute our inability to detect the enemy's radar impulses to his use of extremely short emissions (350). Faced with this tormenting uncertainty, any information which appeared to provide the least clue to the enemy's location methods had to be treated as important. One such case was a report of an experiment carried out by Naval Group Command West's Radar Instructional Unit and *Fliegerführer* Atlantic's aircraft with *Metox* radar search receivers set up on shore, whereby it was established that *Metox* itself emitted radiations which could be detected at 12 miles by an aircraft flying at up to 500 metres, at 18 miles up to 1,000 metres and at 25 miles at a height of 2,000 metres. The question of radiation by electrical equipment of all kinds, including motors and batteries, had already been examined in 1942 and the figures for *Metox*, as then assessed, were far short of those reported by the Radar Instructional Unit. Now the matter was again investigated by the Director of the Naval Communications Division, in collaboration with the German radar specialists, who concluded that enemy aircraft might be using *Metox* radiations to home onto their targets without having recourse to their own radar.

An attachment to the ASV equipment found in a shot-down British aircraft also supported this theory.

"… Only little can be found in the U-boats' reports to support this assumption; moreover, their observations of protracted enemy radar activity in the Bay of Biscay and other areas are still very numerous. The danger of enemy interception of *Metox* radiations exists chiefly when the receiver is kept tuned to a given wave-length and thus radiates at a fixed frequency. The danger appears to be less if the receiver is searching…" (351).

On 31st July 1943 all boats were advised to employ *Metox* with caution and, in areas where the threat from the air was particularly great, to switch off the set entirely if visibility was good enough to permit aircraft to be sighted in good time. In bad visibility *Metox* was to be used, but constantly tuned through the whole wave-band of 120 to 250 cm. In areas where there was less danger from the air, the use of *Metox* was left to the discretion of the U-boat commander.

371. Ban on the use of *Metox*

The U-boat Command at once started an examination of all the U-boat location reports for evidence for or against the *Metox* radiation theory, while the Radar Instructional Unit carried out further experiments to determine the radiation of ship-borne *Metox*, *Grandin* and the new *Hagenuk* receiver. On 13th August 1943, in the middle of these investigations, which as far as U-boats were concerned yielded more evidence against than in favour of the theory but nevertheless confirmed radiation from ship-borne *Metox*, came the startling news that a captured British pilot had stated that ASV was now hardly ever used by British A/S aircraft, since they were able to home onto radiations from a U-boat. He maintained that these radiations could be detected at 90 miles by an aircraft flying at a height of 250 to 1,000 metres and that ASV was now only switched on in order to check the range.

"… Related to the results of the latest experiments, and to events and U-boat losses in the Atlantic in recent months, great importance must be attached to this British pilot's statement. Even if this is a deliberate attempt to mislead us, especially as the alleged range seems improbable and could only be achieved by a very sensitive receiver, the statement must be accepted as true in deciding on further measures in the present situation..." (352).

The British prisoner of war's statement finally decided us, on 14th August, to ban the use of *Metox* and *Grandin*. This was a grave decision, for it deprived those boats not equipped with radar of their only means of detecting the unseen approach of aircraft, but only returning boats were thereby affected, since none had sailed from the Biscay bases since 20th July. Those which became ready for sea subsequent to 14th August were equipped with *Hagenuk* (also known as *Wanze*), whose radiations were estimated to be no more than one-fifth of those of the *Metox* and different in character, so that there was a probability that the enemy would not recognise them as emanating from a U-boat. In view of the recent experience with *Metox*, further and exhaustive experiments with *Wanze* and the U-boat short- and long-range receivers were instituted.

At a conference with Hitler on 19th August, Dönitz reported:

"... With regard to the deplorable and disgraceful matter of the *Metox* radiations, in retrospect these radiations explain all the hitherto mysterious and inexplicable phenomena, such as the enemy's circumvention of the U-boat dispositions and our losses in the open sea, and also point to the fact that our losses in convoy attacks were comparatively few because *Metox* was switched off. The general view is that a large proportion of our losses is due to *Metox* radiations. Whether this is valid, events will show..." (353).

CHAPTER 8

NORTH ATLANTIC SEPTEMBER 1943 - FEBRUARY 1944

SEPTEMBER 1943 ESTIMATION OF THE EFFECT OF ZAUNKÖNIG

372. New weapons and equipment ready to time

Increasingly heavy U-boat losses in the Bay of Biscay and in remote areas from July onwards spurred us to redouble our efforts in order speedily to end the untenable situation in the Atlantic. Special measures had been needed to keep the production of new weapons and equipment up to schedule, in which respect the T5 torpedo (*Zaunkönig*) caused the greatest difficulty. In the normal course of production this weapon would not have been ready for use until the beginning of 1944, which would have upset all our plans, and Dönitz therefore entreated the Armaments Minister to hasten production. The Navy was thereupon allocated additional production capacity, with a number of highly qualified technicians assigned for the manufacture of the complicated components of the acoustic apparatus, and by dint of further stringent measures and at the expense of other armaments commitments, 80 T5 torpedoes were delivered to the western bases, as originally intended, on 1st August 1943.

The T5 torpedo had not yet been tried out in the Atlantic, so that it was not improbable that, at first, serious failures would occur and that the U-boats would receive considerable punishment at the hands of enemy destroyers; but, in the interest of the earliest possible resumption of operations against convoys, Dönitz decided to accept the risk provided that the torpedoes arrived on board the U-boats in perfect condition. However, the least shock during transport from factory to base could throw the highly complicated and sensitive homing device of the T5 out of adjustment. The torpedoes had, therefore, again to be carefully tested and adjusted before being supplied to the boats. This work could only be done by specially trained precision-mechanics and required special testing apparatus, which was not at first procurable. Once again through Speer's intervention, personnel and equipment were made available, and at the beginning of August the first T5 maintenance units were established in the western bases. Units were also established in the Mediterranean, at Kiel and in the Norwegian bases on 21st September, 3rd October and the end of 1944 respectively.

373. Preparations for the resumption of convoy operations

The U-boat crews had not remained in ignorance of our heavy losses in the Atlantic and it had needed the personal influence of Dönitz and the Senior Officers of flotillas to maintain their fighting spirit. Since July 1943, Dönitz had repeatedly pointed out that the introduction of the new weapons would soon change the Atlantic situation in favour of the U-boats and the *Metox* denouement also served to restore the confidence of the U-boat commanders for their impending battles.

"… 23rd August 1943. Recent months have brought severe reverses for the U-boat campaign. Inexplicable losses have occurred among boats in transit and in waiting areas. Our U-boat dispositions have been circumvented by the enemy and our successes have declined. This we attributed to enemy location gear of a new, undetectable type. It has now been established by experiment and confirmed by the statements of prisoners of war, that it was due to the enemy's interception of strong radiation from the *Metox* radar search receiver. This instrument is now being superseded by the non-radiating *Hagenuk*, with which it is possible to detect intermittent radar emissions on all the principal frequencies. The radar question thereby undergoes a decisive change.

At the same time the boats are being supplied with new torpedoes and a heavier AA armament, thus providing the prerequisites for a resumption of the battle, under new conditions, with all its old daring and determination.

This message is to be promulgated forthwith to all commanding officers, but in no circumstances are details of the new torpedoes and the *Metox* revelations to be imparted to the crews..." (354).

Four months having elapsed since the last convoy battle, it was essential, for psychological reasons, that the next one should prove successful. Since success could only be expected if the crews were familiar with the new weapons and the commanders thoroughly conversant with the combined-attack tactics, officers and men underwent special training courses in July and August. The Commanding Officers were instructed at U-boat headquarters, where they were familiarised with the operational possibilities presented by the new weapons (355).

The U-boats' objective was to remain the same, namely to attack enemy merchant ships, while the new weapons were only to be used to force a breach in the enemy air and surface escorts should the boats fail to approach the convoy unobserved. Opportunities for attack would be greatest if the enemy were taken by surprise, so it was essential that the boats should remain unobserved when taking up formation, when seeking to gain bearing on a convoy and also in the first stage of the attack. Lookouts and *Wanze* had therefore to be employed to the best effect, but, in case U-boat commanders should be over-influenced by *Wanze* warnings, it was necessary to remind them that this instrument was only intended as a safeguard against surprise attack and that they should not submerge unless the enemy was actually in sight. In the second stage of the attack, namely before the arrival of the enemy support groups, there was still no need for the boats to expose themselves; only in the last and most difficult stage was this necessary, if, because of heavy opposition from air and sea, they were unable to reach an attacking position unobserved.

In giving battle to the enemy air escorts, all boats in the vicinity of the convoy were, as far as possible, to engage simultaneously. In contrast to former practice, the boats had now to synchronise their tactics, but unfortunately they had no R/T equipment to facilitate this. The fitting of such equipment would have been a lengthy process, quite apart from which the boats were already crammed with radio sets, radar search receivers and other gear of every conceivable kind. It was therefore laid down that the signal "Remain surfaced to engage aircraft" should be obeyed by all boats and that they should then refrain from submerging in the event of air attack.

It was important that the boats should, as far as possible, assemble evenly round the convoy, preferably in groups of two, and larger groups were to be avoided.

"… Should a large bunch of U-boats be located by several escort vessels, all would be forced temporarily to withdraw from the battle. On the other hand, the location of, say, six well separated boats, or of several groups of two or three, would draw at least six escort vessels from the convoy and thereby attenuate the convoy escort… Two boats in company are better able to protect themselves against air attack, besides providing mutual support in engagements with destroyers…" (356).

The requisite concentration of U-boats ahead of the convoy was to be achieved during daylight, the boats using their T5 torpedoes against pursuing escort vessels, with the object of reducing their numbers, and engaging the enemy air escorts on the surface. The actual attack was to take place at night, when the boats would thrust their way to the ships of the convoy with their T5 torpedoes. Every opportunity for firing torpedoes had instantly to be seized, both when attacking and when being pursued, and hence the few T5 torpedoes initially available were carried two forward and two aft. For attacks on merchant ships, four G7a *Fat* and four G7e torpedoes[21] (two *Fat* and two fitted with non-contact pistols) were carried.

"… The convoy battle will demand more from officers and men in the way of alacrity, courage and tactical knowledge and ability

---

21 The G7a was an air-driven and the G7e an electrically-driven torpedo.

than formerly. But the war situation and dire necessity will inspire everyone to do his utmost…"

374. *Wanze* affords greater security in the Bay

The first large boats equipped with *Wanze* and heavier AA weapons sailed from Lorient in mid-August. A few days later the medium boats, each with four T5 torpedoes, sailed for their first convoy operation. Anxiously we followed their progress through the Bay of Biscay, though we observed a definite improvement in conditions in that area, for, despite intensive enemy air activity, there were very few reports of attacks on U-boats, either from the boats themselves or from Radio Intelligence. The danger from the enemy blockade had also lessened, for, following a successful Focke-Wulf attack on British hunter groups on 27th August, in which remote-controlled glider-bombs were used for the first time and HMS *Egret* had been sunk and a cruiser severely damaged, the enemy naval forces had shown a preference for operations further to the westward. The route close to the Spanish coast continued to be reserved for returning boats without radar search receivers, so that outgoing boats had to traverse the dangerous area north of Cape Ortegal. Nevertheless our losses, subsequent to 20th August, remained at a reasonable level, and it can be appreciated that we attributed these changed circumstances to the introduction of *Wanze*. In a message to the U-boats on 13th September 1943, Dönitz said: "Experience in the Bay of Biscay has shown that the radar situation has changed in your favour", an opinion he was later to revise. However, conditions in the Bay did, indeed, continue to improve, for our monthly losses up to May 1944 amounted to only one or two boats, compared to 15 in July 1943 alone.

In conformity with the established practice of commencing operations on the eastern side of the Atlantic, an ONS convoy was selected as the first target in the renewed attack. We had no knowledge of its route, but it was assumed that, like most of the convoys which had crossed the Atlantic since the cessation of U-boat attacks, it was taking the shortest one, and a decision was therefore made to dispose

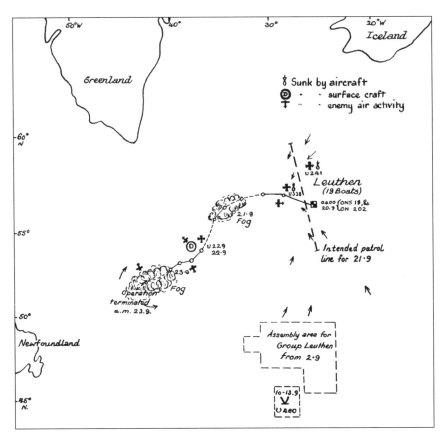

Plan 63. Group Leuthen, 20th-23rd September 1943.
Zaunkönig operation against ON 202 and ONS 18

the boats in line across the great circle in about 25 degrees West, a position which would be reached by the convoy in the afternoon of 21st September. As an additional precaution against treachery, all positions were radioed in the form of reference points which were only known to the commanders concerned. Five boats replenished from U.460 and on 15th September 22 boats, comprising group *Leuthen*, were ordered to take up position by the 20th, unobserved.

375. First use of *Zaunkönig*. Attack on ON 202 and ONS 18

Some of the U-boat commanders were evidently disregarding the order to proceed to their positions submerged, for on the morning of 19th September a British aircraft reported from a little eastward of the intended patrol line *Leuthen* that she had attacked a west-bound U-boat[22] and obtained four possible hits. During the afternoon some indecipherable radio messages came in, which we presumed to have been made by the U-boat attacked. This signal activity was undesirable, since it was bound to betray the presence of the boats.

At 0400 on 20th September, before the line was formed, the convoy was sighted sooner than expected on its anticipated great-circle route. By dawn four boats had reached the vicinity in good conditions of sea and visibility, but only one managed to make a submerged attack during daylight, in which she torpedoed two ships. Contact was then lost because of air activity and the appearance of a surprisingly powerful surface escort. At 1730, U.338 made the prearranged signal: "Remain surfaced to repel aircraft". However, there were insufficient boats in the neighbourhood of the convoy to achieve the desired dispersion of the air cover and U.338 was presumably bombed and sunk shortly after making the signal.

It so happened that ON 202 and ONS 18 had joined company during the day, but as the boats had lost touch we remained in ignorance of this. Contact was regained at dusk, when, despite good visibility only five boats sighted the convoy itself, the remainder being preoccupied with a large number of escort vessels stationed some distance away on the beam and astern. In these engagements the boats carried out no less than fifteen attacks with *Zaunkönig* and reported seven destroyers certainly and three probably sunk. The ships of the convoy were not attacked, because the number of boats which managed to approach it was insufficient to force the inner screen. They merely sank a badly damaged ship which had probably been torpedoed that morning.

We believed that, by sinking so many escort vessels, favourable conditions had been created for a concerted attack on the convoy the next night. But just then the weather came to the enemy's help, fog descending early on the 21st and persisting throughout the day and following night, and though remote touch could be maintained by

---

22 This was U.341.

hydrophone and *FuMB*[23] there were no opportunities for attack, for without radar the boats were blind and could not risk an encounter with the escorts. During the 22nd the fog became patchy and enemy aircraft resumed their activity in the afternoon. Nevertheless, the boats fought them on the surface - their AA fire preventing accurate bombing - and managed to gain bearing in face of these attacks, suffering serious damage to only one of their number in the process.

Just before nightfall, when the fog cleared, five boats were in the vicinity of the convoy and went into the attack, but, coming up against a close screen of remarkable strength considering the large number of escort vessels reported sunk earlier on, they achieved only limited success. Nevertheless, we regarded the reported result - five ships of the convoy and five escort vessels torpedoed - as most gratifying. Visibility deteriorated again in the early hours of the 23rd and, with the convoy close to the edge of the fog area north-east of the Newfoundland Bank and with U-boat crews exhausted after their ninety-hour battle in the fog, the operation was broken off. The convoy was last sighted at noon, but there was no attack.

376. Apparent success of the new weapons

From the boats' radio messages, the result of this four-day battle appeared to be twelve destroyers definitely and three probably sunk by T5 torpedoes, and nine merchant ships sunk by ordinary torpedoes, for the loss of two U-boats.[24] This was undoubtedly a splendid achievement and even better results might have been attained had not fog impeded the second day of the operation. But the real criterion for the success of the whole operation was that, according to their reports, the boats had maintained contact with, and gained bearing on, the convoy in face of an air escort comprising both land-based and carrier-borne aircraft, which encouraged us to assume that the new AA armament had had a satisfactorily deterrent effect. As a result of this apparent success it was decided to employ the same

---

23 *Funkmessbeobachtungsgerät* - see Section 299.
24 Actual figures were; six merchantmen of 36,400 tons and three escorts sunk, and one escort severely damaged, while three U-boats were sunk and three damaged.

tactics in future convoy operations and, in order that the necessary boats should be speedily available for this purpose, on 3rd October nine were transferred from Northern Waters to Western France.

As we shall learn in Section 386, the U-boat Command's conclusions from their appreciation of the boats' radio reports proved wrong, both as regards the efficacy of the T5 torpedo and the effectiveness of the new AA armament. Their mistakes over the former was due to the boats' over-estimation of the number of escorts sunk. According to an appreciation of 24th September 1943, 24 T5 torpedoes were fired, of which 13 were direct hits, three probable hits and seven failures (four of the failures were attributed to their being fired out of range), whereas the actual results, from British post-war records, show three escort vessels (HMCS *St Croix*, HMS *Polyanthus* and HMS *Itchen*) sunk and one (HMS *Lagan*) damaged. The subject of exaggerated claims by U-boats was discussed in Section 251, but their claims in respect of the T5 torpedo arose from new causes which need further explanation.

377. Restrictive effect of T5 firing procedure

As on dark nights, with bad visibility, U-boats and destroyers not infrequently encountered each other unexpectedly at ranges below 1,000 metres, the *Zaunkönig* had to be capable of being fired at very short range. The first of these torpedoes had, therefore, an arming range of 400 metres, which meant that the acoustic mechanism did not become operative until the torpedo had travelled 400 metres. It then reacted to the loudest noise-source detected, principally from the forward sector. At such short range the torpedo constituted a real danger to the firing boat, since it could not distinguish between the propeller noises of friend and foe. Thus, as a safeguard, it was laid down that, immediately after firing an above-water bow shot, the U-boat was to "crash-dive" to a maximum of 60 metres. After a stern shot, she was to proceed for several minutes at her slowest, quiet speed, an instruction all very well in theory but not always possible in practice, for the stern shot was most frequently used against pursuing destroyers and the U-boat had often to "crash-dive" immediately after firing. In either case, if her torpedo missed, the U-boat was likely to be depth-charged and a diving depth of 60 metres was insufficient; the U-boats accordingly sought a greater depth, between 160 and 180 metres. An analysis of the first *Zaunkönig* operation revealed that most of the T5 torpedoes were fired at a range of about 3,000 metres at directly approaching targets, in which circumstances there was no necessity either for a short arming run or for the U-boat to place herself at a tactical disadvantage by having to dive. Accordingly, on 24th September Dönitz put forward a request for a torpedo with an arming run adjustable up to 800 metres, by which the U-boat would not be endangered and should have no need to dive.

378. Reasons for the U-boats' exaggerated claims

As a result of having to dive after firing *Zaunkönig* - an order that remained in force for the first few months of operation with this weapon - the result of a shot could only be assessed by ear and hydrophone. Propeller noises, asdic impulses, torpedo and depth-charge detonations, sinking noises and foxers presented the naked ear with a peculiar, but often impressive, cacophony of sounds. The difficulty of drawing the correct conclusions from these confused noises, in a skirmish with a destroyer and in the vicinity of a convoy, can only be appreciated by one who has experienced it. An examination of the U-boat logs revealed only two incidents from which any valid assessment of the effect of *Zaunkönig* could be made, U.305 and U.666 each claiming to have sunk two escort destroyers, the former in the evening of 20th September and the latter in the night of the 22nd. British records show that HMCS *St Croix* and HMS *Polyanthus* were sunk by U.305 on the 20th and HMS *Itchen* by U.666 on the 23rd.[25]

379. Over-estimation of the value of *Zaunkönig* by the U-boat Command

From the above-mentioned incidents it was perfectly clear to us that the T5 torpedoes had hit and sunk the destroyers. Moreover, the glare

25 More recent research shows that the *St Croix* was sunk by U.305, *Itchen* by U.952 or U.260, and *Polyanthus* by U.952 or U.641.

of the explosion at the sinking of HMS *Itchen* was seen by several U-boats. The remainder of the boats had no opportunity to obtain visual confirmation of their attacks, but the nature and sequence of their hydrophone observations, subsequent to their attacks, corresponded exactly with those of U.305 and U.666. Consequently, Dönitz himself was just as convinced of the success of these attacks as were the U-boat commanders. Hence he also formed too high an estimation of the *Zaunkönig*'s performance.

The fact that the convoy was observed to be still very strongly escorted at the conclusion of the operation appeared to refute the U-boats' claims. On the other hand, the remarkable strength of the escort at the very commencement of the operation led to the assumption that the enemy had been forewarned by French agents of the U-boats' sailing and had provided strong forces in anticipation of the attack, while the additional support groups had been brought up as a result of the sighting of U.341 on the 19th September. The solution was provided, however, by subsequent decryption of enemy signals and the evaluation of the U-boat logs, which revealed that ON 202 and ONS 18 had joined company on 20th September.

For a long time the belief persisted that the *Zaunkönig* had given the U-boats a strong advantage over the enemy destroyers, and it was not until 1944 that Dönitz began to regard the U-boats' claims with reserve. A very great discrepancy existed between the results he accredited to the U-boats and the actual results shown by British records.

SEPTEMBER-NOVEMBER 1943
FAILURE OF ESTABLISHED CONVOY ATTACK TACTICS

380. Brief support from Radio Intelligence

Initially there were fewer boats available for the continuance of convoy operations than there had been in the spring of 1943, so that we had more than ever to rely on Radio Intelligence in finding targets. The requisite data concerning the convoys and their positions was obtained from two high-grade British cyphers, known to the Radio Intelligence Service as *Frankfurt* and *München*. *München* was superseded in April and *Frankfurt* in June 1943, and the breaking of the new cyphers was a laborious task. By the end of September, however, Radio Intelligence had succeeded in breaking into the new *München* and, for the first time, a subsidiary cypher, *Gallien*, so that decrypted material again became available shortly after the resumption of operations.

Let us anticipate here and deal with cryptographical developments up to the end of the war. *München* and *Frankfurt* were again superseded on 1st December 1943 and on 1st January 1944, respectively, with the result that these cyphers were no longer currently decryptable. On 6th December 1943 the British also changed the *Gallien* procedure, whereby the groups, instead of indicating latitude and longitude, gave bearing and distance from reference points with which the ships were apparently acquainted before sailing and which varied from convoy to convoy. Thus, from the beginning of December 1943 no decrypted material was available for current use in operations; in fact, what information there was merely sufficed to provide a convoy's approximate position on the day after sailing, before an impending alteration of route, or during a check on the convoy time-table. But as there were no convoy battles subsequent to February 1944, this absence of radio intelligence was no great disadvantage.

Never again - not even for the shortest period - -did we succeed in re-establishing the same standard of decryption that existed in 1942 and up to May 1943. However, the evaluation and directional fixing of enemy radio messages still enabled us to make deductions concerning the convoys and the strength and location of hunter groups, which were of value to the U-boats.

381. Failure of operations against ON 203, ON 204 and ONS 19
Following the attack on ON 202 and ONS 18, we should normally

have at once formed the remaining boats of group *Leuthen* into a patrol line in the Newfoundland Bank area for the purpose of intercepting the next HX or SC (east-bound) convoy. We therefore assumed that the enemy, knowing our method, would anticipate this and see no cause to divert subsequent west-bound convoys. Weight was given to this assumption by a decryption of 23rd September giving the western part of the ON 203 straggler route (Plan 64) and, as it was only right that we should act contrary to enemy expectations, the remaining boats of group *Leuthen*, reinforced by fresh boats and renamed *Rossbach*, were disposed, on 27th September, across the great circle in 30 degrees West to intercept either ON 203 or ONS 19, which followed.

Several decryptions were received on the 27th, including an amended route for the stragglers of ON 203 running further to the northward, and another, apparently cancelling this and substituting

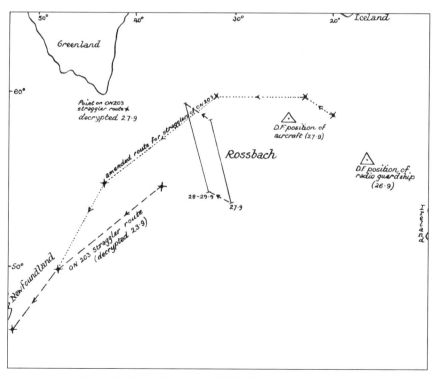

Plan 64. Group Rossbach, 27th-29th September 1943.
Operation against ON 203

a new route still further north, of which only one point - 100 miles south-east of Cape Farewell - had been decrypted. On the other hand, two D/F fixes - of the radio guard ship of ON 203 and of an Iceland-based aircraft which had been attached to the convoy - obtained on the 26th and 27th respectively, indicated a more southerly route. Having learned from previous decryptions that British aircraft were forbidden to transmit information concerning the convoy until they were about 100 miles clear on the return flight, we assumed that ON 203 had lain to the southward of the D/F'd position of the aircraft, but not so far to the north as the point on the straggler route decrypted on the 27th. Accordingly the formation was moved 100 miles to the north-west. Here it waited till the 29th without a sign of the convoy, so that we had to turn our attention to the next objective - ONS 19 or ON 204.

Radio intelligence had shown that for some months past all ONS convoys had been routed far to the northward to allow ships to join from Iceland; for this reason group *Rossbach* was shifted north-eastwards on 1st October and formed into a patrol line between 55 and 60 degrees North (Plan 65). About this time some very valuable data was obtained by radio intelligence. On 30th September two points on the ON 204 straggler route were intercepted and decrypted ((A) on Plan 65); then an intercept of 27th September, decrypted on 1st October, gave a rendezvous for ONS 19 at 10 degrees West for 29th September, this position coinciding approximately with that of ON 204 for 1st October, intercepted on 30th September and decrypted on 1st October ((B) on Plan 65). From ON 204's course of 304 degrees, decrypted at the same time, and from a position intercepted and decrypted on 2nd October, through which stragglers of both ON 204 and ONS 19 were to pass (C) on Plan 65), it was evident that both convoys were endeavouring to circumvent the patrol line to the northward. That the enemy knew the location of the group was simple to explain, for, despite instructions to keep out of sight, *Rossbach* boats had frequently been reported by enemy aircraft during the preceding days and, in conformity with the convoys' northerly deviation, group *Rossbach* was moved in the same direction so that its northern wing reached 63°30' North on 3rd October ((D) on Plan 65). By this time, however, ONS 19 must already have passed to the westward, so, at daylight on the 4th, an easterly movement was commenced with the object of impeding any further northerly deviation by ON 204. During the day, two U-boats reported having observed destroyers and other indications of a convoy on the previous night, but, having been forced to dive at once and remain submerged for a considerable period, they had been unable to report at that time. Thus, the second convoy was also seen to have evaded the group. Pursuit was useless, so the easterly movement was stopped and the boats were sent south-west to form a fresh disposition for the interception of east-bound convoys. Later we learned that, between 3rd and 5th October, three boats had been destroyed, presumably by Iceland-based aircraft. It was most depressing to discover at this radar-dominated stage of the war that, even with the aid of good radio intelligence, convoys could not be located. The war diary of FO U-boats for 4th October 1943 states:

"... This operation provides a further illustration of the difficulty

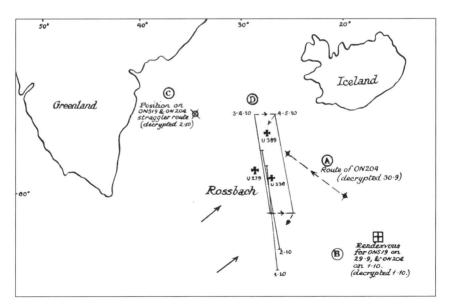

Plan 65. Group Rassbach, 1st-5th October 1943.
Operation against ONS 19 and ON 204.

of interception on the strength of radio intelligence, unsupported by visual reconnaissance. Radio intelligence is very uncertain, firstly because bad weather may cause a convoy to fall behind schedule and secondly because one can never be sure whether or not the convoy route has been altered since the last intercept. Sighting reports provide the only data of value to an operation. Radio intelligence can be of use, but only if it provides more detail than at the present time. Effective reconnaissance by Ju 290, which could have reached the area from Norway, would have had a decisive influence on the operation in question..."

382. Failure against HX 259 and SC 143

HX 259 and SC 143 were expected in approximately 30 degrees West on 8th October, and group *Rossbach* had been ordered to form a reconnaissance line across the 56th parallel by 0001 that day, sweeping south-westwards to meet the latter convoy. During the afternoon and evening of the 7th, while the formation was making for its new position, two east-bound destroyers were sighted on its northern wing and these ships could have been attached to either SC 143 or HX 259, in which case these convoys must have been further east than we had estimated. A search was begun and during the night no less than eight boats sighted destroyers, proceeding singly and in groups, which appeared to be drawing slowly to the north-east. We therefore assumed that the convoy was in the neighbourhood, particularly as a decryption of the 8th showed that stragglers of SC 143 had been routed through the area, and the search was continued and supplemented by air reconnaissance, a BV 222 aircraft being used for the first time. The aircraft reached the area one hour and a half ahead of the expected time of arrival signalled during her outward flight, sighted the convoy at once and commenced to send homing signals, without, however, giving previous warning. Consequently, during her thirty-minute contact with the convoy, none of the U-boats received her homing signals. Group *Rossbach* was ordered to operate in conformity with the aircraft's reconnaissance report, but, despite good visibility and accurate navigational fixes by the

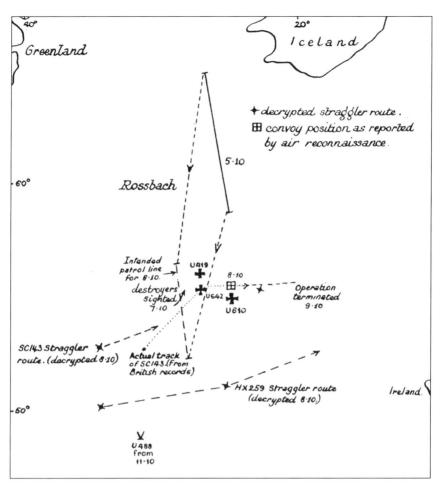

Plan 66. Group Rossbach, 5th-9th October 1943.
Operation against HX 259 and SC 143.

boats, the convoy was not located and the operation was abandoned on the 9th.

Headquarters attributed this failure to a large error in the convoy position reported by the aircraft, but post-war data shows this position to have been exact, so that it can only be ascribed to good co-operation between the enemy air and surface escorts in keeping the U-boats beyond visual range of the convoy itself. Three boats fell victim to air attacks[26] and three further attacks were reported, from which it was clear that the danger from the air was still as

---

26 U.643 and U.419 to Liberators and U.610 to a Sunderland, all on 8th October.

great as ever. The boats claimed two enemy destroyers certainly and one probably sunk. British records, however, show one only - the Polish destroyer Orkan - sunk by U.378. The danger from depth-charge pursuit appeared to have diminished, presumably because of the enemy's respect for the *Zaunkönig*.

383. Failure against ONS 20

On 12th October we decrypted several rendezvous positions for the stragglers of ONS 20 (Plan 67). Assuming that the convoy itself was following the same route, we estimated that it would reach one of these positions - 55 degrees North, 25 degrees West - by the 16th ((A) on Plan 67). In anticipation of this, a patrol line of all available boats - group *Schlieffen* - was to be formed immediately to the westward of this position by 0001 that day. Following the abortive operations against ON 204 and ONS 19, U.584, fitted with *Grenzwellenempfanger*[27], had reported that bearings taken of convoy R/T traffic, on that occasion, actually revealed the direction of the enemy's diversion. So U.413 and U.631 - similarly equipped - were now stationed on either end of the patrol line with orders to report, immediately, the receipt of any such information.

A decryption on the night of 14th showed that ONS 20 was to pass through position 57 degrees North, 20 degrees West the following day, on a westerly course. Group *Schlieffen* was accordingly moved to the northward, but on the evening of 15th, before the boats arrived in position, U.844, outward-bound from Germany, sighted a westbound convoy only 50 miles from the decrypted position. This convoy was presumed to be ONS 20 and U.844 was ordered to use every means to maintain contact, while homing *Schlieffen* onto it. Meanwhile, the group was told to form a new line by 2200 on 16th, calculated to cover the convoy's track, and a few boats, then on their way to join the group and at the time either to the northward or astern of the convoy, were ordered to support U.844. As was to be expected, U.844 was soon located by the convoy escorts and forced

---

27 An intermediate-wave receiver covering the 100- to 200-metre band and fitted with a direction-finding attachment (German codename *Presskohle*).

to withdraw. The finding of the convoy now presented difficulties, for numerous Iceland-based A/S aircraft, which became active on the following morning, kept the boats continuously submerged and contact could only be regained by remaining on the surface. As the boats were widely scattered over a large area and unable to provide mutual support, the question of ordering them to fight it out on the surface needed most careful consideration. At the discussion at U-boat headquarters, in which the author - then Staff Officer Operations - took part, both he and the Chief of Staff expressed the gravest misgivings about taking such action. But the Convoy Specialist Officer, who had recently joined the Staff from sea, and several experienced U-boat commanders just back from operations, were unreservedly in favour of remaining on the surface and were convinced that this procedure would be effective. So Dönitz, who

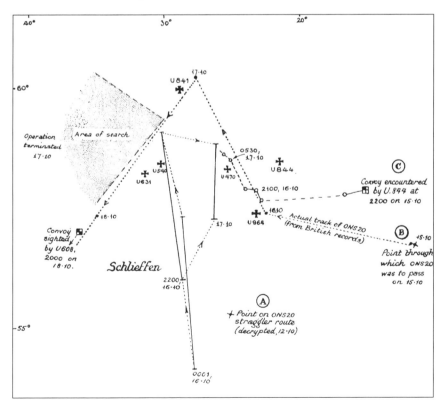

Plan 67. Group Schlieffen, 16th-17th October 1943.
Operation against ONS 20.

valued highly the outspoken opinions of his U-boat commanders, even though they may sometimes have disagreed with his decisions, supported their view, and that morning sent the signal: "Remain surfaced. Shoot your way to the convoy with flak."

Events then took a dramatic turn. Radio messages from U-boats reporting engagements with enemy aircraft, and reports by attacking enemy aircraft (intercepted by Radio Intelligence) began to pour into the Operations Room at Headquarters. Together with reports of air attacks successfully repelled came others of U-boats severely damaged and unfit for action through bombing and cannon-fire, and finally a signal from U.964 reporting that she was sinking. Several boats went to the assistance of the sinking U-boat, but only one - U.231 - managed to pick up four survivors. Despite the gravest fears of further losses, that morning's signal was not countermanded, for the procedure of "fighting it out on the surface" had now to be fully tested.

In the afternoon and evening of 16th October the convoy, which was proceeding more slowly than expected, was sighted for a brief period and attacked, one ship of 6,625 tons being sunk. Group *Schlieffen* was then moved further to the eastward, and the distance between boats closed to 10 miles, but the convoy, instead of maintaining its north-westerly course, altered more to the north shortly after contact had been lost. It was again sighted at 0530 on the 17th, close to the northern end of the patrol line which it was circumventing to the northward, and the whole group was ordered to attack. However, although the boats were favourably situated, contact was lost after two hours and never regained.

Numerous aircraft, which were again in the area during the 17th, continued their attacks on the U-boats as they searched to the north-westward, the boats remaining surfaced to engage them, only if there was no time to dive. In consequence of a convincing report by U.91 of hydrophone contact with a considerable number of ships bearing to south-west, some of the boats turned to the southwest during the forenoon; the convoy, however, was still proceeding northwards and did not alter course to the south until midday. That evening it passed unobserved through the area of the morning's search, by which time the boats were already away to the westward and, to avoid exposing the U-boats unnecessarily to continuous air attacks, the operation was broken off at midday on the 18th. The convoy was sighted once more just before dusk by U.608, which had searched independently far to the south-west, but further pursuit was regarded as pointless.

Of all the U-boats' reports concerning the movement of the convoy during the 17th, two only were correct, and they emanated from U.413, which had twice D/F'd the convoy R/T traffic with her *Grenzwellenempfanger*. Both bearings indicated that the convoy had deviated northwards, which was in fact the case, but no credence was given to these reports, since U.91's hydrophone contact and other data obtained by visual means were considered more reliable.

384. Last operations east of Newfoundland

From information available at U-boat headquarters on 18th October, it appeared that the attack on ONS 20 had resulted in the sinking of one ship for the loss of three - perhaps more - U-boats, but the full extent of our losses would not be known for some days. In the meantime, the U-boats could not remain south-east of Cape Farewell because of strong air patrols operating from Iceland, and those still fit for action were ordered to form, unobserved, a new disposition - group *Siegfried* - by 24th October, 500 miles east of Newfoundland, and to await HX 262 and SC 145. When in position, the boats were to remain submerged during daylight, the intention being to maneuver them so as to gain touch with the convoy in the evening, ready for an attack on the same night. Should the convoy receive strong air protection next morning, the operation was to be broken off.

The boats were in position by the 24th and interception of British R/T traffic and the sighting of carrier-borne aircraft on the 25th led to the assumption that a convoy was passing to the southward of the group. The boats were moved accordingly, but no contact was made. In order to extend the reconnaissance and to mask the disposition on the 27th, the boats were split up into three smaller groups and kept on the move. On the 31st they were re-formed into two larger groups - *Körner* and *Jahn* - and on 3rd November were again redisposed into five small groups - *Tirpitz* 1 to 5; at the same time, four single boats were stationed about 100 miles to the westward to cover the gaps between groups and to give timely warning of increased enemy air activity. Consequent upon the sighting of enemy destroyers and carrier-borne aircraft the groups were shifted several times, but, although an aircraft carrier was once located, no convoy was found, and on 7th November FO U-boats realising that the method of operating hitherto was no longer effective, dissolved the group and ordered the boats back to the Eastern Atlantic.

385. Last refuelling operation north of the Azores

In the period prior to May 1943 - the most successful of the U-boat campaign - the U-tankers had played a decisive role, fuelling as many as 170 U-boats destined for the Western, Central and South Atlantic, and more than 220 engaged on convoy operations - the former south and the latter north of the Azores - without effective enemy interference. Only one U-tanker - U.464 - had been lost in this period, but the severe losses sustained between May and August had reduced the number of U-tankers remaining from 12 to three (two Type XIV and one Type X) and little could be achieved with such a small number.

However, as it was vital that the first convoy operations in September should be a certain success a U-tanker - U.460 - was despatched simultaneously with the operational group - *Leuthen*. U.460 refuelled eight boats of groups *Leuthen* and *Rossbach* in September without incident, and 4th October found her 250 miles north of the Azores refuelling three boats which, having failed to break through into the Mediterranean, had been ordered to join group *Rossbach*. U.264 had just been refuelled when a carrier-borne aircraft attacked down-sun, dropping its bombs harmlessly between the boats.

"... 1205... Aircraft circling the boats at about 2500 metres. Engaged with flak. The commander of U.264 orders U.460 to dive immediately and gives her a rendezvous for 5th October. U.460's upper deck has been cleared except for the 3-7-cm gun's crew. Meanwhile a second aircraft appears on the scene. U.264 repeatedly orders the tanker to dive, warning her that further aircraft were bound to appear.

… 1230. Four more aircraft approach. The commanding officer of the tanker shrugs his shoulders and gesticulates as though not knowing what to do… U.264 dives. Underwater bomb detonations heard and noises as if a U-boat were endeavouring to blow tanks…" (357).

U.460 and, presumably, U.422 were lost in this attack[28], while U.264 and U.455 escaped damage. This was the first tanker loss during refuelling operations north of the Azores and, as the danger of surprise by carrier-borne aircraft appeared just as great here as it was further to the south, FO U-boats ordered that refuelling should in future be carried out only at night; while, in the event of air attack, operational boats in the vicinity should engage the aircraft so as to give the tanker a chance of diving to safety.

After their action with SC 143, some of the U-boats needed fuel for the return passage and, U.460 having been lost, the last remaining Type XIV tanker - U.488 - which had been replenishing some large U-boats west of the Azores, was sent northwards to supply them. The flak U-boats - U.256 and U.271 - were despatched to the refuelling position to provide AA protection. From 12th October, conditions in the area 300 to 600 miles north and north-west of the Azores deteriorated rapidly, and although U.488 made several attempts at different rendezvous to replenish six boats (U.378, U.402, U.584, U.603, U.641 and U.731), some of which were running dangerously low, operations were seriously impeded by bad weather and by repeated daylight air attacks on boats heading for the rendezvous. On 25th October a hunter group arrived at the replenishment area and made a concentrated attack on the tanker, which sought safety by diving to 230 metres and skilfully eluded her pursuers. There was

---

28 Both U-boats were in fact sunk by aircraft from USS *Card*.

now no longer any doubt that the enemy was systematically seeking out the refuelling positions, making it more than ever necessary to avoid the use of radio and homing signals and to proceed submerged by day; yet several boats, particularly U.584, whose refuelling had already been delayed for more than a fortnight, had so little fuel remaining that they were forced to send and request homing signals, regardless of enemy reaction, in order to rendezvous with the tanker in the prevailing bad visibility.

On completion of a minelaying assignment off St John's on 8th October, U.220 was sent to act as a tanker in support of U.488. She arrived in the refuelling area on 20th October, but a week later, having refuelled two boats, she was bombed and sunk.[29] In the event it was not until 8th November that the last of the waiting operational boats could be refuelled for return to base. By that time our casualties through air attack in the refuelling area had reached two tankers - U.460 and U.220 - and five operational boats sunk, and three U-boats, including both flak boats, severely damaged. The refuelling area north of the Azores had therefore to be abandoned. Henceforth, the two surviving U-tankers - U.488 and U.219 - could only be used for occasional refuelling between the Cape Verde Islands and Bermuda (434).

NOVEMBER 1943
EXPERIENCE AND CONCLUSIONS

386. Inadequacy of the new AA armament

Group *Schlieffen*, after searching unsuccessfully for six weeks following the first *Zaunkönig* operation, had on 15th October finally made contact with ONS 20 and in the ensuing attack, during which a further attempt was made to fight it out with the enemy air escorts, suffered a heavy defeat, losing six boats. Whereas the casualties suffered by group *Rossbach* in their encounter with SC 143 early

---

29 By aircraft from USS *Block Island*.

in October were partly attributed to an unfortunate combination of circumstances, those which befell group *Schlieffen* in their attack on ONS 20 could only have been due to some fundamental cause.

On 1st November 1943 Dönitz had been able to write:

"… Group *Leuthen*'s operation as is manifest from the final assessment, was a complete success as regards the assault on the destroyers and the tactics vis-a-vis the aircraft [i.e. remaining surfaced to fight it out]. From the reports of commanders who have returned it is abundantly clear that the air escort was even stronger than was at first supposed. This itself would make the success appear even greater, but it must be assumed that the prevailing fog, which precluded further successes against the ships of the convoy, also protected the U-boats to a very great extent from air attack, and that this was why we lost so few boats in the operation…"

Indeed, reports on the new AA armament, received from sea in September, were very satis- factory, and it was observed that enemy aircraft behaved much more cautiously than formerly, occasionally refraining from attacking a U-boat if she was ready to open fire. As a result, our losses in September dropped to six or 10 per cent of the boats at sea.

From the beginning of October, however, the incidence of air attacks and consequent U-boat losses seriously increased. In contrast to the past, more than 60 per cent of these attacks occurred in the actual operational area - while the boats were surfaced in patrol line, operating against a convoy, or refuelling, it being clear from intercepted enemy aircraft reports, as well as from the reports of the U-boats themselves, that the enemy pilots had overcome their initial fear of the new AA armament and were again relentlessly pressing home their attacks in face of it. True, a number of aircraft had been shot down, while others had probably crashed after making their attacks or during the return flight, but this was of little consequence if they had delivered a successful attack. The AA armament only served its purpose if it was powerful enough to deter or destroy an aircraft before it could attack, and although reports from sea showed that the new twin guns were highly efficient as regards rate of fire and reliability, the 2-cm shell often appeared to be ineffective. There were occasions on which as many as a hundred hits had failed to disable an aircraft, suggesting that enemy heavy-bombers and flying-boats were now more heavily armoured beneath the fuselage. As regards carrier-borne aircraft, the U-boats could apparently hold their own if the aircraft attacked singly, but if two or more attacked simultaneously, the necessary division of the AA armament usually gave one of them the chance to deliver an accurate attack.

The only solution, therefore, was to increase the calibre of the AA guns. Fortunately, heavier AA guns had been under development since 1942 and fitting of the new 3 -7-cm automatic commenced at the beginning of November, with, as far as the author is aware, all boats so equipped after December 1943. They were again in a position to "fight it out on the surface", in an attempt to restore their mobility in attack.

387. Abandonment of the flak U-boat

Experience in October 1943 also permitted a final assessment of the value of the flak U-boat. In addition to U.441 (Section 357), a further six operational boats were converted into flak U-boats in the summer of 1943 (U.211, U.256, U.263, U.271, U.621 and U.953) and used in a few minor operations west of the Bay of Biscay. They had occasionally come into conflict with, and inflicted damage on, enemy aircraft, but had only managed to shoot down two.

Operational conditions had changed since this type of boat was conceived; she could no longer be used in the Bay of Biscay, owing to the strength of the enemy air opposition, nor could she be employed further afield, or against convoys, since she carried insufficient fuel and torpedoes. In fact, compared with the operational U-boat, which in addition to her normal fuel and torpedo-carrying capacity possessed an AA armament nearly as powerful as that of the flak U-boat, the latter was no longer worthy of its title (358). Moreover, the flak U-boat's conversion had made her top heavy and induced a tendency to dip. It was therefore pointless to send the flak boats to sea again, and, on 11th November 1943, C-in-C Navy decided that they should be re-converted for normal operational use.

388. Enemy location and circumvention of U-boat dispositions

Since the resumption of U-boat operations in the Atlantic, every possible precaution had been taken to conceal group dispositions from enemy radar. To this end the boats had taken up their positions either submerged or shortly before a convoy was due to pass, they had remained submerged by day and had changed their location at night, and, finally, the long patrol line had been abandoned in favour of short widely separated lines which were kept constantly on the move. Yet despite these precautions not one convoy was intercepted. At the same time it was established, by Radio Intelligence, that the convoy and straggler routes were being continually altered, some of these route changes occurring in such rapid succession that, by October, we suspected deliberate deception on the part of the British.

With Italy's surrender in September the Italian Radio Intelligence units which, through co-operation with their German counterparts knew of our insight into the British cypher system, were in enemy hands. It was therefore possible that the British were transmitting fictitious routes in an attempt to deceive us, but in the course of the month it became clear that this was not the case, and that diversionary routeing was based on precise knowledge of the location of the U-boats. This applied particularly to ON 203, ONS 19, ON 204 and ONS 20 and to HX 262, SC 145 and HX 263, which had succeeded in circumventing our Newfoundland dispositions to the north and southward. The U-boats had instructions to keep *Wanze* watch while in patrol line and, if radar emissions were detected, to submerge before the enemy radar operator had a chance to identify them; as the enemy, despite this precaution, was still able to establish the exact extent of a given disposition, then he must have been employing a location system which the *Wanze* was incapable of registering.

389. Failure of *Wanze*

Meanwhile, the experience of the boats themselves had indicated the existence of a new enemy location method. In September a group of four boats, bound for the Mediterranean, was frequently attacked from the air without prior warning from *Wanze*. As the boats approached Gibraltar, the surprise attacks increased in number and, as a result of a report from U .667 that she had repelled eight such attacks, including one with rockets - the first experience in the Atlantic - the operation was abandoned. Only U.223, the first to sail, accomplished the break- through.

October saw a large number of surprise attacks, the symptoms in each case being identical to those experienced off Gibraltar; yet it could still not be decided whether all the *Wanze* failures which had occurred since the spring of 1943 had been due to one and the same cause, namely enemy possession of centimetric radar. We had still not recovered from the shock of the *Metox* revelations and were disposed to ascribe these phenomena to an enemy location system of a passive nature. On 5th November 1943 Dönitz commented that enemy radar might have developed on lines as yet unknown to us, or that the enemy might be exploiting electrical or thermal radiations emanating from the boats themselves, but, since there was a similarity between the present phenomena and those observed in the period May to July 1943, the latter possibility was the more likely. That same day, Dönitz, after consulting with the German radar experts, banned the use of *Wanze* and the short-wave W/T receiver, which was also suspected of radiating. Hence, there followed yet another period in which the boats possessed no warning equipment against enemy radar.

Commenting further on 5th November, Dönitz stated that *Wanze* was being superseded by an improved, practically non-radiating set known as *Wanze G2*, the first consignment of which had arrived in Western France that day, and that no further boats would sail with the old type. Simul- taneously, a *Borkum* crystal detector receiver covering the 100- to 250-cm band was, that week, supplied to all outgoing U-boats and also transported by U-boat to those already at sea. The *Borkum* was a primitive instrument when compared to *Wanze G2* but nevertheless gave an adequate performance.

Naxos, an 8- to 12-cm detector search receiver first issued at the end of October, was also primitive in character. At about the same time, a special apparatus, developed for the detection of hitherto undiscovered radar frequencies, was installed in certain boats and manned by additional radar personnel, whose duty it was "to watch for new enemy radar developments". The first of these boats was to sail at the end of November.

In view of the urgency of clearing up the situation, Dönitz, on 7th November, instructed his commanders to seize every opportunity of taking prisoners. He said:

"… Statements by prisoners of war constitute the best and most reliable source of intelligence on enemy tactics, weapons, location gear and location methods. Prisoners from aircraft and destroyers can be of great value to us… Our chief interest lies in the method by which enemy aircraft locate U-boats, as to whether this is done by radar or by a passive system such as the interception of electrical or thermal radiations from the U-boats…"

390. Prospect of future convoy operations

In one respect the new AA armament of eight 2-cm guns had indeed brought a measure of relief for the U-boats by considerably reducing the danger from the air at night; the fire from these guns appeared to have a greater moral effect by night than by day and tended to render a night air attack less accurate. Because of the difficulty of observing the U-boat's course in the darkness, the aircraft's initial approach flight was frequently wide of the mark and, if the aircraft passed close alongside or astern, the U-boat could fire into the unprotected parts of the fuselage at point-blank range to bring her down. At all events the crews had every confidence in the new guns - except in the Bay of Biscay - and Dönitz had no hesitation in continuing operations without the new 3-7-cm gun, provided that every phase of an attack was conducted at night.

Through having to remain submerged by day, the boats needed 15 and 19 days to reach 25 degrees and 40 degrees West, respectively, while their passage to and from the waiting area, alone took considerably longer than their previous average operational period in the Atlantic. Although they put on speed at night, they rarely covered more than 90 to 100 miles a day in Atlantic winter conditions, and this distance consumed two to two tons and a half of fuel, which, in the past, would have taken them twice as far at economical speed. So, now that they could no longer replenish at sea, their sojourn in the operational area would be severely curtailed, which meant, in effect, that still fewer boats would be available in the future.

In these circumstances we had to abandon the Western Atlantic as a theatre of convoy operations and confine our activities to the area east of 35 degrees West, in which the *Luft*waffe could provide support. With the first radar-equipped Ju 290 heavy bomber aircraft at our disposal in mid- November, it would be possible to locate convoys by night as well as by day and to direct the U-boats to their target by beacon signals, while, with radar, the aircraft could carry their reconnaissance into areas dominated by enemy fighter and carrier-borne aircraft.

As regards operational areas, consideration was given to the area west of the North Channel, in which attacks of short duration - one night only - against outgoing and returning convoys were contemplated, and also to the area west of the Bay of Biscay and the Spanish coast. Apart from a few minor fortuitous encounters, no operations against UK-Mediterranean convoys had been undertaken since 1941, for the air and sea patrols in this area had been stronger than anywhere else in the Atlantic and better results could be achieved elsewhere. On 13th November 1943, however, Dönitz commented:

"… Three factors now combine to make a resumption of these attacks appear worthwhile:

1. The introduction of *Zaunkönig*, which will enable the U-boats to remain and hold their own in the area west of the Bay of Biscay

and the Spanish coast, formerly regarded as particularly dangerous on account of the enemy hunter groups there.

2. Long-range reconnaissance by Ju 290s, facilitating the speedy concentration of U-boats on a convoy and hence the possibility of carrying out an attack in a single night.

3. The need to operate in areas close at hand, in order to be able to make fullest use of the U-boats"

391. Withdrawal to the Eastern Atlantic

The withdrawal of the U-boats to the Eastern Atlantic began on 7th November with the dissolution of group *Tirpitz*. Until such time as the boats could be provided with air reconnaissance, it was our intention to try out some other new forms of disposition and group *Eisenhart*, consisting of ten sub-groups of three boats each, in patrol line, was to be disposed so as to cover the area from Cape Farewell to 48 degrees North (Plan 68). This disposition had one disadvantage: there were wide gaps through which a convoy could slip unnoticed. On the other hand it would be very difficult for the enemy to obtain, by radar, a clear idea of its nature and, if a convoy were sighted in a relatively favourable position - e.g. a west-bound convoy on the eastern side of the disposition and vice versa - or if its route were decrypted in good time, two or more sub-groups, depending on the circumstances could quickly combine for a night attack. All this was, of course theoretical, and in practice there were so many uncertain factors that FO U-boats was not over-confident about the results. In the absence of anything better, however, the theory had to be put to the test.

The first disposition, planned for 11th November, covered an area through which 26 out of 28 of the convoy routes decrypted since 1st September had passed, the other two - HX 262 and SC 144 - having passed further to the south. While the boats were slowly forming up, three decryptions were received from Radio Intelligence - a point on the route of ON 210, a rendezvous for ONS 22 and the HX 264 straggler route, decrypted respectively on 7th, 8th and 11th November (Plan 68(A), (B) and (C)). The fact that these convoys were taking a southerly route was significant and it was possible that the Atlantic routes, generally, were being shifted southwards, where they could now be covered by the newly established Allied air bases in the Azores. Certainly, this southward shifting of routes at the commencement of the winter gales was of advantage to the enemy, and FO U-boats therefore deemed it advisable to act on the Radio Intelligence reports, moving the whole of group *Eisenhart* 350 miles to the south-eastward on 12th November and a further 125 miles in the same direction on the next day. Thus the boats wheeled round from north-east to south-east before having assumed the disposition ordered on 7th November. On 15th November we decrypted an approach position for SC 146 and HX 265, 200 miles west of Ireland (Plan 68(D)), while, on the same day, several aircraft escorting these convoys were D/F'd 400 miles north of the Azores (Plan 68(E)). Assuming that these convoys must lie somewhere between these two points, FO U-boats ordered all boats within range to search independently in the intervening area. However, although

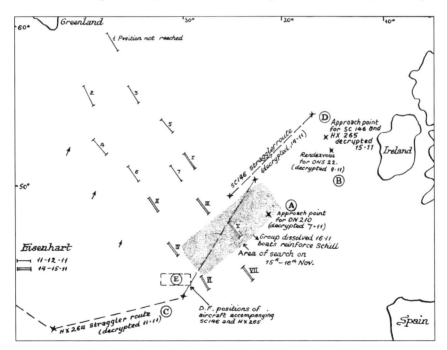

Plan 68. Group Eisenhart, 11th-16th November 1943.
Operation against HX 264, ON 210 and ONS 22.

a few destroyers and aircraft - possibly attached to hunter groups - were encountered, neither convoy was located, and as by this time the boats had insufficient fuel to continue the operation as intended, they were sent on the 16th to reinforce group *Schill* in its attack on MKS 30, to the west of Spain.

392. Operations against MKS 28 and 29

Between 27th October and 10th November two small-scale convoy operations took place to the west of Spain. It was evident, from our heavy defeat in the action against ONS 20, that a mobile attack on a convoy was still beyond our capabilities, and we therefore decided to sail eight boats simultaneously from Biscay bases for a one-night attack on an MKS or a KMS convoy off the northwest Spanish coast. The group - *Schill* - which included three flak U-boats whose fuel capacity precluded their operating on the transatlantic routes, was formed into a patrol line on 27th October, 400 miles west of Cape Ortegal, in readiness for an attack on MKS 28. As radar-equipped FW 200 aircraft were available for reconnaissance, we hoped to receive a continuous series of reconnaissance reports which would enable us to manoeuvre the group so as to make contact with the convoy at dusk on 29th November.

The convoy was sighted by the aircraft on the 27th and 28th, but on the 29th - the vital day - no sighting was made, although reconnaissance was flown both in the forenoon and afternoon. The convoy had made a slight deviation and slipped to the westward. It was again sighted from the air next day to the north-west of the group and, contrary to his original intention, FO U-boats ordered the boats in daylight pursuit, which to our surprise resulted in a contact. At dawn on 31st, U.262 carried out a submerged attack on three large ships and a destroyer and having heard unmistakable torpedo detonations after the appropriate intervals reported four hits. We thus regarded the operation as a success and were encouraged to repeat these tactics; however, it is now known from British records that only one ship of 2,968 tons was sunk in the attack.

From 3rd to 5th November group *Schill* moved slowly southwards between 18 and 23 degrees West, awaiting a KMS convoy. Air reconnaissance in search of MKS 29 commenced on 5th and the first sighting was made on the 7th, group *Schill* thereupon being disposed so that the convoy, if it kept to its last reported course, would pass through the formation in the evening of the 8th. In order to ensure the location of the convoy on that day, reconnaissance was to be flown by three FW 200s, both in the forenoon and afternoon, and on sighting the convoy the aircraft were to direct the U-boats to the target by means of beacon signals. But one aircraft had to drop out of the forenoon flight because of engine trouble, and another in the afternoon because of a radar defect, with the result that, for a second time, the convoy was not sighted on the decisive day. On the evening of the 8th, group *Schill*, in scouting formation, proceeded south-west at high speed, sighting occasional destroyers but no merchant ships, and it became apparent that the convoy had passed through a gap in the line. When air reconnaissance found it again next morning, the U-boat commanders were given a free hand, two boats searching

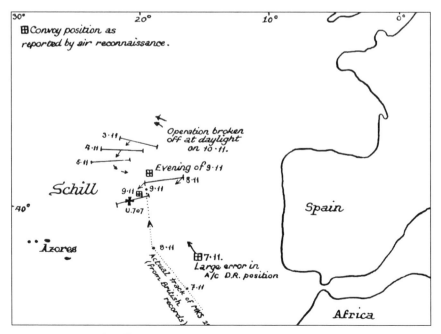

Plan 69. Group Schill, 3rd -10th November 1943.
Operation against MKS 29.

without success until the following morning, when the operation was abandoned. These experiences confirmed our conclusions of 1941, namely, that air co-operation could only be successful if sufficient long-range aircraft were available for prolonged and concentrated reconnaissance, together with adequate reserves of aircraft and equipment.

393. Complete failure against MKS 30 and SL 139

In subsequent operations against MKS and KMS convoys it was intended to form the boats into at least two groups, in patrol lines disposed on a quarterly bearing at distances equivalent to a day's run, and it was thus hoped to have one group drawn up ahead of the convoy, with the other available for searching, should air reconnaissance fail. However, aircraft were available for the next operation, and reconnaissance was flown by up to three machines daily, including Ju 290s for the first time. They first sighted the convoy on 15th November, two days after it had left Gibraltar, and single sightings were made on each of the two succeeding days. Apparently, MKS 30 and SL 139 had joined company, for 67 ships were reported. It so happened that the air shadowing reports took longer to reach FO U-boats than the decryptions of enemy signals reporting the shadowing aircraft and, as the decrypted positions appeared to be more accurate than those reported by our aircraft, FO U-boats based his tactics on the former. Group *Schill* 1, consisting of seven boats, was therefore disposed so that the convoy would reach it in the evening of the 18th. Meanwhile, the remaining boats of group *Eisenhart*, which on 16th November had been sent as reinforcements, were ordered to form groups *Schill* 2 and 3 at the positions through which the convoy was expected to pass on 19th and 20th respectively.

During the forenoon of the 18th, air reconnaissance reported a convoy south-east of group *Schill* 1 at 0945, from which it appeared that our quarry was about to slip by to the eastward, and the boats, which were keeping watch on long wave on a half-hourly routine, were immediately instructed to proceed submerged to the north-east.

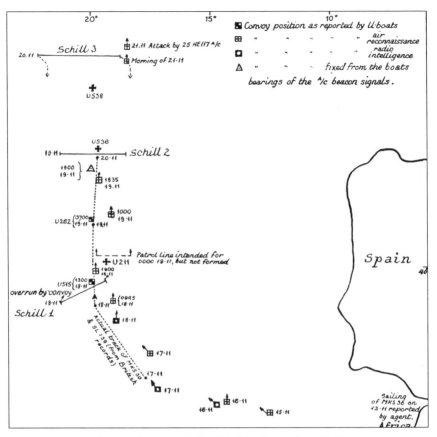

Plan 70. Group Schill, 15th-21st November 1943.
Operation against MKS 30 and SL 139

At 1500 the convoy was reported by air reconnaissance to be still further to the eastward, whereupon the boats were ordered to surface at 1830 and search at high speed, in broad zigzags, to the north-east, forming a new east-west patrol if no contact had been made by midnight. The convoy's 1930 position, given by the relief aircraft, lay further westward than the two positions previously reported by its predecessor, which persuaded us that the convoy had passed through the patrol line during the day. This indeed proved correct, for at about 2300, U.515 reported having been overrun by the convoy at 1300. The convoy was therefore already far ahead and, although the boats followed up at high speed, they were greatly impeded by night-flying aircraft, only one boat - U.262 - making contact just

94

before dawn and being immediately driven off. The remainder were so far astern that further pursuit was pointless and they were ordered to submerge.

On receipt of U.515's message, group *Schill* 2 was moved farther north to ensure its being ahead of the convoy on surfacing on the evening of the 19th. This time air co-operation worked well, for when the boats surfaced at 1830 a Ju 290 was in contact with the convoy and her homing signals were picked up by six boats, cross D/F bearings giving them an accurate fix 20 miles south of the centre of the patrol line. Yet, despite these favourable initial conditions the night ended with complete failure, for the enemy, by the skilful employment of his escort vessels and incessant night air attacks, had kept the U-boats at a distance and forced them to submerge for long periods. In anticipation of intensified enemy air activity, the boats of group *Schill* 2 were ordered to dive at dawn and so our intention of using one group of U-boats to direct another on to the target - the basis of the whole operation - could not be realised.

Air reconnaissance flown on the moring of 20th November, in support of group *Schill* 3, failed to locate the convoy. Of the two aircraft of the morning flight, one was shot down near Cape Ortegal, while the other developed a radar defect. The evening reconnaissance also failed, the one available aircraft being shot down over the Bay of Biscay. The two aircraft lost had been victims of a well organised system of heavy fighter patrols. A strong northerly wind, which had been blowing since the morning, was expected to slow down the convoy on its passage north and so, after surfacing in the evening, group *Schill* 3 was ordered to make towards the convoy, first on a south-easterly and later on a southerly course. During the night the boats sighted occasional destroyers, which fired starshells, and numerous aircraft, of which two, a Sunderland and a four-engined bomber, were shot down while attacking. But the convoy itself was not found and we presumed that it had passed through a gap in the line allocated to two boats which, unbeknown to us, had been lost weeks previously. The group submerged again at daylight.

When, on the morning of the 21st, the convoy was again located, *Fliegerführer* Atlantic sent 25 He 177s to the attack, the aircraft, two of which failed to return, claiming to have sunk two large ships and to have damaged three others.[30] Considering that these aircraft were operating for the first time at a range of 800 miles from base, we regarded the attack as a complete success; moreover, it revealed possibilities of practical co-operation between aircraft and U-boats in convoy attacks. Although there was little prospect of this in the subsequent months because of the limited range of the He 177, we hoped that this first successful attempt would inspire the *Luftwaffe* to further operations of the same nature; but this was not to be, for the He 177s were transferred shortly afterwards to the Mediterranean.

Group *Schill*'s operation ended in complete failure, one boat of each sub-group being lost for the torpedoing of only one ship - HMS *Chanticleer*[31] - and the destruction of two enemy aircraft. Though the boats had had bad luck and had suffered through inadequate air reconnaissance, the chief reason for their failure lay elsewhere:

"… The second, and particularly the third, night of the attack showed that in this area the enemy, having once located the U-boats, is able to engage them speedily and effectively with numerous night-flying aircraft and strong surface escort forces… The next operation in this area must therefore be planned for one night only, the disposition being as close as possible, so that a large number of boats may be concentrated round the convoy…"

394. Lessons of the MKS convoy operations

This last operation again demonstrated the impossibility of conducting proper reconnaissance and U-boat direction with only a handful of aircraft. The convoy's position had to be established not once or twice in 24 hours, but every four hours at least, otherwise it was impossible to maneuver the submerged U-boats ahead of the convoy in time, or to counter a diversionary change of course. While

---

30 One ship of 4,405 tons was sunk and one other damaged, both by glider-bombs.
31 HMS *Chanticleer* was seriously damaged aft by an acoustic torpedo and was towed to Horta, Azores, where she became depot ship under the new name of *Lusitania II*.

it was gratifying to confirm that our aircraft were able, with their radar, to maintain contact with a convoy at night, it was unfortunate that beacon signals alone did not indicate the convoy position with sufficient accuracy for the U-boats, which at night had to rely exclusively on visual sighting. A visual aid was needed, such as a marker-bomb, which could be recognised by the U-boats but could not be imitated by the enemy; moreover, a signal of this kind was the only means of countering the enemy's diversionary starshell fire. The U-boats' successes against enemy aircraft were remarkable, particularly on the last night of the battle, when quite a number of air attacks were repelled and two aircraft were shot down, with one or two sending out distress signals on their return flight. In summing up the battle, we presumed that, in order to preclude attacks on damaged ships of the convoy, enemy aircraft in the vicinity had been instructed first to identify their target as a U-boat. Since this required a preliminary approach flight, the U-boats had been well prepared to receive the aircraft on its second run.

The reasons for the poor results against the ships of the convoy were obvious. The U-boats had been seriously impeded by air and sea escorts of unprecedented strength and, in the nocturnal melee, had failed to gain bearing through having to take avoiding action against air and surface radar, diving because of the approach of aircraft or destroyers, fighting off aircraft, operating *Aphrodite* and so on. The convoy's outer screen had doubtless been reinforced by units of the hunter groups operating in the western part of the Bay of Biscay, and none but U.262 managed to force it, despite the use of the T5 torpedo, which had, however, failed to come up to expectations. It was now decided that subsequent Atlantic-bound U-boats should be sent to the west of the British Isles, where enemy surveillance was less intense, in an attempt to carry out further "one-night" attacks.

395. Operations against MKS 31 and SL 140

On the evening of 23rd November the remaining fourteen boats of groups *Schill* 1 to 3 were drawn up in patrol line - *Weddigen* - between 18 and 22 degrees West. On 22nd and 23rd November air reconnaissance was flown in the area to the north of the group, in search of KMS 33 and OS 59, but one of the two aircraft which took off on the 23rd had to return because of engine trouble and the other had a radar defect, so nothing was sighted. The convoy could still have been to the northward of the disposition, but it was thought more likely to have hauled farther to the westward to keep out of range of the He 177s, and group *Weddigen* was therefore moved at high speed to the south-west. During this movement a considerable number of enemy destroyers were sighted, which we presumed to have been attached to a hunter group and, when no indication of the convoy's approach had been received by the next evening, the group was shifted to the south-eastward in readiness for an attack on MKS 31 and SL 140.

This convoy was sighted by air reconnaissance on 26th November steering a westerly course, and the group was moved accordingly, but

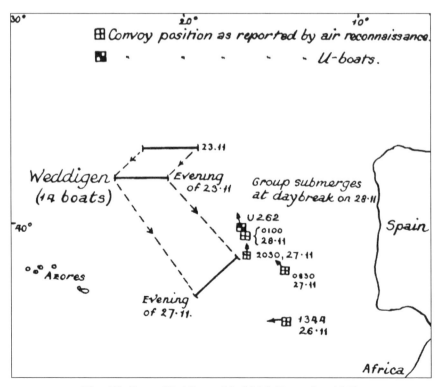

Plan 71. Group Weddigen, 23rd-28th November 1943.
Operation against MKS 31 and SL 140.

as soon as the aircraft had headed for the base the convoy apparently altered course to the north, for when sighted from the air at 0830 next day it was to the eastward of the formation. The boats now proceeded submerged to the north-east, surfacing in the evening to take up the pursuit at high speed, and a BV 222 aircraft shadowed the convoy from 2030 to 0130. However, although her homing signals were picked up, the bearings were too acute for an accurate fix. Weather conditions were favourable, but the boats, harrassed by enemy aircraft and destroyers, made little headway, many of them presumably being misled and delayed by large numbers of enemy starshell, which, it was now obvious to us, the enemy deliberately used to create a diversion. Just before dawn the convoy passed over U.262, which surfaced between the lines and carried out an attack. On the strength of her report she was credited with four ships; British records, however, show that no ships were sunk in this attack. The operation was broken off on 28th November, when the remaining boats of group *Weddigen* were moved in patrol line to the north-west as far as 25 degrees West, and, after an unsuccessful minor operation on 6th December against a southbound convoy sighted fortuitously by a returning U-boat, the group was dissolved.

DECEMBER 1943-FEBRUARY 1944
ABANDONMENT OF OPERATIONS WEST OF THE BRITISH ISLES

396. Last use of patrol line and scouting formation

At the beginning of December 1943 a large number of U-boats, chiefly from German bases, had assembled off the North Channel and from 5th to 15th December they operated between 20 and 35 degrees West, as group *Coronel*, against ONS 24, HX 268 and ON 215. Air reconnaissance, flown during this period by a maximum of two to three aircraft daily, failed to locate any of the expected convoys. On the 15th all available reconnaissance aircraft were sent west of the

Bay of Biscay to reconnoitre for three returning blockade-runners. In order to make use of this reconnaissance, group *Coronel* 3, which had gone far south in search of ONS 25, was moved - as group *Borkum* - into the area west of Cape Ortegal (Section 397). The remaining boats continued to search for convoys west of the British Isles, initially in three groups - *Sylt*, *Antrum* and *Föhr* - and from 22nd December in six sub-groups of three boats each - *Rügen* 1 to 6. Instead of remaining in one position, these groups kept constantly on the move, changing their relative positions and opening out and closing in, so as to prevent the enemy from establishing the exact extent of the dispositions and leaving him only to perceive that the boats were scattered over a wide area. Actually this procedure brought some success, for as soon as the groups started to open out several convoys were encountered - two westbound, on 23rd and 30th December, and an east-bound on the 26th - but in no case could we achieve our object of attacking with a minimum of three boats. Thus the sole remaining argument in favour of disposition in small groups was disproved (359).

On 7th January 1944 these groups were dissolved and the boats were allocated, singly, to attack areas west of the British Isles. This step signalled the abandonment of the patrol line and scouting formation for convoy interception, except when air reconnaissance was available. The fact that the virtual discontinuance of pack attacks would further diminish our prospects of success had to be accepted, and henceforth the individual U-boat would generally have to cope single-handed with the entire convoy escort and bear the brunt of its counter-attack.

It was to be expected that convoys everywhere in the Atlantic would be preceded by strong air reconnaissance forces, so that, as the U-boats had no means of evading their radar, the enemy would detect and avoid them no matter what their disposal. In future, therefore, pack attacks by existing and projected types of U-boat could only be carried out with any prospect of success if continuous air reconnaissance were available to direct them on to their objective (360).

397. Success against hunter-killer groups

From 20th December air reconnaissance was flown daily, west of the Bay of Biscay, for the returning blockade-runners *Osorno*, *Alsterufer* and *Regensburg*, and as a KMS convoy was expected to pass through the area at this time, group *Borkum* was drawn up in patrol line 400 miles north-west of Cape Ortegal. Reconnaissance by four FW 200 and one BV 222 aircraft on the 20th produced no result, three of the aircraft having developed radar defects, but on the 22nd and 23rd several sightings were made of an escorted aircraft carrier, apparently on patrol and, in view of this threat to the blockade-runners, group *Borkum* was ordered to attack the carrier. The boats sighted her on the night of the 23 rd and managed to carry out several attacks on the escorting destroyers, of which they claimed to have sunk four. British records show, however, that only one escort - HMS *Hurricane* - was sunk on 24th. Three days later, on 27th December, the destroyers and torpedo-boats which had been sent to escort the returning blockade-runners met up with a force of British cruisers, 200 miles north-west of Cape Ortegal, and in the ensuing action we lost one destroyer and one torpedo-boat, from which 55 survivors, including the commanding officer of T.25, were picked up by four U-boats.

Group *Borkum* was subsequently shifted from one position to another between 20 and 25 degrees West and made several contacts with hunter-killer groups, the U-boats using their T5 torpedoes to good effect in torpedoing five destroyers, of which two were reported sunk.[32]

On 8th January 1944, on completion of their reconnaissance on behalf of the blockade-runners, the aircraft operated once again in support of group *Borkum* in its search for MKS 35 and, by a strenuous effort *Fernaufklärungsgruppe* 5 managed to provide two Ju 290s daily for four successive days. The convoy was sighted once on the 9th, but on the 10th - the vital day - the aircraft's radar broke down and there was no further sighting. That evening, U.305 at the extreme

---

32 No Allied destroyers were sunk in these engagements.

end of the patrol line made chance contact with the convoy and the group was ordered to attack, but as the boats had been disposed at wide intervals none succeeded in closing the enemy. The dissolution of group *Borkum* on 13th January marked the end of our attempts against convoys proceeding north and south between Spain and the Azores.

398. Further plans for U-boat / *Lufwaffe* co-operation

In none of the combined U-boat/*Luftwaffe* operations carried out since October 1943 had the U-boats been successfully directed to their objective. A paucity of aircraft was the root cause of this unsatisfactory state of affairs, as can be appreciated from the fact that the forces at the disposal of *Fliegerführer* Atlantic in mid-November comprised two BV 222s, six Ju 290s and 19 FW 200s, of which only part were operational at any one time, while the FW 200, owing to its inferior armament, could only be used at night. As a result, a mere 68 reconnaissance flights were made in the period 15th November to 18th December - an average of two a day - which was less than the RAF Coastal Command often flew in a single day (361).

Although it was clear to Dönitz that, even with air support, the current-type U-boats could no longer achieve any consequential results, he notified *Fliegerführer* Atlantic and the *Luftwaffe* that he intended to continue with these combined operations in the succeeding weeks. His reasons for this were, firstly, that experience of co-operation with aircraft had to be gained in order that it could be applied to the training of the new-type U-boats and secondly, that, having for the past year impressed upon Göring the need for air reconnaissance and persuaded Hitler to prevail upon him to develop aircraft suitable for the purpose, he could not possibly declare that he did not at the present time need air reconnaissance since the U-boats were unequal to their task. Had he done so, Göring, whose resources were also strictly limited, would have welcomed such an excuse for restricting his efforts on behalf of the Navy, with the result that, when the U-boat campaign was resumed at the end of 1944, there would be a dearth of long-range reconnaissance aircraft and trained air crews.

399. Reduced stability restricts U-boats' range of vision

The execution of our projected operations had to wait until *Fliegerführer* Atlantic had sufficient aircraft for sustained reconnaissance to the west of the North Channel, lasting for several days. Meanwhile the boats on patrol (group *Rügen*) remained disposed singly, in 20- to 40-mile wide attack areas between 50 and 61 degrees North and 18 and 24 degrees West, moving by day at periscope depth, or at a suitable depth for hydrophone listening, so as to be able to receive W/T messages on long wave. The commanders had the following order:

"… If by day the enemy is sighted through the periscope or located by hydrophone, boats are either to attack at once, or surface to gain bearing and make an enemy report. Contrary to previous practice, however, they are to break off the operation and submerge on the appearance of strong enemy air forces, or if weather conditions are such as to hinder the fighting of the anti-aircraft armament or expose the boat to danger of surprise attack through low cloud. If there is a possibility of catching up with the target that night, boats are to pursue at high speed.

If a sighting is made at night, boats are to press home their attack regardless of enemy radar or air opposition.

On receipt of an enemy report by day or night, all boats favourably situated are to make every effort to gain contact with the enemy, operating in the manner laid down for the single boat" (362).

The additional AA armament and bridge armour had made the Type VIIC U-boat top-heavy, and in bad weather the average roll reached 30 degrees each side, with a maximum roll of 60 degrees not unusual, which imposed a severe physical strain on the crews, particularly the bridge personnel, while also considerably diminishing the range of vision from the boat at night.

On 14th January 1944, after several changes of position, the boats were brought closer in to the North Channel, where the enemy air and sea defences proved tolerable and the boats managed to close in slowly as far as 15 degrees West. From the few sightings and Radio

Intelligence reports, it was apparent that the enemy forces were evenly distributed over the whole area and not concentrated at specific points and that convoys were circumventing the U-boat disposition to the north and south. For this reason the boats on the northern and southern wings of the disposition were wheeled, respectively, to the south-east and north-east, so as to form a semicircle round the North Channel covering the presumed outward and return routes of the convoys. Yet, despite this precaution, contacts with the enemy remained few, and it is certain that many single ships and convoys passed the U-boat disposition unnoticed.

400. Failure against a KMS convoy because of inadequate air support

In January 1944 *Fliegerführer* Atlantic received reinforcements bringing his force up to 11 Ju 290s, two BV 222s and four long-range Ju 88s, and air reconnaissance was started on the 20th of that month to the west of the British Isles. On the 26th a KMS convoy was sighted west of the North Channel, and eight of the southern boats of group *Rügen* were formed into a patrol line - *Hinein* - at the position through which the convoy was expected to pass at sunset on the next day. As there could also have been an ONS convoy to the westward of the British Isles, the remainder of the *Rügen* boats were hurriedly assembled - as group *Stürmer* - in a smaller area north-west of the North Channel. *Fliegerführer* Atlantic was requested to report the convoy's position at regular intervals, so that we could detect any deviation in good time, but the radio transmitter of the Ju 290 that flew the night reconnaissance on 26th/27th January broke down, and it was not until 1600 on the 27th that we received the convoy's 0450 and 0955 positions, indicating a pronounced westerly course. Had the first position been transmitted when it should have been, we could have had time to move the patrol line ahead of the convoy under cover of darkness; now, on receipt of a radio message from the relief aircraft, giving the convoy's position at 1529 as still further west, those boats carrying 3-7-cm AA guns were ordered to surface and close the convoy at high speed, so that they should

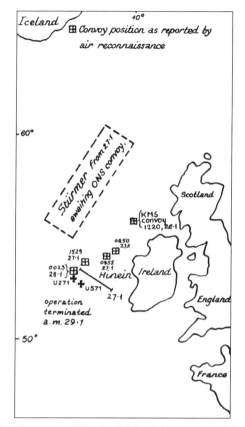

Plan 72. Group Hinein, 26th-29th January 1944.
Operation against a KMS convoy.

be favourably situated to receive the aircraft's homing signals at dusk. But bad luck again intervened. The BV 222 that had taken off that morning for the evening reconnaissance returned at midday because of engine trouble and so there was no contact at dusk. At 0023 on the 28th contact was made by the next aircraft, which gave an approximate position, but owing to a technical defect she was unable to send homing signals and the boats searched throughout the night without gaining touch in the prevailing bad weather and visibility. Few enemy aircraft were encountered, apparently owing to fog at their bases.

The operation was abandoned on the morning of 29th, because of a suspected Allied invasion, following an aircraft report of 200 to 300 landing-craft about 120 miles west of the Gironde estuary.

Although this seemed improbable, boats outward-bound from Biscay bases were sent at high speed to intercept, and at 0800 one of these boats - U.302 - reported sighting an air-escorted convoy steering a north-westerly course near the position reported by the aircraft. It appeared, therefore, that the aircraft's report was correct and that an invasion was indeed intended, although this was most unlikely in the absence of air attacks on Western France and as the landing formation had appeared in the early afternoon. At 0830 all boats in the North Atlantic, including groups *Hinein* and *Stürmer*, were ordered at full speed to the Biscay coast, but two hours later U.302 reported that the ships which she had taken for a convoy had turned out to be Spanish trawlers, whereupon the boats were instructed to submerge and reoccupy their previous attack areas. Summing up in his war diary, Dönitz stated:

"… The failure of the KMS operation and of most of the joint operations of recent months was due to too few reconnaissance aircraft and to defects in their radar and radio equipment…"

401. Last operation against an ONS convoy

The last day of January found the boats of groups *Hinein* and *Stürmer* again disposed on a semicircle round the North Channel (Plan 73). On 3rd February a number of them operated unsuccessfully, to the west of Ireland, against a convoy bound south-westward, while on the 8th an attempt to concentrate on a north-bound convoy, reported by air reconnaissance west of the Bay of Biscay, also failed. In both these cases we refrained from forming a patrol line and merely concentrated the boats in the convoy area.

From the beginning of February, a strengthening of the enemy defences became perceptible, particularly at the southern part of the disposition, and on the 4th of the month the boats began to withdraw slowly westward, being renamed groups *Igel* 1 and 2. It was soon evident, chiefly from frequent enemy tactical signals, that several hunter-killer groups were active to the south-west of Ireland, and when, after the sinking of a steamship between Scotland and Iceland on 8th February, enemy A/S activity was also intensified in the

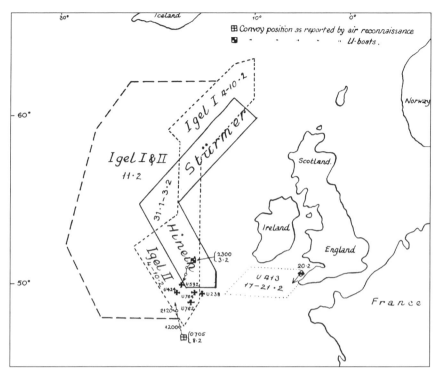

Plan 73. Groups Stürmer, Hinein and Igel, 31st January-11th February 1944.

northern part of the operational area, the whole disposition had to be withdrawn still further west.

This westward movement was necessary anyhow, since we intended carrying out an attack on an ONS convoy between 14th and 18th February in co-operation with *Fliegerführer* Atlantic. There were IS aircraft available for this operation, and when ONS 29 was first sighted from the air on 14th February just westward of the North Channel all U-boats to the west of the British Isles were quickly concentrated in an area 600 miles south-west of Ireland. Further sightings were made by air reconnaissance on each of the next three days, and on the 18th the boats were drawn up ahead of the convoy's line of advance in two parallel patrol lines - *Hai* 1 and 2 - *Hai* 2 being disposed to the south-west and behind *Hai* 1, since some of these boats had not reported for several weeks and we were not sure if they still survived. Subsequently it was established that three of the 19 boats of *Hai* 1 and four of the seven boats of *Hai* 2 had already been lost.

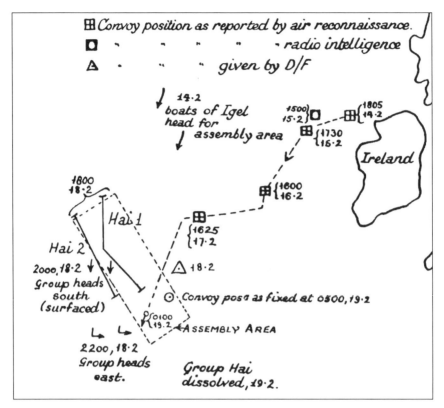

Plan 74. Group Hai, 14th-19th February 1944.
Operation against an ONS convoy.

We intended waiting for the air reconnaissance report of the night of 17th/18th before deciding on the final position of the patrol lines, but, owing to defects, the two aircraft detailed for that night's reconnaissance had to return before reaching the area. On the 18th, D/F bearings of what we presumed to be the convoy W/T guard ship gave a position much further south than would have been the case had the course indicated by the air reconnaissance reports been maintained, and it appeared that the convoy had turned south on 17th, after the last shadowing aircraft had headed for base, so circumventing the patrol lines to the eastward. Both groups were, therefore, immediately sent south at first submerged and from 2000 at high speed on the surface, with orders to get ahead of the convoy at all costs. The take-off times of the 10 aircraft then available were adjusted so as to ensure continuous shadowing from dusk till dawn, but the first two aircraft to reach the area missed the convoy, probably because of navigational errors. They made only brief contact on the return flight at about 0100 on the 19th and, although the homing signals sent by succeeding aircraft were received, cross-bearings were too acute to give an accurate fix. It was not until 0500 that a good fix could be obtained, and it then became apparent that some of the aircraft had been far out in their estimated positions. Theoretically, about eight boats could have reached the convoy by daybreak; in practice, however, they merely sighted a few destroyers and established enemy radar activity. The operation was finally broken off at daylight, when the boats had to submerge owing to the presence of an aircraft carrier in the convoy.

402. Lessons of the air reconnaissance

The following extract from the final summing up of the operation, taken from the war diary of FO U-boats, reveals the paucity of air reconnaissance resources available to us:

"... *Number of aircraft employed:*

2 Ju 88s, 17 Ju 290s, 3 FW 200s and 2 BV 222s

Total 24, of which the following dropped out:

4 Ju 290s and 1 BV 222 through engine trouble

2 Ju 290s through radar and radio defects

2 Ju 290 through compass failure

1 FW 200 through other causes

Total 10

Three Ju 290s overdue, of which two were probably shot down by carrier-borne aircraft and one by Mosquitoes in the Bay.

Conclusions:

The large number of aircraft defects which developed, especially towards the end, were caused by lack of proper maintenance, in turn due to the high pressure under which the aircraft were operating. Reconnaissance was only made possible by doubling the number of aircraft in a flight and sending out one as a reserve. That so many flights were made, particularly on the last night, was due to the most strenuous and devoted efforts on the part of the maintenance personnel.

The only way to eliminate all these difficulties is to increase the number of aircraft…"

These conclusions also proved the validity of the argument with which Dönitz had sought the aid of Hitler and Göring in this matter, namely,

"that most of the past U-boat operations against Atlantic convoys had failed because of a certain lack of training amongst the aircrews and the difficult conditions under which the U-boats were operating."

The above is quoted from a memorandum dated 7th February 1944, addressed to the Supreme Command of the German Armed Forces and the C-in-C *Luftwaffe*, in which the Naval Staff reiterated their demand for adequate air reconnaissance. This memorandum was occasioned by a report that the *Luftwaffe's* current building programme allowed for the construction of four Ju 290 aircraft a month, while additional aircraft of this type, which were to be built from June 1944 onwards, were to be used for military purposes. The memorandum continued:

"… The revival of successful operations by new-type U-boats in the autumn of 1944 stands or falls by the adequacy of the air reconnaissance. In view of the immense importance of this matter generally, the Naval Staff again request that the production of Ju 290 aircraft be stepped up to the utmost limit and that, as they become available, these aircraft and all available FW 200s and He 177s - even those equipped with glider-bombs - be allocated for reconnaissance on behalf of the U-boat Command. Further, that steps be taken to ensure the fulfillment of C-in-C Navy's request for the provision of twelve long-range reconnaissance aircraft daily…" (363).

The Air Staff's reply, dated 1st March 1944, which attributed the shortage of Ju 290 aircraft to production difficulties, gave evidence of its inability to appreciate the importance of the U-boat campaign:

"… We cannot share the view that the failure of most of the past

U-boat operations was due to the paucity of *Fliegerführer* Atlantic's forces. Convoys were often accurately located and continuously shadowed by the *Luftwaffe*, yet the U-boats were unable to achieve any worthwhile results…" (364).

Reconnaissance with breaks of eight hours or more might, perhaps, be described as "continuous" when considering the wide reconnaissance range of radar equipped aircraft, but not from the point of view of the U-boat, which at night could barely scan a strip of seven miles and whose speed of advance in an area dominated by enemy aircraft was 10 to 12 knots.

The last reconnaissance flown between 14th and 18th February provided valuable, if chiefly negative experience. The loss of two aircraft in the vicinity of the convoy showed that the enemy could fly off his carrier-borne fighter aircraft at night and also demonstrated the amazing efficiency of his fighter-direction organisation. In addition, we found that a single Ju 290 was insufficiently powerful to shadow a carrier-escorted convoy; in future, therefore, either a faster and more powerful type of aircraft had to be used, or the Ju 290s must operate in strength. Another surprising discovery was that the enemy ships were able to jam our aircrafts' radar. Thus we had learnt valuable lessons for use in air reconnaissance at a later period, while further experience of U-boat/aircraft co-operation could be gained in Northern Waters, in operations against PQ convoys carried out during the succeeding months. Any further such operations in the Atlantic were, however, precluded by the development of the overall war situation.

The author having spoken so often of the lack of air support for German naval operations feels that he should point out that FO U-boats, *Fliegerführer* Atlantic and their respective forces always worked well together. The latter was fully cognisant of the need for a strong naval air arm and had done his utmost to induce the *Luftwaffe* to provide the necessary forces. The personnel under his command had done their best with the inadequate material at their disposal, fighting bravely and with self-sacrifice, and their failure to achieve the results we desired was not their fault. Satisfactory results could only have been obtained by a strong naval air arm, the creation of which had been omitted because, inter alia, the Supreme Command of the German Armed Forces and the Air Staff lacked an understanding of maritime warfare and the significance of the U-boat campaign. By the time that they had digested the true state of affairs, it was already too late.

SEPTEMBER 1943-FEBRUARY 1944
REMOTE AREAS

403. Shortage of boats curtails operations

The following is an extract from the conclusions reached by the U-boat Command in their review of U-boat operations in remote areas dated 23rd August 1943:

"… Several boats were attacked by enemy aircraft at night without previous warning from their *Metox*. It must therefore be assumed that the enemy is making extensive use of *Metox* radiations for the purpose of location and attack and that this is one of the chief causes of our heavy losses. The cause of these losses having been established and eliminated, at least temporarily, by the introduction of the *Hagenuk* radar search receiver, we shall be able to resume the battle in these remote areas. The Type VIIC boat will be used only if refuelling facilities can be provided…"

With the loss of U.460 and U.220 in October 1943, these refuelling facilities had ceased to exist, so that from then on we could only employ large boats - Types IXC and IXD - based on Western France, but we had lost so many of these boats in recent months that there were now only just enough to maintain an average of four actually on operations. Concentration was therefore out of the question, and by the autumn of 1943 circumstances had compelled us to aim chiefly at tying down and dispersing the enemy forces in all remote areas except the Indian Ocean.

Our hope that the introduction of the *Hagenuk* search receiver would alleviate the situation appeared to be realised, for of more than 30 boats which operated in remote areas between 1st September and 20th November, only two - U.161 and U.533 - were lost, the former off the Brazilian coast at the end of September and the latter in the Gulf of Aden in mid-October. Later we realised that our heavy losses were not due to the *Metox* radiations but to the enemy's introduction of centimetric radar, which the *Hagenuk* could not register. It was remarkable, therefore, that our losses had been so low in the four weeks following the introduction of the *Hagenuk*.

The following minelaying operations were carried out in this period:

Date	Position	Mines	Mine	Laid By
8th October	Colon	15	SMA	U.214
8th October	St. John's	66	SMA	U.220
8th October	Trinidad	12	SMA	U.218
8th October	Takoradi	8	TMC	U.103

Of the torpedo operations during the autumn, three were regarded as successful: U.68 and U.515 each sank three ships in the Gulf of Guinea and the former also sank the escort trawler Orfasy, while U.516 achieved excellent results in the Caribbean - principally in the Panama area - sinking five ships aggregating 30,067 tons.

404. Difficulty in refuelling U.516

The sinkings off Panama evoked the strongest enemy reaction and U.516 was systematically hounded by aircraft bent on exhausting and destroying her. At Headquarters, intercepted enemy aircraft sighting and attack reports enabled us to follow her return through the central Caribbean with accuracy, and we eventually came to the conclusion that if the boat kept on this route she would be unable to shake off her pursuers. A signal was therefore sent permitting her to take avoiding action either by withdrawing to the north-west, or by seeking radar cover under some suitable island until the hunt had subsided. To compensate for the additional fuel consumption, she was to oil from an operational boat at a later stage of her return passage.

U.516 managed to escape without taking avoiding action, but she still needed a small quantity of fuel to take her back to base, and arrangements were made to supply this from U.544, a Type IXC boat which had been weather reporting in about 35 degrees West since the beginning of January 1944. This boat was to rendezvous with U.516 and U.129 - the latter returning from the US coast - 360 miles north-west of the Azores at dusk on 16th January and to supply each boat with *Borkum-Gerät* before refuelling U.516 during the night. Approaching the rendezvous submerged, just before dusk on the 16th the returning U-boats heard the detonation of aircraft bombs and the propeller noises of two destroyers; nothing more was heard of U.544 and we presumed her to have been sunk at the rendezvous by carrier-borne aircraft.[33]

U.129 continued her return passage while U.516 made rendezvous on the 19th with U.539, 150 miles further to the north, where they were attacked by carrier-borne aircraft and U.516 was depth-charged by two destroyers. The two U-boats again joined company on the 21st and, after many attempts in which the oil hoses repeatedly carried away in the seaway, the refuelling was finally accomplished on 4th February.

These incidents reawakened our suspicion - never completely allayed since 1941 - that the enemy was obtaining details of our rendezvous positions through treachery or decryption, yet, despite every precaution and the tightening up of security, we were still unable to prevent the recurrence of such incidents in the year 1944.

405. Disappointing results in the Indian Ocean
Group *Monsun* reached the Indian Ocean without further trouble (Section 363) to rendezvous on 11th September 450 miles south of Mauritius with the tanker *Brake*, which had been sent from Penang.

---

33 U.544 was sunk on 16th January by aircraft from USS *Guadalcanal*.

On the same day we received news from Japan that the Italian armed merchant cruiser Eritrea had escaped from Penang (Italy had capitulated on the 9th) and, since the officers of this ship were aware of *Brake*'s assignment, there was a danger of compromise. Our fears proved groundless, however, for the refuelling went off without incident.

We had originally intended that group *Monsun* should open a sudden attack in the Arabian Sea, sometime towards the end of September, but as the enemy had meanwhile been alerted in this area by Japanese U-boats, which had been operating there since August 1943, the group was permitted to commence its attack at once. While the boats were proceeding to their respective attack areas, the Japanese requested that they should not be permitted to operate north of 17 degrees South in order to preclude the possibility of incidents with Japanese U-boats. Such a restriction would, however, have been detrimental to the operation, and the German Naval Staff replied that the U-boats would occupy the Arabian Sea as originally intended, pointing out that no incidents would arise if the boats of both nations were expressly forbidden to attack other U-boats. They also requested assurance that the small reconnaissance aircraft, which were carried by some of the Japanese U-boats, should be forbidden to attack U-boats. The Japanese agreed to these proposals.

The results of the *Monsun* operation were disappointing. The commanders of U.168 and U.183, operating between British East Africa, the Seychelles and to the south of Bombay, had apparently been unequal to the mental and physical strain of the long voyage and failed to exploit their opportunities. U.533 was lost in the Gulf of Aden, U.532 sank five ships between the Chagos Archipelago and Southern India, while U.188 sank three ships off the Arabian coast in the Gulf of Oman and also unsuccessfully attacked a convoy as it was leaving the Gulf of Oman. It was subsequently established that the hot climate had caused the batteries of U.188's electric torpedoes to deteriorate, with the result that her torpedoes were running slow. By the beginning of November the four boats had entered Penang.

406. Heavy U-cruiser losses

It was clear from the *Monsun* boats' reports that the A/S situation and opportunities for attack in the northern part of the Indian Ocean were far more favourable than in the Atlantic. Hence it was decided that, as soon as they became operational, all subsequent Type IXD boats (U-cruisers) should first be sent to the Indian Ocean. Never did any scheme fail so badly as this. The commanders of the U-cruisers which became operational in 1943 were experienced officers, being generally selected from those who had distinguished themselves in the North Atlantic or Mediterranean, and nearly all of them had been awarded the *Ritterkreuz*; in the age of radar, however, experience counted little, and they all perished with their boats on their first operation, mostly through air attack while outward-bound.

The first victims were two old Mediterranean commanders, *Kapitänleutnant*s Schonder and Kraus, the former going down with U.200 on 24th June south of Iceland and the latter with U.199 on 31st July off the Brazilian coast. There followed *Kapitänleutnant* Kuppisch (U.847) on 27th August south of the Azores, *Kapitänleutnant* Rollman (U.848) on 5th November west of Ascension, *Kapitänleutnant* H. O. Schultze (U.849) on 25th November east of Ascension , *Korvettenkapitän* Evert (U.850) on 20th December south of the Azores, and *Korvettenkapitän* Buchholz (U.177) on 6th February 1944 east of Ascension. Before sailing, the commanders of U.847, U.850 and U.177 had been expressly warned of the clanger of attack by carrier-borne aircraft in the open sea, so that we had to assume that they had trained their lookouts to a high degree of proficiency. Nevertheless, as far as we could judge, most of them had fallen victim to the first air attack. Finally, we concluded that the enemy had a system of plotting the boats as they moved southwards, occasionally checking their positions by radar and then awaiting favourable conditions of cloud and sun to carry out a decisive attack without using radar. The commanders of subsequent outgoing boats were informed accordingly and warned against steering a straight outward course; instead, they were told to make occasional alterations and to vary their times of surfacing in an attempt to delude the enemy.

407. Operations from Penang

Our U-boat base at Penang was constructed in 1943 by the Japanese and by German naval personnel landed from various armed merchant cruisers and blockade-runners. It was at first administered by a former executive officer of an armed merchant cruiser, but at the beginning of 1944 this officer was superseded by *Korvettenkapitän* Dommes, the commander of U.178, who had had to relinquish his appointment because of ill health. Generally, the Japanese co-operated well, although on occasions difficulties were caused by the Oriental's distrust of the Occidental, which was only overcome after long personal association. While the Japanese navy did everything to assist us, the Japanese army, with whom they stood in keen rivalry, created much difficulty on those occasions which required our working with them. The U-boat crews were comfortably accommodated in disused schools and hotels administered by the base commander, and during refit they were able to spend several weeks recuperating in convalescent homes in the hills, where it was cooler. As it was almost impossible for Europeans to exist on the provisions allowed to the Japanese U-boats, necessary victuals such as tinned bread, preserved meat, vegetables and fruit were prepared in a well-equipped factory at the base. At the beginning of 1944 there had been no air attacks on the harbour, so that we had no qualms about allowing the boats to lie in unprotected berths at Swetten-ham Pier, but concern was caused by the lack of any form of harbour defence against enemy submarines or surface craft and also by the absence of an A/S organisation, together with the appropriate vessels. As it was, we did our best to rectify this by ourselves manning the few Arado 34 aircraft, which had been turned over to the Japanese, and employing them against the Allied submarine patrols in the Malacca Strait.

The size of the Penang flotilla was limited by the capacity of the dockyard, which just sufficed to maintain the five German and two or three Japanese U-boats. Extension work was in hand, however, so that heavier commitments could be accepted at a later date. With the available dockyard personnel and plant, all normal repair work could be undertaken with the exception of docking, which had to be done at Singapore. Compared with German standards the work was slow, although well done. Delays were caused by a lack of materials which could only be obtained from Japan, and great difficulty was experienced in obtaining consumable stores, the Japanese standard allowance being niggardly even to their own boats; large quantities had therefore to be brought by the boats joining from Western France.

Torpedo stocks, which were small, had been derived from German armed merchant cruisers and blockade-runners and some of the torpedoes had deteriorated badly through long storage in the tropics, with the result that there were frequent failures in the ensuing months. To relieve this situation, additional stocks of torpedoes and spares were shipped in two Type VIIF torpedo-transport U-boats - U.1062 and U.1059 - the first of this type to become ready for service. It was a modification of the Type VII, with a larger torpedo compartment and a displacement 400 tons greater, and could carry 39 torpedoes besides other essential stores. U.1062 sailed in January and U.1059 by the end of February; in view of the urgency of their mission, they were ordered to refrain from seeking action while *en route* and to exploit only exceptionally favourable opportunities for attack.[34]

The first German boat to operate from Penang was U.178, which sailed from that port at the end of November 1943. The two *Monsun* boats, U.188 and U.532, sailed in January 1944 and U.183 in February, so that with U.510, which was coming from Western France, we had five to six boats in the operational area from February 1944, disposed in the Gulf of Aden and between the Indian coast and Mauritius. Of six ships totalling 38,751 tons sunk and one of 7,283 damaged in January, and seven totalling 44,857 tons sunk and two

---

34 U.1062 reached Penang on 19th April, but U.1059 was sunk of the Cape Verde Islands on 19th March by aircraft from USS Block Island. The latter was caught hove-to on the surface, with some of the crew having an early-morning bathe.

totalling 1,977 tons damaged in February, seven were accounted for by U.188 alone, which had encountered considerable traffic in and to the eastward of the Gulf of Aden. Results would have been higher but for the above-mentioned torpedo failures.

U.178 and U.510 refuelled on 28th January from the tanker *Charlotte Schliemann*, 100 miles south-east of Mauritius, and U.178 afterwards remained in the vicinity of the island in order to be able to return to Western France on completion of her operation. U.532 was also to return home after refuelling from *Schliemann*, 900 miles east of Mauritius, where she made rendezvous with the tanker on 11th February, but owing to bad weather refuelling could not take place and they lost sight of each other. The tanker never appeared again and, since flying-boats were twice sighted near the rendezvous at the time, we had to assume that the enemy had located and destroyed her.[35] Meanwhile U.532's fuel had run very low and U.178 had to supply as much as she could spare without having to refuel on the return passage, so as to enable U.532 to last out until the tanker *Brake* arrived.

---

35 The *Charlotte Schliemann*'s refuelling activities were known to the British. The cruiser *Newcastle*, destroyer *Relentless* and a Fleet Auxiliary, together with seven Mauritius-based Catalina flying-boats, were detailed to search for her (Operation "Canned"). ON the afternoon of 11th February the *Schliemann*, with a U-boat in company, was sighted by one of the Catalina, which, for lack of fuel, had to return to base after reporting the tanker's course and speed. The *Relentless*, at that time about 100 miles to the westward, closed at speed and, after a well-conducted search, intercepted the *Schliemann* shortly after midnight 11th/12th, destroying her with torpedo and gunfire.

- C H A P T E R   9 -

FEBRUARY-MAY 1944

CONTAINING THE ENEMY

408. A more cautious strategy required

For five months the U-boat arm had toiled relentlessly at the task of intercepting convoys on the North Atlantic routes, all reverses being borne in the belief that the new weapons and devices gradually coming into operational use, helped by air reconnaissance, would once again turn the convoy war in the U-boats' favour. But the last attack on a convoy, carried out against ONS 29 from 16th to 19th February 1944, had also ended in heavy defeat, the loss of U.406 and U.386 finally demonstrating that all the new weapons together could not give back to the old-type boats their striking power.

While it was important that U-boat operations should continue, if only because of their value in tying down enemy forces which might otherwise be used elsewhere, in present circumstances the U-boat Command was faced with the danger of there being insufficient boats left to sustain the war, and it became necessary to place greater value on conservation. Costly convoy attacks were therefore abandoned and, beginning in March 1944, U-boats were operated singly and concentrated upon tactics designed to contain the enemy's enormous resources until such time as a strong U-boat arm of new types was ready to resume the battle with, it was hoped, greater prospect of success.

409. Greater percentage of U-boat losses caused by naval forces

Prior to the last months of 1943, U-boat commanders had used every opportunity to despatch a situation report and this continual stream of incoming signals had enabled the U-boat Command to maintain an up-to-date record of losses and their probable causes. Now, however, the efficiency of the enemy D/F organisation[36] deterred commanders from using their radio, some boats remaining completely silent for over six weeks on end, and without these vital situation reports it was almost impossible to make an accurate assessment of losses (365). In the event, the U-boat Command estimated that seven boats had been lost in December 1943, nine in January and 18 in February 1944 - whereas the actual losses were five, 13 and 14 - and the resultant loss curve showed an alarming rise for February, which was taken as a danger signal.

The situation was further obscured by uncertainty about the enemy's mode of attack, for there was no indication at all how four of the boats in January and nine in February had been lost. However, it was believed that a large number of all the casualties must have occurred within an area bounded by the meridians 15 and 25 degrees West and the parallels 48 and 53 degrees North, which lay across the south-western UK-USA traffic route and was also the area through which the U-boats most frequently passed on their way to and from operations. So, with radio intelligence showing an unusually large concentration of surface A/S forces there in February, it was assumed that enemy naval forces had been responsible for a larger proportion of losses than heretofore.

From a great mass of individual observations sifted by the staff officer responsible for intelligence, the following picture of enemy A/S measures had been formed by the Spring of 1944.

410. Better equipment for intercepting U-boats - the mystery of the noise-boxes[37]

All enemy vessels were equipped with excellent listening gear, either installed onboard or towed, some of which could be operated at speeds in excess of 20 knots. Some ships proceeding independently also carried listening gear, which they mostly used to outmanoeuvre torpedoes, on occasion with marked success. Asdic equipment was

---

36 German radio-intercept information showed that each signal was picked up and ranged by an average of twenty D/F stations situated round the Atlantic and Indian Oceans,

37 The content of this section is mostly imaginary, well illustrating the general German ignorance of British A/S measures.

fitted in almost all vessels engaged on A/S operations and, although its range was limited, destroyers had frequently been known to make direct for submerged U-boats from as far away as 10,000 to 15,000 metres, and then to drop depth-charges with reasonable accuracy in their first attack. It therefore appeared that some reliance could be placed upon agents' reports claiming that supersonic equipment, or long-range instruments operated on electromagnetic principles, were being used. One Mediterranean boat had actually picked up supersonic pulses, when submerged, with the aid of a special receiver, and further observations were in progress.

On the subject of location by explosive ranging - *Knallortung* - which continued to be used frequently, more information was available. The A/S vessel fired small canisters of explosive, from special guns, in the vicinity of a submerged U-boat; then, by comparing the time elapsed between the explosion and receipt of the echo reflected from the U-boat, the latter's position was fixed and marked by different coloured-smoke floats. This explosive-ranging technique was used only for close-range location.

Evaluation of the numerous, extremely varied reports concerning acoustic buoys used by the enemy entailed considerable work and thought. However, U-boat Command finally divided them into the following categories, according to shades of sound and probable purpose, and issued a comprehensive report on the state of enemy A/S measures, dated 1st June 1944:

"*Decoy buoy.* A noise is produced similar to that of the screw and asdic of an A/S vessel. The buoy is probably laid by A/S vessels and aircraft acting as convoy escort, in order to keep the U-boats submerged… Objects sighted by two U-boats in Northern Waters were probably noise-boxes of this type; they were black containers in the shape of a mine, but without horns, and with one vertical spike. The noise of screws and faint asdic transmissions were heard, although no surface vessels were to be seen.

Rattle buoy. A rattling, knocking sound has been observed coming from A/S vessels, especially when they are aware of the presence of a U-boat, and when a sound record of the German GBT acoustic sweep was played over to U-boat commanders, they recognised this as the same noise. The sound of screws is completely drowned and bearings of the source cannot be taken at short range, but it is possible to do so from a distance. Whether the source of the noise is installed in the vessel, or is towed, has not yet been established. It is probably a noise-box designed as a defence against the T5 torpedo, a conclusion drawn from the fact that it was first encountered about one month after the original T5 operation, and also from the manner in which it is used...*[38]*

Musical saw. Since the introduction of the rattle buoy, a noise has been observed which at long range sounds like the buzzing of a bee, then, on approaching, rather like a mosquito. At close range it changes to a pure, musical note similar to that of a musical saw. It is not clear whether this is a new type of location equipment or a noise-box. This particular noise has only been observed with A/S vessels around... " (366). [39]

411. Enemy's anti-submarine weapons become more effective[40]

Three different types of depth-charge were being used in enemy A/S vessels at this time: the normal 180-kg type, an extra-heavy type weighing from 250 to 340 kg, and the so-called "Killer" weighing 450 kg. Normally, the method of firing was to roll them off the stern or over the side. The 180-kg type could also be catapulted forward and laterally by means of compressed air and rocket propulsion to a distance of from 80 to 250 metres. Detonation was generally effected by water pressure, but sometimes magnetically, and could be set for depths of between 15 and 180 metres. Presumably it was also possible to adjust for greater depths, as a U-boat proceeding at 220 metres had received serious dents on her pressure hull from depth-charge blast.

In the spring of 1942 the Japanese had captured a secret British

---

38 Probably refers to the Foxer.
39 Possibly refers to the humming of tripped Foxer wires.
40 The information in this section is also generally inaccurate.

Admiralty report entitled "A/S Defence, January 1942", and at the end of 1943 they had sent this report to Germany in the blockade-runner *Osorno*. Among other important information it contained a picture and description of Hedgehog, the existence of which had been known to German U-boat authorities since 1942, through decrypted messages and agents' reports. It was a gyro-stabilised multiple-rocket battery for 24 small depth-charges, these being detonated either by water pressure or magnetically.[41] Detonation and angle of spread could be set by a common gear, so that depth-charges detonated at different depths and at fixed distances apart; in this way a cube-shaped area of specific length was comprehensively covered, the Hedgehog being fired in such a way that the U-boat came within this area.

The assumption that the enemy had received information from Polish sources about German homing torpedoes, even before the T5 was used, was confirmed by verbal reports from U-boat prisoners of war, who had returned home under the sickness exchange scheme, while, on the German side, the enemy was known to have been working for some time on a homing torpedo. In this he had probably profited from the information transmitted via Polish sources, as well as in the design of defence measures, and U-boat commanders were therefore instructed to report immediately any phenomenon which might indicate the use of homing torpedoes or other related devices.

Agents' reports referred to a device called Oscar which steered itself independently towards U-boats under water.[42]

"… 1st June 1944. As a large number of prisoners have been reported taken from different types of boat recently, it is considered unlikely that these boats were destroyed by a weapon of this nature, which would cause total loss with no survivors, but rather as a result of systematic A/S patrolling and blockade…"

---

41 Not so; they were contact charges.
42 The American Mk 24 mine, codename Fido.

412. Less uncertainty about surface location

So many and varied were the species of underwater sound produced by the enemy from 1943 onwards, that it was difficult for U-boat men to form a clear picture of the equipment in use. It was therefore fortunate that, at about this time when confidence under water was beginning to waver, any remaining doubts about enemy surface radar should have been finally dispelled, *Naxos* equipment, introduced in November 1943, having revealed that the enemy was using the 8- to 12-cm waveband in his Rotterdam set. As a direct result of this discovery, the number of incidents where U-boats were taken unawares by air attack immediately decreased although interference and limited sensitivity prevented the *Naxos* from providing a completely infallible warning system and impulses were frequently picked up too late to risk diving.

The British ASV was still being used by aircraft and naval forces in the North Atlantic. The increasing number of bearings obtained on *Naxos*, however, showed that the change-over to the more efficient Rotterdam, with its greater range and better definition, was progressing rapidly and that this radar set could shortly be expected in all aircraft and naval vessels. There were, indeed, interesting reports to the effect that both ASV and Rotterdam were used in quick succession by the same aircraft, and this tallied with the report from one agent, who observed aerials for both sets fitted to a Liberator aircraft which had made a forced landing in Portugal. The ASV had a blind-spot at close range, and it appeared probable that Rotterdam was sometimes switched on during the final run in, allowing bombs to be dropped blind; in most cases, however, Allied pilots preferred to illuminate a U-boat immediately prior to attack, either by flares or Leigh light.

At the beginning of 1944, serially numbered 3-cm instruments - Meddo sets - had been found in aircraft shot down over Germany, and it was expected that this equipment would soon be fitted in A/S planes, if it were not already in use. The most urgent requirement was, therefore, for a sensitive warning instrument which would also cover this frequency; although it was equally important to overtake the advances made by the enemy and develop German active radar equipment in the centimetre band.

Other reports and radio intelligence confirmed our suspicions that the enemy was very busy on research into methods by which aircraft could detect submerged U-boats. One such procedure, known as ERSB[43], required three floats - the name of which was later deciphered as "gonio buoys" - to be laid in a triangle around the suspected position of a submerged U-boat, whereafter, listening gear or asdic, fitted to the floats, would pick up sounds from the U-boat and radio this information back to the aircraft. The first report from a U-boat concerning the possible use of this device was made in March 1943, and on 5th March 1944 an aircraft in the Caribbean was overheard reporting that it had a "sound" contact. Few grounds remained, therefore, on which to discount agents' reports that aircraft would soon be able to take magnetic or radio bearings of submerged U-boats.

These new discoveries concerning enemy location methods were considered so important by the C-in-C Navy that he informed Hitler on 13th January 1944:

"… Apparently it is not a question of passive location, where the U-boats themselves radiate something, nor is it the radiation of the exhaust. British location is based on the centimetre wavelength.

Prisoners' statements show that the new radiolocation equipment was first installed in British aircraft in March 1943 and was effective in May. This date coincides with the steep rise in U-boat losses…" (367).

At this time Dönitz stressed the need for a general re-organisation in the field of radar research and development. Hitherto, work in this field had been the responsibility of Göring, in his capacity as Commissioner of the Four-Year Plan, but he had completely misjudged the manpower requirement and during the first years of the war allowed many radar scientists and technicians to be released

---

43 The American expendable radio sonobuoy.

for military service, which thus seriously depleted this important reserve. The greater part of radar research activity had, in any case, been directed towards air force requirements. Dönitz, after a number of talks with Göring, Speer and Hitler, succeeded in getting the responsibility for radar research transferred to a specialist - Dr Lüschen, the Director of the Central Board of Electrical Engineering - who was granted far-reaching powers in research matters (368).

413. Production faults in the 3-7-cm gun

Apart from *Naxos*, U-boats had practically nothing to measure against the enemy's progress in A/S measures.

The 3-7-cm automatic AA gun, which had been installed in some boats from the beginning of December 1943 and on which U-boat men had pinned great hopes, was not yet regarded as operationally reliable, breakdowns in the automatic system occurring continually, due either to errors in manufacture or to careless work - a defect as much attributable to the harassment of well established gunmakers as it was to the use of inexperienced firms. Furthermore, the material used was very sensitive to sea water, which necessitated continual servicing and frequent test firings to prevent the formation of rust. Neither could, however, be carried out very often, because boats proceeding to and from the operational area surfaced only to charge batteries, and those actually in the operational area only at night, and a commander could not be expected either to allow his artificers to work on the gun with lights, or to range the weapon in the dark.

Measures had already been taken to correct production faults and to minimise rust formation by the use of a material which would resist sea water, but several months were bound to elapse before matters could be rectified, and by then, in the opinion of FO U-boats, the old conventional-type U-boat would be quite unable to surface in daylight.

414. Morale undermined by surface location

Since December 1943, an average of some 20 per cent of the boats at sea had been lost each month. First-hand experience of the merciless hardship of U-boat warfare, the crises arising from the prohibition of *Metox* and *Wanze* and, most of all, the months of uncertainty concerning enemy surface location, were bound, in the long run, to tell upon the morale of even the best-trained men.

Even the outward and return voyage through the Bay of Biscay, which in 1944 took 10 to 12 days as against an earlier three to five, entailed heavy physical and mental strain and meant remaining submerged for 20 to 22 hours a day, with restrictions on the use of all facilities. The knowledge that the boat might at any moment be caught by enemy A/S forces, and the frequent explosion of bombs and depth-charges, created an atmosphere of continuous nervous tension. Commanders were constantly weighing their chances of charging batteries and compressed air flasks to capacity at the next surfacing, and when a boat did surface, the short charging interval was spent in standing by for air attack, or for the next alarm from the radar search receiver. Finally, after action might come the repair of heavy damage, and a cramped and unpleasant existence in the presence of men wounded by small-arms fire, for whom there was little help and only limited medical equipment.

Out at sea beyond 15 degrees West conditions were somewhat better. If, however, the boat was intercepted by enemy A/S forces, which commenced their cat-and-mouse tactics, possibly lasting for hours until the boat was exhausted, it could be as bad as in the Bay of Biscay. But in the long run it was the uncertainty of how to act when intercepted which had the worst effect on commanders.

"... 1st March 1944. In the operational area, also, the boats must always be on their guard against surprise air attack. Their entire activity is therefore largely conditioned by the radar search receiver, which, unfortunately, records only the fact that the boat is being located and not the type, range and direction of the radar source.

At night, for instance, a boat may dive on the assumption that it is being intercepted by an aircraft, but in many cases a hydrophone bearing soon reveals the source to be a destroyer or corvette, fast approaching the diving position. It is now too late to resurface, the boat is forced to remain on the defensive and a depth-charge attack generally ensues. If this boat profits from its experience on that occasion and remains on the surface the next time it is intercepted, it is bombed. Wrong again!

Surprise attacks by aircraft and surface vessels continue frequently to occur without previous warning from the radar search receiver, because some of the emissions which should have been spotted are missed. The main reason for this is that the receivers at present in use do not cover all the enemy's radar frequencies, but technical faults and sea damage to aerials are also responsible in part.

With this ever present danger of being surprised and the uncertainty prevailing about enemy location methods, it is little wonder that many U-boats, especially those under the younger, inexperienced commanders, are very much defensively inclined. Time and again individual commanders deliberately refrain from pressing home attacks against convoys or stragglers, for fear of being intercepted. This defensive state of mind will probably disappear when radar search equipment, or our own active radar, make it possible to determine the .direction, range and nature of the enemy…" (369).

ANTI-INVASION PREPARATIONS

415. U-boat losses strengthen the need for containment

The decision, taken in March 1944, to abandon the attack on Atlantic convoys and to adopt a strategy of containing the enemy was unavoidable. Ever since the end of 1943, the number of Type VIIC boats operating in the North Atlantic had been falling and this trend was expected to continue. In plain fact, there were just not enough boats left to form and maintain packs of an adequate size.

The strength of the enemy's A/S defence was mainly responsible for this decrease in the number of U-boats available. From the summer of 1943, on average, only 70 per cent of Atlantic boats returned from operations, some of them seriously damaged and needing long periods in dockyard hands. But a steady diversion of boats and experienced crews to the Mediterranean had also been taking place since 1943, and the difficulty of this undertaking was apparent from the time which it took them to reach their new station. On an average, U-boats sailing from France during 1942 had made their "passed" signal from the Mediterranean after a week at sea, while in the spring of 1944 the voyage took at least three, and in one case five, weeks, some boats accomplishing the breakthrough only at the second or third attempt. The following table shows the number of boats attempting the passage and the losses incurred between September 1943 and May 1944:

Month	Attempted	Successful	Lost	Abandoned Attempt
September 1943	4	1	-	3
October 1943	4	2	2	-
December 1943	1	1	-	-
January 1944	3	3	-	-
February 1944	4	3	1	-
March 1944	4	2	1	1
April 1944	1	1	-	-
May 1944	2	-	2	-
Total	23	13	6	4

In December 1943, certain other boats which had been destined for the Atlantic were allocated to SO U-boats Northern Waters for attack on the revived PQ convoys, the destruction of these supplies to Murmansk being of supreme importance to land operations on the German arctic front. By this time it was clear that U-boat operating conditions were better in the Arctic than in the Atlantic, there being strong German air reconnaissance and bomber formations available in Norway, and on 26th December 1943 Dönitz ordered the number of U-boats in Northern Waters to be increased from 18 to 24. On 10th January 1944 this number was further increased to 33. Making allowance for casualties, this meant that some 20 U-boats went to Northern Waters at the expense of the Atlantic theatre.

416. Anti-invasion planning

Anti-invasion planning also played a part in denuding the Atlantic of U-boats.

Early in 1944, the Naval Staff foresaw that the danger of an enemy invasion of southern Norway or Denmark must increase as the weather improved, and it was decided to hold a certain number of U-boats in readiness against such an eventuality. Hence, on 16th February 1944, 10 of the Type VIIC boats about to sail from Kiel were ordered to stand by at ports in southern Norway - four at Bergen, four at Kristiansand and two at Stavanger. These boats were to form group *Mitte*, commanded by Captain U-boats East, *Fregattenkapitän* Schütze, and would come under Naval Command North in an emergency. In March the strength of group *Mitte* was increased from 10 to 22 boats and, as a consequence, from January to mid-May only about 30 U-boats reached the Atlantic from German ports, more than a third of them Type IXC.

From March 1944 there were also many indications of an Allied invasion of western France. If such an enterprise were to succeed, Germany would be faced with a European war on two fronts, which she could not hope to withstand indefinitely. Whereas in *Wehrmacht* circles it was generally believed that an invading army could only be defeated comprehensively by land warfare on the Continent itself, the Naval Staff regarded the coast as the principal line of defence and was resolved to oppose any invasion forces offshore and at the beachheads.

U-boats had little prospect of success in anti-invasion operations and were almost certain to incur serious losses; nevertheless, plans were made to use them as part of the general effort to prevent the enemy from gaining a foothold, and on 22nd March 15 Type VIIC boats were ordered to be held in operational readiness at the French bases. These boats were known as group *Landwirt*, but it was too early to foresee how they should be deployed - whether they should be sent to penetrate the English Channel or merely afford protection to the Brittany coast and the Bay of Biscay by their presence. At the beginning of April it was thought that 15 boats would be sufficient for the task and, in order to effect a rapid reinforcement, six U-boats which had just reached the Atlantic from Germany were told to head for the Biscay ports immediately. From the middle of April all medium-sized U-boats in the Biscay bases, as they became operational, were held back, and this reduced the number of boats at sea from 70 (32 of them Type VIIC) on 16th March, to 44 (13 of them Type VIIC) on 1st June. During May an average of only four to six U-boats were operating in the Western Approaches to Britain.

417. In the North Atlantic

Turning now to operations in the Western Approaches to the British Isles, after the end of Operation *Hai* (20th February 1944), the U-boats concerned had first hauled westward and then formed up as group *Preussen*, 400 to 500 miles north of the Azores. On 25th February the position of the convoy ON 225 was estimated, from a radio intelligence report, as just west of the North Channel at 1300 on 24th and, on the strength of this information, from 27th to 29th February the group was concentrated between 22 and 30 degrees West, ahead of the general track deduced from the report. However, no contact was made with the convoy and the boats were dispersed again, continuing to retain the formation of a loosely knit group. A few days later, on 2nd March, another decrypted message disclosed that ON 225 had received new course instructions and had presumably made a wide detour; as it was known that other convoys had also used this route, on 6th March the group hauled to the northward.

U-boat Command had already enlarged the attack zones of individual U-boats, so that a sufficiently wide front could be covered by an ever-decreasing force, but now, as strong A/S patrols had to be avoided, they were allowed even greater freedom of movement and individual attack zones were extended to 100 miles. With such dispersion there was no point in disposing the U-boats primarily for attack on convoys, and the sole remaining purpose was to discomfort the enemy while at the same time providing the boats with sufficient freedom to escape the concentrations of A/S forces. On 22nd March, therefore, FO U-boats disbanded group *Preussen* and allocated large patrol lanes about 100 miles wide to the few remaining units, commanders positioning themselves in these lanes according to their own estimation of the current A/S situation between the coast of Britain and 40 degrees West. Concurrently, one or two boats patrolled independently in the southern portion of the USA-UK convoy route as far as 400 miles east of Newfoundland.

Losses remained very high, despite the freedom allowed to commanders, and as it was again believed that most of these losses had occurred in the area 600 to 800 miles south-west of Ireland, on 27th March FO U-boats closed this area to all U-boats (Section 409). It was not until 10th April that it was declared free again, after radio bearings had indicated that the A/S forces had also moved to the south and westward because of lack of work.

During April and May the number of operational boats in the Atlantic continued to fall until there were only five remaining to the west of the British Isles, all employed on transmitting weather reports for the OKW and OKL. As weather information was of vital importance, both for air warfare and for assessing the chances of an Allied invasion, U-boat commanders were instructed to make their reports without regard to self-compromise, but, after each transmission, evasive action was to be taken, either by leaving the area at full speed or by remaining submerged for a long period. Although commanders carefully followed this routine, U.342 and U.765 had to be presumed lost as a result of enemy forces following up bearings taken on their reports.

418. Some coastal operations

In a further effort to tie down enemy forces, a few U-boats were ordered to attack shipping close in to the enemy coast. One of them - U.744 - was presumed to have been lost before reaching her operational area off Reykjavik, but the others - U.621 north of the Minches, U.333 off the North Channel, U.413 off Lizard Head and

U.448 off the north-west coast of Iceland - succeeded, with great difficulty, in taking up their positions for a few days during February and March. But, in general, enemy countermeasures were too strong to allow the boats to operate on the surface, while submerged they were too slow to close the majority of targets, and the only claims to success amounted to the sinking of the destroyer *Warwick* off the north coast of Cornwall on 20th February and of an escort vessel north of the Minches. British records, however, make no mention of any loss in the latter area.

On 12th February, in an encounter between U.413 and the escort of a convoy to the south of Ireland, that U-boat's intercept party was able to give valuable assistance to the commander, by watching the convoy R/T wave:

"12th February 1944. 0420… more starshells. Destroyers, talking to each other on convoy R/T wave about having continuous bearings on the U-boat, are going over to the attack.

0424. Visibility 1,600 to 8,000 metres. Fired T5 torpedo from tube V at southerly destroyer. Torpedo launched on surface; heavy explosion after 11 minutes 25 seconds.

0435. Destroyer not seen. Obscured by diesel exhaust and bad visibility. Radio intercept of convoy R/T indicates hit obtained. One destroyer briefly and excitedly reports condition, then nothing more. Another destroyer goes to her aid and later reports incident to a third; sinking of the destroyer may therefore be taken as certain.[44] Move away, altering course repeatedly and using *Aphrodite* on several occasions. Intend switching off *Naxos* and regaining a favourable position.

0535. Closed in to scene of sinking on course 345 degrees; strong smell of fuel oil; star-shells fired at us through haze.

0540. Continuous *Naxos* location; R/T intercepts show that another destroyer has arrived.

0630. R/T intercepts show that aircraft are now coming out to the convoy…"

---

44 British sources record no sinking or torpedoing.

On 20th February 1944, in shallow water north of the Scilly Isles, the same boat sank the afore-mentioned destroyer, HMS *Warwick*, which was on convoy escort. Surprisingly enough, the U-boat was not pursued after the attack, probably because the British thought the destroyer had struck a mine.

419. Better German radar and radar search equipment

Several important radar and search equipments, which should have been introduced into service in the autumn of 1943 and would probably have reduced losses, were not delivered until March 1944 because of production difficulties; even then only one or two sets were available.

In the active radar field there were now available the 80-cm *Gema* and the 43-cm *Hohentwiel* sets,[45] the latter as a result of constant pressure from the Naval Staff. Two boats which had been equipped with *Hohentwiel* in March - U.743 and U.311 - found that they were able to pick up attacking aircraft at ranges of between 10,000 and 12,000 metres; they could thus man and range their guns in good time and in one or two instances managed to open fire before actually sighting the plane. In later engagements it was observed that, on more than one occasion, aircraft using radar flew by at 6,000 to 12,000 metres, which confirmed the FO U-boats' suspicion that U-boats often dived prematurely on receipt of radar transmissions when in fact they were not being picked up by the enemy's radar. It also seemed to suggest that the enemy used planes to transmit haphazard radar impulses to compel the U-boats to dive, a procedure which, in relation to convoy protection, rendered the U-boats harmless, and in the transit areas denied them sufficient time to charge their batteries, so threatening them with low battery capacity in the event of further attacks.

From April 1944 onwards, the *Hohentwiel* set in particular brought great relief to the few boats equipped with it. It showed:

"... the exact direction and range of a plane, thus making it

---

45 *Gema* was a surface gunnery set of little use in U-boats. *Hohentwiel* was adapted from an aircraft radar and functioned quite adequately.

possible to decide whether or not it was making a direct line for the boat and, if so, whether diving was practicable. The whole routine of the boat was therefore made much calmer and a safe yardstick provided for diving and AA defence…" (370).

The presence of *Hohentwiel* also contributed to the gradual disappearance of the defensive attitude shown by one or two commanders.

As for radar search equipment, *Naxos* was gradually replaced in the 8- to 12-cm band by *Fliege*, the latter being fitted with a cavity aerial which was much more sensitive than the 'single-finger' antenna of *Naxos*. *Fliege* still required manual training, but this disadvantage was amply offset by a greatly increased interception range of 40 to 60 km and by the ability to obtain a rough bearing of the source. In order to cope with the 3-cm American Meddo radar, a special set - *Mücke* - was introduced, in most respects similar to *Fliege*.

Although experience over the last few months had shown 80 per cent of detected enemy radar transmissions to be within the 10-cm band, i.e. emanating from Rotterdam or Meddo, it was still considered imprudent to dispense with *Wanze* and *Borkum*; room had therefore to be found on a U-boat's bridge for the aerials of *Wanze*, *Borkum*, *Fliege* and *Mücke*. In order to relieve this most unsatisfactory situation, a combination of the latter two sets - *Tunis* - was at once devised and first installed in May 1944.

420. The schnorkel and first experience of its use

Plans of a device to enable a U-boat to proceed submerged on diesels were originally submitted by Professor Walter in November 1942. It consisted of two pressure-resistant flexible hoses secure together by metal bands, with their lower ends secured rigidly to the boat and their upper ends terminating in a raft-like float, which housed a non-return valve. One hose was designed to supply air to the diesels, the other to conduct away the exhaust gases. Such a device was clearly of great potential value at a time when enemy aircraft and surface radar were progressively forcing the U-boats to spend more and more time submerged, and in mid-1943 Dönitz ordered experiments to commence. Professor Walter's original design proved impracticable, but further experiments and trials, in which the Professor and U-boat Acceptance Command co-operated, a satisfactory installation was produced, to which the name *Schnorchel*[46] - a somewhat vulgar term for nose - was given.

The first installation was known as the Klapp*schnorchel* (folding snort), in which the air intake and gas exhaust pipes were housed in a thick mast, raised and lowered from inside the boat. When not in use, the mast lay in a housing in the deck; when in the raised position, a flange at the lower end of the mast made a pressure-tight joint with a corresponding flange surrounding the air intake and gas exhaust from the diesel room. On being raised, water in the mast drained into the boat and contact was established with the outer air. A floating valve at the head of the mast prevented the ingress of water in a seaway. Ultimately the Germaniawerft developed an installation which dispensed with the dangerous joint flanges.

Research into the schnorkel had largely been completed by the end of 1943. However, serial production meant a further burden on the shipbuilding industry, which it was in no position to meet, and sub-contractors with little experience of shipbuilding were therefore called upon to manufacture individual parts, in particular the very complicated pressure-tight casting at the foot of the schnorkel. In some cases their work was far below standard. Moreover, a fair proportion of the schnorkel sent to bases in France during the spring and summer of 1944 was damaged *en route* by bombing, adding to the delays and difficulties of installation.

The first operational boat equipped with schnorkel - U.264 - was lost on 19th February in the group *Hai* operation, before she could make a report on her experience. The second boat - U.575 - radioed her experience report and was then lost. Her commander considered that it was impracticable to operate schnorkel in an area where a submarine hunt was in progress, because the din of the diesels made listening impossible. There was also a danger that the schnorkel

---

46 The anglicised spelling "Schnorkel" is used throughout this publication.

exhaust fumes might be located, or the sound of the boat itself be picked up at long range.

No more reports were available for a time, because the schnorkel-equipped Type VIIC boats were being held in readiness for the anticipated invasion, and it was not until 19th May 1944 that the commander of U.667 reported, on his return, that during the voyage back from 15 degrees West he had proceeded submerged for nine days and was most enthusiastic about the schnorkel. Special training in the schnorkel was, however, required, and in future all boats coming from Germany were detailed to carry this out at Horten, Norway. Similar special training could not be carried out by the boats converting in the French bases because of shallow water and the danger of mines just outside the harbours, so these boats had, perforce, to gather the necessary experience during their first operation.

In due course precise schnorkel orders were introduced, containing sections under the headings: Stand by to proceed schnorkel; Change from proceed submerged to proceed schnorkel; Battery-charging; Change from proceed schnorkel to proceed submerged; and Action stations when proceeding schnorkel. Normally, boats used the schnorkel for three to five hours during the night, schnorkelling being interrupted every 20 minutes, when the diesels were switched off and all-round listening carried out. If the U-boat proceeded with one diesel on screw and one on pure battery-charging, at a speed of three to four knots, then in three hours snorting the batteries received a sufficient charge to operate for one day submerged.

The schnorkel was also very useful for ventilating the boat. To accomplish this the outer diesel air-intake valve was closed slightly, so that some air was sucked out of the compartment by the running diesel; then, as soon as pressure dropped sufficiently, the air was renewed from outside by reopening the air-intake valve. If the interior of the boat became foul as a result of heavy seas or bad depth-keeping causing the schnorkel head to dip below the surface for any length of time, escape apparatus was donned at once, while the boat was brought to periscope depth and ventilated by the method just described. If the presence of the enemy made this impossible, the crew was gravely imperilled by the foul air and it is fairly certain that one or two boats were lost in this way.

421. Increased Coastal Command activity

As the enemy was well aware of the decrease in U-boat activity in the North Atlantic, it was astonishing that he in no way relaxed his A/S measures. In fact, he actually increased them. During March and April the 19th Group of Coastal Command flew about 40 to 50 sorties a day, but these patrols met with little success because those U-boats equipped with *Fliege* were able to detect the approach of the planes in time to dive. Determined to achieve some success, between 25th and 27th March enemy planes attacked one or two boats at the points where they made rendezvous with their escorts, or even attacked them while under escort.

"… This seems to mark a change of tactics. The enemy has apparently deduced the fact that in the Bay of Biscay, which all our U-boats cross submerged, there are comparatively few targets to be found. The fact that he has obviously been deceived on numerous occasions by the *Thetis* buoys[47] laid in the Bay of Biscay, has probably also been in part responsible for a change of tactics. It appears that more planes are now being sent to points where U-boats are obliged to proceed on the surface, i.e. in the swept approach channels to the bases…"

The first of these surprise attacks was carried out on 25th March 1944 by a large number of Mosquitoes and four-engined bombers, and resulted in the loss of U.976, while she was entering St Nazaire. Our immediate reaction was to strengthen the escort for returning U-boats, but these extra escorts had to be taken from the forces allocated to outgoing boats, which were forced thereafter to sail mostly unescorted, by night. As a further precautionary measure,

---

47 Radar decoy buoys designed to defeat metric radar. Post-war tests show that these buoys gave little or no response to centimetric transmissions, and it is therefore unlikely that they had any success.

patrols of heavy fighters were either sent out, or held back in readiness, whenever U-boats were being escorted inwards. On 11th April an attack similar to that of 25th March was made on the unescorted U.255, and in the ensuing air battle four out of 15 attacking Mosquitoes were shot down for the loss of three of our machines; another plane was brought down by an escort. While a search was in progress for the crews of the aircraft shot down, another Ju 88 *Staffel* engaged six to eight Mosquitoes, shooting down two for the loss of three more of our planes.[48] These additional, rather serious losses apparently deterred the enemy from repeating such attacks.

It was apparent that 18 Group Coastal Command, patrolling in Northern Waters, had also been reinforced. In the second half of May, after group *Mitte* had been brought up to strength and U-boats were once again sailing for the Atlantic, the number of machines on patrol rose from an average of 10 a day to 25 or 30 a day. On 25th May U.476 was attacked by a Liberator off Bergen. The plane was shot down, but the U-boat received such serious damage that she had to be sunk by U.990, which, while putting into Bergen with the crew of U.476, was herself sunk by another Liberator pressing home its attack in the face of AA fire from escort vessels. In June it was discovered that 18 Group's intensified operations during the second half of May had caused the loss of a further four boats proceeding to the Atlantic. (371)

REMOTE AREAS

422. Success in distant areas

U-boat Command estimated that, between 22nd February and 1st June 1944, U-boats had sunk, in the North Atlantic, nine ships totalling 27,000 tons (British figures give four of 26,373 tons), in the Central and Western Atlantic, 13 ships totalling 92,600 tons (British figures give 12 of 67,913 tons), and in the Indian Ocean,

---

48 British records on the day claim a total of seven Ju 88s destroyed for the loss of four Mosquitoes.

11 ships totalling 78,700 tons (British figures give seven of 44,461 tons sunk and two of 16,963 tons damaged). Thus, more than 80 per cent of all successes had been obtained in distant areas, but it was not possible to send reinforcements of suitable boats to cover them more densely.

On their first operation, the Type IXC boats, coming from Germany, could reach no farther than the waters off the eastern seaboard of the USA, south of Nova Scotia and Newfoundland. There, traffic was organised into heavily escorted convoys, despite only a remote danger from U-boats, and it was deduced from the Radio Intercept Service that two of the boats operating in this area - U.856 and U.550 - had been lost in encounters with such convoys, somewhere between Halifax and New York.

The success of U.66 in sinking five ships in the Gulf of Guinea in March prompted FO U-boats to send three more boats to the same area in April, but these boats encountered no shipping and returned without a single sinking. Two more boats sent to the Caribbean sighted, like their predecessors, a number of fast-moving tankers, but because of continuous air patrols were unable to manoeuvre into an attacking position, either on or below the surface. Nothing was heard of the effect of the minefields laid by U.218 off Port Castries and San Juan and by U.214 off Casablanca.

423. Central Atlantic worse than the Bay of Biscay

Painful and unnecessary losses occurred in the Central Atlantic. At the beginning of March 1944 the last remaining U-tanker at sea - U.488 - was standing by, west of the Cape Verde Islands, to carry out emergency refuelling. The first boat to require that service was U.801, destined for the Indian Ocean, but on 16th March, while 200 miles west of the Cape Verdes and not far from the tanker, she was attacked on several occasions by carrier-borne aircraft. Her commander reported by W/T that he had suffered heavy casualties from machine-gunning and would need crew replacements from the tanker. Nothing further was heard of U.801.[49] After this, two

---

49 She sank on 17th from damage inflicted on the previous day by aircraft from USS *Block*

refuelling operations were carried out smoothly - U.843 on passage to the Indian Ocean and U.123 on her way back from Freetown - and on 21st April the tanker was to fuel three outward-bound U-boats - U.543, U.68 and U.S15 - 900 miles WNW of the Cape Verde Islands. Then, without sending an intermediate report, she was to proceed to a second rendezvous, where, on 26th April, she was to supply U.66, which was returning from the coast of Guinea. On 25th April, at the second rendezvous, U.66 observed several carrier planes, and during the night of 25th/26th April heard through her listening gear the sound of numerous depth-charge explosions followed by sinking noises. These noises could only have come from U.488, which failed to arrive at the fuelling point and made no reply when called by the U-boat Command.

In the meantime, U.66 had become precariously short of fuel, and on 29th April a rendezvous was arranged for her with U.515, a boat which should have refuelled from U.488 on 21st. This boat, too, failed to arrive, and neither she nor U.68 made any reply when called by the U-boat Command. In actual fact, both had been sunk by carrier aircraft south-east of the Azores. The next operational boat available was U.188, which was returning from the Indian Ocean and was at that time just south of the Cape Verde Islands. She was ordered to transfer fuel and provisions to U.66, 500 miles WNW of the islands, and thereafter to accompany her on the return voyage. On 5th May U.66, after being attacked by carrier planes, made a signal: "Central Atlantic worse than Bay of Biscay…" Next day, when about 90 miles south of the new rendezvous square, U.188 heard the sounds of a heavy depth-charge attack, which presumably resulted in the sinking of U.66. The signal from U.66 was no exaggeration; subsequent research has shown that, at this phase of the war, a greater percentage of boats was lost on passage through the Central Atlantic than in crossing the Bay of Biscay.

Events west of the Cape Verde Islands had indicated that, in the Atlantic, even occasional fuelling from operational boats was now

Island.

too dangerous, and the breakdown of this supply system seriously compromised plans for U-boat traffic to East Asia. But some way of fuelling in patrolled areas had to be found. One solution proposed was that of underwater fuelling, an evolution in which two boats connected pipelines on the surface, then dived and carried on pumping underwater. After this procedure had been tried out in the Baltic and considered practicable, the necessary equipment was installed in a number of boats, including Type XXIs, but it had not been used operationally by the time the war ended.

424. Another supply ship lost in the Indian Ocean

Up to the end of March 1944 an average of four to five U-boats were operating in the Indian Ocean, and of the 11 ships claimed as sunk in this area, eight were torpedoed by U.510. On 23rd February she sank two ships totalling 16,566 tons and damaged another of 9,970 tons from a convoy in the Gulf of Aden.[50]

The Gulf of Aden and the west coast of India offered many opportunities for attack, but they could not now be fully exploited, for at the beginning of March it was necessary to send three boats into the almost-deserted waters to the south-east of Mauritius, there to take on fuel and stores before returning home. In fact, no provision had been made for these boats to remain on patrol off the Indian coast for any length of time, as they had already taken on cargo of important raw materials for transport to Europe. Furthermore, there were insufficient torpedoes left on station to allow of protracted operations. Two transport U-boats were at that time *en route* to Penang, carrying a new supply of torpedoes, but this consignment would have been barely adequate to meet the requirements of the Type IXs of group *Monsun* and, in the event, one of them - U. 1059 - was lost in the Atlantic even before she had reached the equator.

During February the tanker *Brake* had been loaded with fuel, lubricating oil and provisions in Singapore and had then sailed for a position between Madagascar and Australia, where she was to

---

50 This attack was carried out on convoy PA 69, which consisted of 19 ships escorted by two minesweepers.

remain for two months, supplying 12 U-boats on their way to and from the Indian Ocean.

As the tanker *Schliemann* had been sunk in the same area in mid-February (Section 407), the first three *Monsun* boats to replenish carried out a preliminary reconnaissance, U.532 round the supply point 1,000 miles south-east of Mauritius, U.188 at a point 200 miles to the north and U.168 at a point 200 miles to the west. They found no sign of air reconnaissance and, on 11th March, made rendezvous with the *Brake* as arranged. On the 12th, after U.188 and U.532 had been replenished, operations were interrupted by bad weather and the four vessels proceeded in company to the south-westward. At 1056 on the same day, U.188 sighted an aircraft and crash-dived:

"… 1116. Surfaced.

1128. Two aircraft port beam.

1135. Flying-boat starboard quarter. Remain surfaced to stand by *Brake*. Column of smoke bearing 140 degrees. Two planes over it. Gunfire from direction of smoke column. Cannot yet identify vessel. Am about 500 metres astern of *Brake*. Have no torpedoes, so dive. From 1218 to about 1330, 148 shell bursts and 14 heavy explosions heard. Boat sometimes violently shaken, as we are in immediate vicinity of *Brake*.

1320. Loud sinking noises, followed by about 30 minutes of fairly loud and minor explosions. Tanker *Brake* is sunk.

1503. Surfaced just after sunset and proceeded to scene of sinking…"

The crew of *Brake* was picked up by U.168. The sinking of this second tanker, in an area far removed from all air and naval bases and at the exact time that replenishment was in progress, was indeed remarkable.[51] Once again FO U-boats and the Chief of Naval Communications made a thorough investigation to find out whether the enemy had taken bearings on U-boat signals and kept the reckoning, or whether there were other reasons for the appearance of the enemy force. During the course of this investigation it came

---

51 The *Brake* was first sighted by searching aircraft from the escort carrier *Battler* and later sunk by gunfire from the destroyer *Roebuck*.

to light that, between 28th February and 8th March, UIT 24, which was scheduled to refuel after the other three boats, had made several radio signals south of Mauritius (Section 430). These signals were not picked up in Germany, but from them it would have been possible for the enemy to deduce the course of a U-boat proceeding eastwards towards a supply point. This, however, could hardly be the full explanation, for the most that could be obtained from bearings was information about the course of the boat and not the exact time of supplying, while the enemy had started up his air reconnaissance only one day before the replenishment operation was due to begin and must have had some idea of the programme. Treason, compromise of the U-boat codes, or interception of radio traffic to Japan may have been contributory causes, but nothing definite could be established.

RETROSPECT

425. Containing tactics prove costly

"… 1st June 1944. U-boats' own observations, agents' reports and radio intelligence have shown that the policy of 'tying down enemy forces' has so far been successful. The number of enemy planes on operations, the number of A/S vessels, aircraft carriers and miscellaneous vessels engaged on A/S patrol or escort work has increased.

For the officers and men of the U-boats, the task of tying down enemy forces is a particularly heavy responsibility. In the past, more than with any other branch of the Service, success has been the personal reward of the entire crew and has endowed them with extra keenness and powers of endurance. Now, chances for attack are comparatively remote, while those of not returning from operations are very high. In the past few months an average of only 70 per cent of all boats has returned from operations…"

In these words FO U-boats outlined the events of the three months prior to June 1944, during which, despite cautious containing tactics, losses had not fallen. Indeed, the struggle for survival in operational areas was now extremely hard.

On 13th May 1944 an order was issued to the effect that no Type VIIC boats were to be at sea for more than eight weeks at a time, and on 1st June 1944 five U-boats, sailing from Norway, were ordered to put into French Atlantic bases to fit schnorkel and *Hohentwiel*. In future no boat was to put to sea without these two valuable installations, but further heavy losses were still anticipated, and those in authority were obliged to consider carefully if it was correct to continue with the U-boat war as hitherto or whether some other course should be taken. Very serious thought was given to this matter, the conclusion drawn being recorded in the War Diary of 1st June 1944, which, in order to afford a better understanding of subsequent developments, is quoted in some detail in the following section.

426. Reasons for continuing the U-boat war

"… Our present successes, and those which we may expect to gain in the future with the older type boats, are not sufficient by themselves to justify either the high expenditure of manpower and material at present being lavished on the U-boat arm at home or the heavy toll taken of U-boats in the Atlantic, but for various reasons both operations and expenditure are inevitable.

It is imperative to continue the U-boat war, because once it has come to a standstill we shall be unable to resume. To keep the enemy on his toes is of absolute importance from the standpoint of tactics, technology and, not least, morale. The U-boat arm has shown that it can survive the darkest hours. Equipped with new weapons, it must face the battle ahead with that same unshaken confidence that it has even today, however serious may be the losses.

It is known for certain that the enemy have used several thousand aircraft and many hundreds of escort vessels, from destroyers down to fishing smacks, to protect their shipping against U-boats…"

British Coastal Command Chart

15 Group	200 aircraft	80 flying-boats
15 Group	200 aircraft	-
15 Group	320 aircraft	30 flying-boats
15 Group	580 aircraft	40 flying-boats
Total	1,300 aircraft	150 flying-boats

Anglo-American Naval Forces

From destroyer downwards in the Atlantic, Arctic, Mediterranean and Indian Ocean. All ships listed are either for use as escort vessels or are used as such in emergency:

Coastal Convoys and General Escort Work

	Destoyers	Frigates	Escorts Vessels	*Total*
Britain	205	160	600	965
USA	120	85	130	335
	325	245	730	1,300

Coastal Convoys and Routine A/S Patrols

	Small Escorts Vessels	A/S Vessels	*Total*
Britain	850	540	1,390
USA	310	340	650
	1,160	880	2,040

To abandon U-boat warfare would mean:

a. That a large number of enemy aircraft, including many four-engined bombers, would be released for operations over Germany and that many aircraft, with crews specially trained for flying at sea, would be free to attack German shipping along the entire coastline of Europe.

b. That that section of the Allies' aircraft industry devoted to the construction of A/S aircraft (flying-boats, bombers, torpedo-planes, carrier planes), together with numerous air bases

147

and their ground staff, would be directed towards further intensification of the enemy air offensive against Germany.

c.   That a large number of destroyers and light escort forces would be released for operations against German coastal shipping.

d.   That, in the event of invasion, these air and naval forces could be employed in the assault of our shores.

The effect of this diversion of forces must not be underestimated. In fitting out the new boats, training their crews and developing new U-boat tactics, full account must be taken of the enemy's current A/S developments in interception and attack. This is only possible if U-boats continue to collect experience from actual operations. In this way our own equipment will be completely up to date when the new offensive is ready to begin.

The only conclusion to be drawn is that U-boat warfare must continue with the resources available and that losses, which are at present disproportionately heavy, must be borne, however bitter. Most of the industrial capacity engaged on U-boat construction will be devoted to the building of the new Types XXI and XXIII. There will be no further serial construction of existing types, even though the flow of older-type boats from Germany, to replace losses, may .cease before delivery of the new boats begins. Every effort will be made, within the competence of the U-boat Command, to ensure that the new boats are commissioned with properly trained crews. To this end, experienced commanders, officers and men will be recalled from sea, even though this may mean temporarily reducing the fighting efficiency of operational boats. It will probably be necessary to pay off the old Type VIIC boats and draft whole crews with operational experience to commission the Type XXIs..." (372).

U-BOATS AS BLOCKADE-RUNNERS

427. The end of surface blockade-running

Although Germany had gained a fair measure of self-sufficiency through her conquests in the east and west, the Ministry of Food and Economics had declared that, to maintain the German war economy, annual imports of raw materials must reach 400,000 tons, but, taking into account the situation at sea and the availability of merchant vessels suitable for blockade-running, there was no hope of reaching this figure. Nevertheless, by stretching available shipping resources to the limit, between 1941 and the end of 1943 the Naval Staff succeeded in shipping to Europe a total of 110,800 tons of raw materials - 49,000 tons of fats, 44,000 tons of rubber, 4,800 tons of ore and 13,000 tons of mixed cargo - and a further 56,000 tons to East Asia. Thirty-five ships sailed from East Asia, of which 16 reached Europe; outward bound, six out of 21 ships were lost (373, 374).

Particularly heavy losses were suffered during the blockade-running season which started in the autumn of 1943, in the course of which the enemy's screen of long-range aircraft and carrier groups trapped seven ships returning from the East, all of them destroyed. However, in view of repeated calls from the Economics and Armaments Ministries for more raw materials, the Naval Staff felt obliged to make a further attempt at blockade-running from Japan during the next dark season, beginning in the autumn of 1943. Out of five fast ships - the *Osorno*, *Alsterufer*, *Rio Grande*, *Weserland* and *Burgenland* - only the *Osorno* reached Europe, putting into Bordeaux on 25th December 1943. The *Alsterufer* was sunk by British forces off the west coast of France and the others by US forces in the South Atlantic. Following these failures, Hitler on 18th January 1944 cancelled the sailing of four ships standing by in Bordeaux with cargoes for Japan, which signified the end of organised large-scale blockade-running, for there were no ships left in East Asia fast enough to attempt the breakthrough. Now, the only vessels with any chance of running the blockade were U-boats.

428. Building programme for transport U-boats falls through

The Naval Staff had been considering, since 1942, the feasibility of using U-boats for the transport of raw materials from abroad, and, following the heavy losses incurred during the 1942 blockade-running season, a start was made on the construction of transport U-boats and also of underwater barges. In the meantime Italian, and subsequently German, operational U-boats were called upon to assist in the shipment of raw materials. The various methods employed are examined separately.

The expanded fleet-construction programme, which Dönitz had submitted to Hitler on 11th April 1943, contained provision for the building of three Type XX transport U-boats a month (Section 338). These had a displacement of 2,700 tons, with a calculated cargo capacity of 450 tons of rubber outside the pressure hull, 190 tons of tin in the keel and on the upper deck, and 110 tons of ore and other cargo inside the pressure hull. Thirty boats - U.1601 to U.1615 and U.1701 to U.1715 - were to be commissioned successively, the first being ready by the summer of 1944. The minimum quantity of cargo to be carried in 1944 was fixed at 20,000 tons and, to achieve this figure, 25 to 30 boats would have to complete two voyages a year (375). However, increasing difficulties in the general field of arms production resulted in delays to the building programme, and at the beginning of 1944 it became clear that the first Type XX boats would not be commissioned before January 1945 at the earliest, with a subsequent completion rate of only one or two a month (376). In March of 1944, therefore, the Naval Staff began to give serious thought to the idea of scrapping the Type XX transport U-boat and replacing it with the Type XXIE, which was the Type XXI redesigned for cargo carrying; and on 27th May, after hearing that completion of the first Type XXs would be subject to a further three months' delay, Dönitz cancelled the whole programme (377). Exceptionally, the three Type XXs in the most advanced stage of construction were to be completed and used for the carriage of fuel between Germany and Norway, but they were never delivered. Finally, a decision on the conversion of Type XXI into Type XXIE transport boats - 65 tons of cargo in the keel and 95 tons inside the pressure hull - due to be taken in the autumn of 1944, was at first postponed and subsequently shelved.

429. Towing of underwater barges impracticable

The Naval Staff had also been studying the problem of using underwater barges for the transport of raw materials. The idea of building such a means of transport had been first mooted in 1943 when supplies to North Africa had been virtually cut off owing to the utter failure of the Italian convoy organisation (378).

The first attempt to tow a barge of 90 tons displacement was successfully accomplished by a Type VIIC, the U.1163, in October 1943 (379). The U-boat contrived to tow the barge, both on the surface and under water, without upsetting her depth-keeping while increasing or decreasing speed, or while turning. However, it was found that the towing boat must maintain a speed through the water of at least 4-1 knots when at periscope depth, for at 3-9 knots the barge lost the dynamic force necessary to hold it under water. In the spring of 1944, contracts were placed for 50 such 90-ton barges, to be towed by tugs in European waters (Norway and the Italian and Dalmatian coasts). At the same time, further attempts were made to provide a barge with a better aerodynamic form and with additional fittings, such as equipment which would allow it to be slipped or sunk from the towing U-boat. Should these efforts prove successful, the Naval Staff seriously considered:

"… organising a towing service between Europe and East Asia, surface vessels covering the stretch from East Asia to the South Atlantic, while outward or homeward bound operational U-boats negotiated the final leg from the South Atlantic to Europe…" (380).

But, as FO U-boats expected, further trials proved that it was impossible to reduce the minimum towing speed. And as German U-boats had insufficient battery capacity to proceed submerged at four knots for any length of time - and it was already dangerous enough in 1944 for a U-boat to proceed at normal speeds without towing anything - the idea was abandoned.

430. Failure of the *Merkator* boats

On 8th February 1943, in his first conference with Hitler as Commander-in-Chief of the Navy, Dönitz had suggested using the few serviceable Italian Atlantic submarines for cargo-carrying to and from East Asia, and compensating for this by sending extra German U-boats to the Mediterranean. After one or two difficulties, the Supramarina sanctioned the use for this purpose of the last 10 Italian boats operating from Bordeaux, and these were given the code name of *Aquila*; however, two of them were lost on their last Atlantic operation - *Archimede* on 15th April and *Leonardo da Vinci* on 23rd May 1943.

Although the first two *Aquila* boats to take on cargo - *Barbarigo* and *Enrico Tazzoli* - disappeared after sailing from the Bay of Biscay in May, by the end of August the *Reginaldo Giuliani, Commandante Alfredo Cappellini* and *Luigi Torelli* had all reached Singapore. At that time there was considerable doubt about the future of the Italian armed forces and the Japanese authorities used every pretext to prevent these three boats from leaving; the *Giuseppe Finzi* and *Alpino Attilio Bagnolini* were similarly delayed at Bordeaux until after the Italian capitulation, when all the Italian boats were taken over by German crews. The *Ammiraglio Cagni*, however, which was still on her last Atlantic operation at the time of the capitulation, surrendered to the British. The code name *Aquila* had thus to be considered compromised and changed to *Merkator*, while the five remaining boats were designated UIT 21 to UIT 25.

In the event, it was some time before the German crews became acquainted with the unfamiliar layout of the Italian boats and could complete the necessary machinery overhauls. The first Bordeaux boat to sail - UIT 22 (*Bagnolini*) - did not leave until January 1944, and on 22nd February she was machine-gunned by an enemy plane 900 miles south-west of Ascension Island, this attack causing such loss of oil from her outer bunkers that it became necessary for her to refuel before reaching Penang. U.178, then returning from the Indian Ocean to Europe, was detailed to carry out this task, and a rendezvous was arranged for 12th March at a point 500 miles south of Cape Town, but on arrival at the given position U.178 found only a large patch of oil. It was clear to U-boat Command that UIT 22 had been sunk by the enemy on the day before, which was borne out by radio intelligence. The second Bordeaux boat - UIT 21 (*Finzi*) - had so many engine defects that she was paid off and eventually scuttled in August 1944.

Of the Far East contingent, UIT 23 (*Giuliani*) was torpedoed and sunk by an Allied submarine on 14th February 1944 while on passage from Singapore to Penang. UIT 24 (*Cappellini*), *en route* to Bordeaux with a cargo of 115 tons of rubber, 55 tons of tin and 10 tons of miscellaneous goods, was forced to refuel from U.532 and return to Penang following the sinking of the tanker *Brake* on 12th March 1944. Because of engine trouble, she was then sent to Japan for overhaul, together with UIT 25 (*Torelli*), and was not ready to return to Europe until August; then, as there was no possibility of refuelling the boats *en route*, their sailing was cancelled and they were subsequently handed over to the Japanese. Thus, not a single ton of cargo was brought to Europe by the *Merkator* boats, another indication of the difficult situation in the Atlantic. When one considers the amount of effort which was expended on manning these Italian submarines with German crews, overhauling their faulty machinery and installing radar and radar-location equipment, one cannot but conclude that it was misplaced. Measured against the Allied A/S situation in 1943, these Italian submarines belonged not to the sea, but, as German U-boat men used to say, to the scrap-heap (381).

431. Plans for the import of raw materials finally frustrated

As early as the summer of 1943, the Naval Staff, anxious to seize every opportunity to exchange freight with East Asia, has arranged for all operation boats assigned to the Indian Ocean - those following group *Monsun* - to carry cargo in place of keel ballast. The principal cargoes for Japan were mercury and lead and, on the return journey, tin and wolfram ores. Boats returning home were also required to find further cargo space for rubber, molybdenum, opium and quinine. With careful stowage it was possible for the Type IXC or IXD to carry 110 to 130 tons of cargo in the keel and outside the hull, and 20 to 30 tons inside the boat (382).

When surface blockade-running ceased in January 1944 the shipment of raw materials to Germany became a prime responsibility for U-boats returning home from Penang; but even with every available boat loaded to capacity, only a fraction of the originally planned shipments could be carried, and it thus became necessary to review the raw material demands of the German economy and to scale them down considerably. No doubt it would have been better, from 1941 onwards, to have chosen a different distribution of gross imports - for instance, instead of 50,000 tons of nutritive fats, which represented only 2-4 per cent of Germany's total consumption of this commodity, it would have been better to have imported larger quantities of rubber and other raw materials - but at the same time the Ministry of Food had first call on the blockade-runners and, owing to over-optimism in regard to the expected duration of hostilities, the supply of rubber already imported was considered sufficient to Germany's future war needs.

A review of imports carried out in January 1944 showed that, by stretching available stocks, extra requirements of rubber, tin and wolfram would be covered until 1945, if at least 1,000 tons of cargo were to be shipped by the end of 1944 and 1,000 tons a month thereafter. The Naval Operations Division therefore drew up a comprehensive long-term plan aimed at attaining this target and providing for the *Monsun* and *Merkator* boats, together with one or two Japanese submarines, to carry "on shipments until the more suitable Type XX transport boats became available (383). This plan, however, proved to be purely theoretical, not only due to the failure of the *Merkator* boats but also to the heavy losses sustained by U-boats both *en route* to and in the Indian Ocean (Sections 406 and 457), and to difficulties arising from the loss of replenishment vessels. The sinking of the *Brake*, for instance, prevented the return of both U.168, which had taken the survivors of *Brake* back to Penang, and U.532, which had had to carry out the emergency refuelling of UIT 24.

Even though the import quota was reduced in January 1944, the U-boats could only carry a fraction of it and, after the building of

154

transport U-boats had been cancelled in May 1944, the Director of Naval Armaments and the Director of the German Planning Office - President Kehrl - were ordered by the C-in-C Navy in June to determine afresh what raw materials were really essential to maintain the German war economy. The astonishing conclusion of this new review was that, except for fuel, existing stocks and home production were sufficient for the time being. However, U-boats would be required to import, monthly, from June 1945, 240 tons of rubber; from September 1945, 200 tons of wolfram concentrates; from April 1946, 35 tons of molybdenum concentrates; and from June 1947, 200 tons of zinc (384). Additionally, miscellaneous goods - bismuth, selenium, cassium, quinine and opium - were required immediately, to a total of 12 tons a month. By using all operational boats returning from East Asia for cargo-carrying - which meant only two torpedoes and no guns - the deadline dates might be extended until sufficient Type XXI and later Type XXIE boats, were available for the full shipment programme. The Navy therefore need take no further special steps.

Up to the end of the war, the part played by U-boats in respect of raw-material shipments was limited. Instead of 14 U-boats, as laid down in the Naval Staff's 1944 plan, only three reached Bordeaux from East Asia during 1944 - the Japanese submarine *Kiefer*, U.178 and U.188. In April 1945, the U.843 and U.861, each carrying 100 tons of zinc, reached the coast of Norway and, while proceeding thence to Germany, U.843 was sunk by air attack in the Belts. In the same month, U.510 put in to St Nazaire, because she had insufficient fuel to reach Norway. U.532 was proceeding home at the time of the capitulation and she took her cargo of 100 tons of tin, 60 tons of rubber, eight tons of wolfram and 5 tons of molybdenum to Loch Eriboll.

It was only pressure of circumstances that was responsible for the expenditure of so much effort on a project for which U-boats were little suited and in no position to fulfill after May 1943, and, in fact, their failure to achieve the target set for raw material imports made no appreciable difference to Germany's prosecution of the war.

JUNE-SEPTEMBER 1944

JUNE 1944
THE NORMANDY INVASION

432. Prospects of the schnorkel boats

For some weeks prior to the beginning of June, the Biscay-based Type VIIC U-boats, on becoming ready for sea, had carried out deep-diving and trimming trials and then returned to base, remaining at six hours' notice. It had been our intention to equip most of these boats with schnorkel during May; but production delays occasioned by the Allied bombing offensive in Germany prevented this from being done. Moreover, the progressive disruption of traffic in France led to loss of much of the equipment which was despatched. In the event, only eight boats were equipped that month, of which five were formed into group *Dragoner* and sailed, between 17th and 25th May, for the western part of the Channel to operate, with the support of the shore radar service, against the enemy cruiser and destroyer formations which made occasional excursions into that area. Although valuable experience was gained during the operation, both in the use of the schnorkel and in the tactics to be adopted in an area heavily patrolled by aircraft, results were disappointing in that no contacts resulted from a steady stream of information passed to the U-boats. At the same time we were dismayed to discover from radio intelligence reports that the enemy was very soon aware of the location of the boats through detection of the schnorkel by airborne radar.

As group *Dragoner*'s operation had shown that schnorkel-fitted boats were able to remain in an area dominated by enemy aircraft, it was possible to plan for their future employment in the Channel against the enemy's invasion forces. Indeed, consideration was given to moving them at once to bases on the French north coast; but this idea was rejected, since, with no bunkers available at Cherbourg, Le Havre or Boulogne, the U-boats would have fallen easy victim to air attack, even before the invasion occurred. Operational control of Channel U-boats was, however, transferred to the SO U-boats West since he was thoroughly conversant with the minefields in that area and also for fear of a breakdown of communications between Germany and western France at the beginning of the invasion.

433. Initial operations against the Normandy landings

At 0001 on 6th June, U-boat dispositions in Home Waters were:

(a) Group *Mitte*, comprising 22 non-schnorkel boats, lying at six hours' notice at Bergen, Stavanger and Kristiansand.

(b) Ten non-schnorkel and seven schnorkel-fitted boats *en route* from Norway to the Atlantic, some of them already 300 to 500 miles south of Iceland. Actually, five of these boats had already been destroyed and one damaged, but we were unaware of this.

(c) Three Type IX boats on weather reporting duty in 30 degrees West.

(d) Group *Landwirt*, comprising 37 boats all told. Of these, eight schnorkel-fitted and nine non-schnorkel were at Brest; while the remaining 19, of which only one was fitted with schnorkel, were distributed between St Nazaire, Lorient and La Pallice. All were at six hours' notice.

First information of the landings reached U-boat headquarters at 0305 on 6th June, and groups *Mitte* and *Landwirt* were brought to immediate notice; the five schnorkel boats which were already in the Atlantic were ordered to make for Western France at high speed, while those still to the west of Norway were halted and told to remain in their present positions until further orders.

In this hour of crisis the role of the U-boats was decisive to the outcome of the war and every available boat had to be flung into the battle, regardless of cost. Clearly, their primary task was to attack the invasion fleet off the Normandy coast. But this area was only accessible to schnorkel boats and even they would have great difficulty in reaching it, since the enemy would surely devote a large proportion of his uncommitted A/S forces to the protection of his western flank. However, should the eight *Landwirt* schnorkel boats succeed in forcing their way into the central English Channel, their prospects of success against the great weight of shipping to be found there might be good. The chances of their effecting a breakthrough would certainly be enhanced if further boats were transiting the area at the same time; so, with the additional knowledge that a number of enemy supply convoys were coming from the direction of the Irish Sea, Dönitz was compelled, against his better judgement, also to send the nine Brest-based non-schnorkel boats into the danger area on the first day in order to attack traffic passing through the western Channel on its way to Seine Bay. For the rest, since the enemy had complete air superiority and we were thus unable to discover whether or not he intended to land elsewhere, the remaining non-schnorkel boats of group *Landwirt* were sent to cover the approaches to the Biscay coast, while those boats which had been halted west of Norway were assigned specific patrol areas and group *Mitte* remained in harbour at short notice.

434. First U-boats in the Channel

Despite a shortage of local escort vessels and frequent interruption of Headquarters communications, SO U-boats West managed to sail 35 of the 36 boats of group *Landwirt* on the first day of the landings. The eight schnorkel boats were sent to the area north of Cherbourg, where they were expected to arrive in five to six days, and the nine non-schnorkel boats from Brest to the area between Lizard Head and Hartland Point. They were ordered to proceed at high speed on the surface and consequently had to fight their way through against enemy air opposition. But there was no alternative to this, since it was essential to bring our forces to bear while the invasion was still young and the enemy therefore at his weakest; besides which the boats had to be out of Brest and well away from the coast that night, in order to get out of range of the enemy A/S forces patrolling just off the harbour. As was to be expected, this mass exodus of U-boats evoked the strongest enemy air activity hitherto encountered, nine boats reporting having been attacked, while double that number of attacks and sightings were reported by the enemy aircraft engaged. Subsequently it appeared that more than 50 air attacks occurred on that first night, while four large aircraft were shot down. The drama of some of these incidents is illustrated by the log of U.415:

"... 7th June 1944, 0140. Sea 1 to 2, swell, moonlight, good visibility. Dropped escort off Brest. Course 270 degrees, full speed (15 knots).

0145. Next astern attacked by aircraft. I open fire with her. Aircraft shot down by U.256. Radar audible on all bearings, strength 3 to 4.

0220. Radar no longer audible to starboard, so assume aircraft on run in. Sunderland approaches from green 40. I open fire. Four bombs fall just ahead and detonate under the boat. Liberator attacks simultaneously from the starboard beam, firing her guns which hit my bridge. She drops no bombs. The Sunderland's bombs have brought my diesels to a standstill. The boat rises high in the water and settles by the stern, so that water enters the conning-tower hatch. Order 'Clear lower deck; clear away rubber dinghy'. Radio out of action so cannot report. Manned emergency radio transmitter on bridge. Rubber dinghy and life-buoys are being cleared away. Boat remains afloat, so order all ammunition on to the bridge. Rudder jammed to starboard.

1228. Sunderland renews attack from starboard, firing her guns and dropping bombs from low altitude. Bombs straddle us amidships. Directly afterwards the Liberator flies in from the port bow. I open fire. My twin machine-guns shoot well and the aircraft crashes in flames. My *Wanze* and *Fliege* have been shot out of action. Some time later the Senior Engineer reports all clear for diving on one electric motor, so I order all hands below and commence return passage..."

On that first night, one schnorkel and five non-schnorkel boats reported that they were returning because of damage, while U.970

and U.955, the latter returning from the Atlantic, were sunk. Towards the morning of the 7th we deemed it necessary to allow the boats to proceed to their stations submerged, and their daily run was thereby reduced to 50 or 60 miles; however, despite this relaxation, two more boats - U.629 and U.373 - were lost and two others damaged on the following night. By 10th June, two of the nine non-schnorkel boats which had left Brest for the Plymouth area had been sunk, while five had been forced to return damaged, and it was clearly impossible for U-boats without schnorkel to reach the western part of the Channel. On the following day, therefore, the two boats still at sea - -U.740 and U.821 - were advised to return, but they failed to do so and were assumed to have been destroyed on their outward passage.[52]

435. Problem of employment of the non-schnorkel boats

The non-schnorkel boats which left Lorient, St Nazaire and La Pallice on 6th June were drawn up in a double reconnaissance line between the latitudes of Brest and Bordeaux, conforming roughly to the 200-metre line. On 8th June one of our meteorological aircraft sighted a south-bound convoy 120 miles west of Brest and, since this could have been an enemy landing force, the boats were moved in to the 100-metre line, whence they could engage more speedily. Some hours later these ships were identified as fishing vessels; nevertheless, the boats were retained on the 100-metre line, for here they could lie on the bottom for long periods and thereby shorten the time needed for recharging batteries. Normally they were forbidden to bottom in less than 100 metres of water; but this ban was now lifted, since the danger from ground mines was regarded as less than that from air attack while on the surface. Although this procedure reduced to a minimum the time spent on the surface, the boats were still located and attacked on almost every night; but we dared not recall them to harbour, because a further enemy landing, or the mining of the approach channels, could have trapped them there. We therefore chose the lesser evil and left them exposed to the danger of air attack at sea. By 12th June it was evident, from the strength in which the

---

52 U.740 and U.821 were sunk by aircraft on 9th and 10th June respectively.

enemy had landed in Normandy, that the danger of an immediate landing on the Biscay coast had passed and the boats were recalled to harbour, where they remained at six hours' notice.

Their future employment was the subject of long discussion, and the question arose as to whether it might not be more expedient to send them into the Atlantic rather than keep them idle in harbour, even though their prospects against convoys would be extremely poor, for their appearance in the Atlantic might well induce the enemy again to employ his independent hunter groups in that area, from where they had been withdrawn to the Channel. However, FO U-boats believed that the enemy possessed sufficient A/S vessels to render such a withdrawal unnecessary and that he was still able to provide his Atlantic convoys with, at least, close escorts and escort carriers. In the Flag-Officer's opinion, therefore, the sending of non-schnorkel boats to the Atlantic would result only in further heavy losses, whereas, by keeping them in western France we still had some prospect of inflicting damage on the enemy in the event - still a possibility - of his invading the Biscay coast.

"… Two years ago it was true to say that Norway had to be defended in American waters; that is, where we could sink the greatest tonnage. This precept is no longer valid. Today it is more important to sink one LST in the invasion area than, say, one Liberty ship in the Atlantic…" (385).

The boats therefore remained in their bases, while the work of equipping them with schnorkel was pressed on with the utmost vigour.

436. Precautions against an enemy landing in Norway

In the opinion of the German Naval Staff, the British invasion forces still remaining in Scottish and English coast ports on 8th June were sufficient for a secondary landing on the Norwegian coast, and hence they considered that the threat to Norway persisted.

By virtue of the rugged nature of the Norwegian coastline, the boats of group *Mitte* were in less danger of being trapped in their bases through an enemy landing, or by minelaying, than those of group *Landwirt*. However, there were too few reconnaissance aircraft available in the area to guarantee the sighting of an approaching landing force in sufficient time, and so a large number of U-boats had to be used for reconnaissance duties in Norwegian waters, for which they were ill suited. Between 8th and 10th June, 11 boats of group *Mitte* put to sea and, together with those boats already on patrol, formed a reconnaissance line from Trondheim to Lindesnes. Additional boats from Kiel later brought the strength of the flotilla up to 30, of which 16 were kept at sea. The patrolling boats suffered from frequent air attacks and they were therefore ordered to remain submerged, except when recharging batteries; the depth of water was too great to permit lying on the bottom, but some of them took advantage of density layers to drift, stopped and trimmed. Nevertheless, despite all precautions, two boats from group *Mitte* and four Atlantic-bound schnorkel boats fell victim to enemy aircraft during the month . Towards the end of June, as it became obvious that the threat to Norway had greatly diminished, the number of boats on patrol between 57 and 61 degrees North was reduced to five. Concurrently, nine boats of group *Mitte* were paid off and their crews drafted to the 23rd and 24th Flotillas, for manning the new Type XXI U-boats.

437. Considerations concerning the use of schnorkel boats in the Channel

Since the enemy had chosen to establish his bridgehead in Seine Bay, it was abundantly clear that only schnorkel boats had any chance at all of attacking his supply traffic, and that even they would be running a grave risk in so doing. FO U-boats, although outwardly confident, was haunted by the fear that he had demanded the impossible from his crews. We had had too little operational experience with the schnorkel to lay down hard and fast instructions for its use, or to state what procedures should be adopted in the presence of numerous A/S vessels; we did not even know if the boats would find the time to schnorkel-charge their batteries while operating in such a limited and populated area. No operational experience had been gained in the shallow waters of the Channel since 1940; it was a year since we had operated in American coastal waters; and, for all we knew, the enemy might now possess depth-charges or other weapons of such devastating effect in shallow water that a U-boat's detection would ensure her destruction. Thus the boats, fitted with a schnorkel installation with which they were still unfamiliar, were being sent to face an unknown threat in an area considered, even in 1940, as too dangerous for such operations.

Operational control was rendered difficult and onerous by the problem of communicating with U-boats, even in normal operations, and during group *Dragoner*'s brief sortie into the Channel in May there had been many instances of boats missing important messages through having to schnorkel, despite careful timing of long-wave routines. It was most likely, therefore, that in the present circumstances the boats would have few opportunities to transmit, and that the Command would have to rely entirely upon radio intercepts and the reports of returning commanders for a picture of the situation. Such intelligence could be long out of date, and it is not surprising that we were unable to make up our minds on the viability of U-boats in the Channel, either before or after the invasion.

438. Twelve schnorkel boats against the invasion

The absence of an accurate assessment of the situation imposed an additional burden of responsibility on FO U-boats. His decision to use the schnorkel boats was influenced by the fact that, of all the weapons at our disposal, the U-boat was the only one capable of destroying any considerable quantity of the enemy's invasion supplies before they had been landed; and, when balancing the amount of ammunition carried in a supply ship, or the number of tanks in an LST, against the cost in German lives and material needed to destroy these once they had been landed, there could be only one conclusion, namely, to attack the supply traffic with every available U-boat.

This requirement overruled our reluctance to use those schnorkel boats joining direct from Germany, which were on their first operational cruise and usually reached the approaches to the Channel only after a strenuous three- to four-week passage; indeed, to reduce this transit time, four of these boats were ordered to proceed surfaced, at high speed, as far as the latitude of the south of Ireland and then to continue into the Channel on schnorkel. One other was sent to the North Channel and another to the Minch, with the object of tying down enemy forces in that area.

In the early stages of the Normandy landings only 12 schnorkel boats were able to take an active part against the enemy's seaborne forces - eight from group *Landwirt* and the four mentioned above.

439. Experience of enemy countermeasures

"... Every enemy vessel supporting the landing, even though it may be carrying only 50 men or a tank, is a target. Press home your attack, even at the cost of your boat. Should it be necessary to close the enemy landing fleet, pay no regard to the danger of shallow water, mines or other hazards.

Each soldier and weapon destroyed before reaching the beachhead diminishes the enemy's chance of victory.

A U-boat which inflicts losses on the invasion forces fulfils her highest mission and justifies her existence, even though she herself may be destroyed." (386)

This grim order was carried by the boats when they sailed from Brest on 6th June. On the way out, that night, most of them came under attack from enemy aircraft and the next day brought them into contact with the surface groups, which were waiting for them just off the coast. The difficulty experienced in forcing a way through the ring of enemy warships was brought home to us by a report from U.984, which returned to Brest on 9th June. U.984 had been located on 7th, 30 miles north-west of Ushant, by a surface group which subjected her to a 24-hour depth-charge pursuit and almost exhausted her. She finally shook off her pursuers by heading for the French coast, and an extract from her log is of interest:

"... 8.6.44. 2000. Six miles west of Ushant. Although enemy radar is still audible, I decide to schnorkel a little to ventilate the boat. We have now been submerged continuously for nearly 42 hours without a change of air, and for the last 12 hours breathing conditions have been extraordinarily bad. The men have literally been gasping for breath. A certain amount of relief has been obtained by breathing through potash cartridges, with the aid of escape apparatus mouthpieces.

2212. I am now close to the coast, my batteries completely exhausted, so decide to return to Brest to recharge and top up with torpedoes..."

Similar experiences were reported by U.953, which entered Brest on 18th June, and by U.269, U.27S and U.984 (again), which all put into St Peter Port, Guernsey, between 13th and 18th. On 8th June, when 40 miles north-west of Ushant, U.953 had an encounter with a group of three destroyers, one of which bore the number H90, and claimed to have sunk all three;[53] but, after developing a defect in her periscope, she was forced to return before reaching the operational area. Apparently the enemy had set up several patrol lines between Lizard Head and Ushant, and between Start Point and the Channel Islands, besides keeping a particularly sharp watch on French waters.

The use of St Peter Port by the three U-boats, for battery-charging, served to provide interesting proof of the excellence of the enemy's intelligence system. Up to that time the harbour had been left unmolested by enemy aircraft; but a few hours after the arrival of each boat an attack was delivered by fighter-bombers, resulting in the loss of one patrol vessel and damage to two others.

We were greatly concerned at reports that boats had been bombed - and perhaps fired at - while schnorkelling at night, indicating that the schnorkel could be located and recognised by radar. In these circumstances it became even more difficult for the boats to find time and space for recharging their batteries, and we could only hope that no such accurate location and recognition would be possible amongst the dense traffic to be found in the actual area of operations. In view of these schnorkelling difficulties we refrained from restricting the boats to specific attack areas and merely detailed

---

53 No ship was sunk in this attack, nor was H90 - HMS *Broadway* - present.

three to operate to the north and three to the south of the parallel 50° 10' North, with freedom to cross this line if A/S and traffic conditions so demanded.

440. Great uncertainty over the situation in the Channel

Enemy radio intercepts on 11th and 13th June indicated that one or more boats had reached mid-Channel. But, as there was no further intelligence of this nature, and in the light of the reports of those boats which had returned, serious doubt soon arose as to whether the intercepts had referred to actual asdic contacts, or merely to the suspected presence of U-boats. This lack of further intercepted enemy action reports was particularly worrying, as it pointed to the possible destruction of any boats which had managed to reach Seine Bay. Because of this uncertainty and our lack of knowledge of the operational possibilities in the assault area, we examined the question of recalling to base those four boats approaching the Channel from Germany, which were now approximately south of Ireland, and of diverting the next four - at this time north and north-west of Britain - to attack areas to the west of the British Isles. However, in view of the necessity to exhaust every possible means in combating the invasion, we determined to keep to our original plan and send them all to the Channel.

On 17th June FO U-boats reluctantly decided that the next four Biscay-based schnorkel boats to become operational should be used to transport anti-tank and machine-gun ammunition to Cherbourg, which was now cut off and seriously threatened.

"… The U-boat is a complicated and highly developed instrument of war, wholly unsuited to transport purposes. My decision to employ them on this task is made easier by the fact that we are completely ignorant of the operational possibilities in the landing area…" (387).

The four boats duly sailed from Brest and La Pallice, between 20th and 22nd June, with 8,000 rounds of anti-tank and 350,000 rounds of machine-gun ammunition, only to be recalled on 23rd, because the entrance to Cherbourg harbour was blocked.

441. The recall of the U-boats from sea

The first positive information of conditions in the actual operational area was provided by U.621 and U.764, both of which returned to Brest on 22nd June. The former had, on 15th June, penetrated the screen of a convoy of six LSTs, to the north of Seine Bay, and had fired a spread of three torpedoes which all detonated prematurely; however, she later sank a straggler - LCP 280 - with a T5 torpedo. On 18th, in the same vicinity, prematures again robbed her of success, this time against a Valiant and a King George V class battleship. U.764 had, on 15th June, attacked and sunk the frigate *Blackwood* to the north of Jersey, but had then to return on account of damage.

Operational conditions appeared to correspond generally with our original expectations, the approach to the operational area proving very difficult, while the area itself offered considerable opportunity for successful attacks, with little enemy opposition because of poor conditions for asdic and radar location. However, these opportunities could not be fully exploited on account of torpedo failures and the U-boat's low speed, and both boats reported being frequently passed over by convoys without an opportunity to attack them.

No further reports were to be received from the operational area until the beginning of July; so when, on 25th June, a four-day series of intercepted enemy U-boat sighting reports suddenly ceased, we wondered whether the A/S situation might have deteriorated since U.621 and U.764 left the area or, alternatively, whether these two boats might not have struck a particularly favourable period. Worried by this uncertainty, we decided, on 2nd July, to send no more boats to mid-Channel, and five, then passing through the western Channel *en route* to the operational area, were recalled to Brest, where they were to remain until the situation in the invasion area became clearer. Two of these, however, failed to arrive, and we presumed that they had been lost to the south of Ireland or while entering the Channel.[54] In order to clarify the situation as soon as possible, the five boats which

---

54 British records show that both were sunk in the Channel.

167

had been longest in the operational area were instructed either to transmit a situation report or to return to base forthwith.

442. Use of schnorkel boats justified by results

The first and, as it turned out, the only boat of the five to return from the Channel was U.894, which arrived on 5th July, and her Commanding Officer confirmed that operational conditions in the Seine Bay area were every bit as favourable as indicated hitherto. He reported that on 25th June, while 40 miles north of Jersey, he had sunk a frigate in an encounter with a surface group, British records showing that the vessel in question - HMS *Goodson* - was in fact damaged and towed back to harbour. He also claimed to have sunk two large ships and damaged two others from among a group of transports which he attacked on 29th, 30 miles north of Cape Barfleur; in this case British records show that he actually sank three ships totalling 21,500 tons and damaged one of 7,240 tons.

"… This proves conclusively that the U-boat is able to operate in the Seine area, and that introduction of the schnorkel has restored her efficacy in areas heavily patrolled by aircraft. Nevertheless, we must not lose sight of the fact that a schnorkelling U-boat is likely to be taken by surprise…" (388).

On 5th July, U.671 put into Boulogne. This boat was one of those which came direct from Germany and, in accordance with her instructions, had kept well in to the English coast on the final eastward run. She had reached the middle part of the Channel without difficulty; but on 4th July, while lying bottomed 20 miles south-west of Beachy Head, was detected - probably through an oil trace - and attacked with depth-charges, the resulting damage compelling her to make for the nearest port. As there were no U-boat technicians at Boulogne, a party of 30 was sent from St Nazaire and these men, working under great difficulties, had her ready for sea before the month was out.

In a contemporary assessment of the results of U-boat operations during the first four weeks following the Normandy landings, we found that of 12 boats which left Brest for the Channel in June - -10 with torpedoes and two with mines - three had been destroyed and two had failed to reach the operational area. Judged by conditions prevailing in 1944, these losses were quite tolerable, but matters were entirely different in the case of those boats arriving direct from Germany; of these, only two had survived - U.671 and U.480 - while two were presumed to have been destroyed in the Bay of Biscay and four in the western Channel. It has since been established that one was lost in the Bay, three in the western Channel and two in the centre part of the Channel. Such heavy losses proved that we had given too difficult a task to these inexperienced crews and quickly scotched any idea of routeing boats from Germany via the North Sea and Dover Straits, a step which was being seriously contemplated.

The factual reports from U.984 and U.671 decided us to continue operations in the Channel, but only with boats based in Western France. During the first four weeks of Channel operations, U-boats had sunk five ships totalling 30,994 tons - including an LSI(H) - and two frigates, and had damaged one ship of 7,240 tons and one corvette, for the loss of a good 500 men of the U-boat arm. Expressed in terms of supplies lost to the enemy, these sinkings, alone, would have warranted an even greater sacrifice on behalf of the German army in its grim, bloody defensive battle. Furthermore, as, from now on, only experienced crews would be sent into the Channel, it was reasonable to expect that losses might remain within tolerable limits.

JULY 1944
TIGHTENING OF THE ENEMY BLOCKADE OFF THE BISCAY COAST

443. Conditions in the Channel continue favourable

The capture, at the beginning of July, of an enemy track chart and an accurate appreciation of our U-boat, E-boat and air activity, furnished us with a fairly good picture of the enemy's supply organisation. Nine convoys left from each side of the Channel daily and, of those bound for France, four sailed from Portsmouth, three from the West of England and two from the Thames, following buoyed routes and times to arrive in the unloading area between 1400 and 1800, while it was still light. There were no night sailings. The routes were protected on their flanks by destroyer patrols, while the convoys themselves were usually escorted by motor-launches. Ships and escort vessels often towed kite-balloons as protection against low-flying aircraft, and these balloons sometimes enabled our U-boats to spot a convoy, through the periscope, at long range.

The A/S defences in the area lying between Seine Bay and the Isle of Wight were far less dangerous than in the western Channel and, during the last two weeks of June, after three successive boats had been pursued almost to exhaustion in the latter area following attacks on surface groups, orders were given to refrain from attacking A/S vessels and to concentrate on invasion supply ships.

Throughout July schnorkel boats continued to be sent to the Channel, as they became ready for sea; but, since we had no idea of when losses occurred, the number of boats in the operational area was overestimated at about six, whereas the actual figure had been between three and four. By 21st July four more boats had returned and, between them, claimed to have sunk three ships totalling 20,000 tons and two destroyers, with a further three ships and one destroyer damaged; but British records show only two ships totalling 3,426 tons and a trawler sunk. Mines had been laid by two of these boats, U.214 laying 16 SMA off Plymouth, which damaged one ship of 7,177 tons, and U.218 a similar number off Land's End. Only two of the boats had encountered strong enemy opposition, the others practically none. All four Commanding Officers were optimistic in regard to prospects in the unloading area, where the great concentration of shipping made detection less likely, and considered that the effect of the enemy defences depended chiefly on the luck and skill of individual U-boat commanders.

444. Schnorkel routine and disposal of refuse
Only through the verbal reports of individual commanders did we

learn of the hardships suffered by the crews during their three- to four-week sorties. In daylight, which lasted for nearly 20 hours out of 24, they dared not raise the schnorkel to ventilate the boat; consequently the atmosphere, which was always pretty foul in a schnorkel boat, was further polluted by the stench of decaying waste food and other refuse. A few boats had been equipped with a new type of air-pressure WC, which included a sump and large-bore discharge pipe through which waste matter could be evacuated after being chopped up; others tried to solve their problem by packing refuse into tins and laboriously disposing of them at night through the *Bold*[55] discharge tube. But in July one commander hit upon the idea of stowing all his refuse, including packing cases, in an empty torpedo tube and firing it every three or four days. Of course, the tube could no longer be used for its proper purpose and had to be isolated so as to avoid fouling the remainder; but this procedure, known as a *Müllschoss* (rubbish shot), was subsequently adopted by most of the boats, and thereafter, when a boat returned to base, the first dockyard workmen to arrive on board no longer recoiled from the open hatch.

Since every man's movement consumed oxygen, a boat's routine was usually adjusted to the schnorkelling pattern - clean ship, torpedo maintenance and meals being put off until the night schnorkelling period, when there was sufficient fresh air for all. For most of the time and unless on watch, crew members generally lay on their bunks, and a few commanders even extinguished the lighting to discourage conversation and other oxygen-consuming activities.

445. Ordeal in the Channel

This last mentioned measure was psychologically unsound, since it allowed the minds of the crew to dwell too much on outside noises. In these Channel operations, the din endured by the U-boat crews surpassed anything experienced hitherto; the buzzing and screaming of various types of noise-box, the pinging of asdic and the whirring of propellers were continuous, while the detonations of innumerable

---

55 *Bold* was the asdic decoy.

bombs and depth-charges shook the boat as a constant reminder of the enemy's presence. It was almost impossible to estimate the range of a noise-source; the faintest humming could spell danger, and a sustained noise often drowned the whirr of approaching propellers. On occasion, a destroyer would suddenly be heard directly overhead, or depth-charges would explode nearby without warning. Even the bravest - and one must grant that these pale-faced U-boat men were brave - could not fail, eventually, to become adversely affected by such conditions.

A U-boat could find herself in very serious straits if hunting vessels remained in her vicinity and gave her no opportunity to ventilate between decks, as illustrated by the following extract from the log of U.763, for 6th July 1944:

"… 1645. South of Isle of Wight. Bottomed again in 55 metres. Enemy still has contact. I shall wait here till night. Depth-charges are now fewer and further between. Thirty-four detonated in our near vicinity between 1600 and 2000. Despite the addition of oxygen and the use of potash cartridges, the air has become perceptibly fouler. A very great quantity of air was consumed by members of the crew who had to be moved in order to keep trim during my attempt to shift position. The crew are becoming more exhausted. It is nearly 30 hours since the boat was last ventilated. The first cases of vomiting occur, and I issue each man with a potash cartridge. Breathing becomes distressed. The enemy search group is still active overhead… The intervals between depth-charges are getting longer, but detonations are nearly all very close… During the 30 hours of the pursuit, 252 depth-charges were counted in the near vicinity, 61 at medium range and 51 at long range…"

A schnorkel failure or defect could also cause serious difficulty, as is illustrated by the experience of U.218, on 20th June, during her minelay off Land's End:

"… 0400. Bomb or depth-charge concussion has apparently fractured a tappet lever on the port diesel. Starboard diesel started; but owing to insufficient exhaust pressure the safety valve lifts and the exhaust gases escape into the boat, filling all compartments and necessitating the wearing of escape apparatus.

0500. Surfaced to ventilate the boat.

0503. *Naxos* gives three separate warnings, amplitude 4 to 5. Dived to 80 metres.

1200. Several men suddenly taken ill during the forenoon. By noon two-thirds of the crew are suffering from severe headache and stomach-ache, nausea and retching and are no longer fit for duty. The remainder, also complaining of bad headache, keep things going. There are several cases of fainting through over-exertion and carbon-monoxide poisoning.

1230. Rise to periscope depth in an attempt to ventilate with the port diesel.

1240. Port diesel starts, but exhaust pressure is too low to empty the schnorkel mast. The safety valve lifts again, filling the boat with exhaust fumes which cause further cases of poisoning.

1250. Electric compressor started in an attempt to draw out the fumes and replace them through the schnorkel valve. The state of the crew continues to deteriorate.

1400. Surfaced to change the air in the boat. I cannot wait until dusk.

1406. Dived. The boat is thoroughly ventilated. By evening there is only a slight improvement in the state of the crew. Milk is issued to counteract the effects of the poisoning. Six men, in a state of collapse, given injections of lobelyn sympatol to stimulate heart action..."

446. Difficulties of navigation in schnorkel operations

The constant battle against the enemy defences called for the greatest determination and physical and mental toughness on the part of the U-boat commanders. This meant the employment of younger men, and in 1944, with most of the senior commanders either dead or forming the backbone of training establishments and shore commands, their ages ranged between 23 and 26. These young officers had received their commands after only four to seven years' service and few of them had any experience of navigation in difficult tidal waters; the same was true of the navigators, nearly all of whom joined their boats direct from training school. Moreover, in these Channel operations and, later, in operations in British inshore waters, commanders and navigating officers had to cope with the added difficulty of continual submergence.

The periscope could, of course, be used for terrestrial navigation, but with the object lens so close to the surface it was necessary to approach very near to the shore; the commanders fought shy of this, for the risk of destruction by mine or A/S forces was greater in depths of 15 to 30 metres.

A device for taking star sights by periscope was only in the development stage. To obtain a fix by radio beacon, the boat had to surface sufficiently to bring her frame aerial above water, in which state the conning tower was exposed to location and attack from the air. Speed in operation was therefore vital, but, as a number of these beacons had been destroyed by bombing and others were frequently out of action for various reasons, it usually took some time to obtain a fix and commanders understandably, seldom ventured to expose their boats for so long. In these circumstances they had generally to navigate by dead reckoning - a difficult task, since, apart from Hurd Deep, there were no well defined depth lines in the Channel; furthermore, the tidal rates and directions given in the Tidal Atlas were primarily for surface navigation and not for the water strata between 30 and 50 metres below the surface in which the boats normally operated. The tides were sometimes so strong that the boats had difficulty in intercepting a convoy, or even remaining in a selected position, for a submerged U-boat could not anchor to prevent herself from drifting and only around the time of slack water could she rest on the bottom, trimmed by the bow, allowing her stern to swing with the tide. On occasions when their batteries became exhausted, commanders were compelled to seek bottom regardless of the state of the tide and to risk damage to rudder and screws, by dragging.

Despite all these difficulties, the boats would probably have managed to fix their positions with reasonable accuracy, had not navigation frequently to be sacrificed to tactical need. If A/S vessels happened to be searching in the vicinity, gyro-compass and echo-sounder had both to be switched off to reduce noise, and after some hours of dodging here and there neither commander nor navigator had any idea of their position; consequently the U-boats sometimes found themselves in awkward situations.

447.U.763 drifts into Spithead

The experience of U.763, between 7th and 8th July 1944, will probably remain unique in the history of the U-boat. The following is an account from her log:

"… 7.7.44.1200. After having been pursued with asdics and depth-charges for nearly 30 hours, our greatest worry is the fixing of our position. No echo-soundings could be taken during that time and our alterations of course and the set of the tide have taken us a considerable distance. Dead reckoning puts us 20 to 30 miles north of Cherbourg…

1654. Touched bottom (40 metres).

1902. Bottomed in 40 metres. This shallow depth makes me wonder if we are actually further to the southward. There is a 9-knot current there. Though we are trimmed by the head, the boat is lying very badly. Rise to periscope depth. Course 330 degrees. Land in sight to port, bearing 300 degrees true…

2258. It is beginning to grow dark. As visibility is bad to starboard, I can make no further check. There are no stars. From a study of the chart it appears certain that the current has carried us between the Channel Islands. Sounding continuously and utilising the northerly set, I try to schnorkel clear to the northward. Visibility ahead is good enough…

8.7.44. 0041. The soundings do not agree with the chart. An attempt to fix by radio beacon produces one position only (Brest), which passes through the area in question and, together with the soundings, appears to confirm our estimated position. So long as I have sufficient water and visibility there is no point in surfacing.

Carry on schnorkelling in order to have the batteries sufficiently charged, by daylight, to enable me to obtain a fix at periscope depth.

0337. Touched bottom (16 metres). Stopped schnorkelling. I determine to surface, since our estimated position cannot possibly be correct. The farther we proceed to the north-west the shallower the water becomes, whereas according to the chart it should become deeper. I wonder if the echo-sounder is reading correctly.

0356. It is almost a flat calm, moonlight and misty. Surfaced... About two and a half miles on the port quarter, four destroyers are lying in the moonlight. Land lies on both beams. The shapes of several steamships are visible to port. I turn off to the north-west, assuming that I have the enemy-occupied Cotentin Peninsula to starboard and the Channel Islands to port. The echo-sounder must be out of order and the current must have carried us into shallow water.

0433. Submerge again when the echo-sounder shows 30 metres. Bottomed at 35 metres. After pondering over what I have seen, it suddenly occurs to me that we have fetched up close to the English coast. The direction of the Brest position line on the chart shows that in all probability we are at Spithead, however unlikely that may sound..."

That night and the following forenoon U.763 remained bottomed a few miles north-west of the Nab light.

"... 9.7.44 1525. Left bottom.

1548. Periscope depth at silent running speed. Using the periscope sparingly and just awash, I discern three small vessels anchored in the stream.

1605. An anchored landing craft - US 264 - lies on the starboard beam, and ahead of her the hospital ship, No. 62. I pass between them to the other side where, on the port bow, I sight two old 2,000- to 3,000-ton steamers, in ballast, lying at anchor. On south-easterly courses the water becomes shallower. A fix by cross-bearings shows that I am in danger of being left high and dry by the tide. I therefore turn about and make for a 20-metre patch.

1802. Bottomed again in 17 metres. Low water is at 2204, so that I am no longer in danger of being stranded…"

Despite the opportunities that presented themselves - though there were no really worth-while targets - the Commanding Officer could not attack for fear of his *Lut* torpedoes running ashore and falling into enemy hands.

"… We have inexplicably got the boat in here unnoticed and will get her out intact, for she must not fall into enemy hands.

2220. Action stations…

2250. Leave bottom. Rise to periscope depth. I keep to the starboard side of the fairway. Returning landing craft and what I presume to be two destroyers, pass us on the opposite course…

2338. Course 140 degrees. We have not been observed. The water gets gradually deeper…

From the Commanding Officer's observations we saw the possibility of penetrating into this area to lay mines. Indeed, such an operation was planned, but it had to be dropped because of the subsequent evacuation of the Channel.

448. Enemy starts close blockade of the Biscay coast

At the end of June, enemy light naval forces operating at the western entrance of the Channel transferred their attention nearer to the Biscay coast and, on 6th July, a small force of destroyers attacked one of our outgoing U-boat convoys off Brest, sinking two of the escorts. Thus began a gradual enemy infiltration into the Bay of Biscay coastal waters and, since our own defence vessels were too weak to give battle, there was nothing we could do to stop it; moreover, we had no air reconnaissance at our disposal. Having encountered no opposition, enemy squadrons gradually felt their way southwards, until by the end of July they were operating off La Pallice and Bordeaux with the same immunity. In these circumstances, rendezvous positions for U-boats and their escorts were shifted back into those areas covered by our coastal batteries, but even so the enemy continued to sink so many of our escorts that, eventually, the U-boats had to sail and return from operations unescorted. The Senior Officer U-boats West made some attempt to counter these surface attacks by stationing two schnorkel boats off Brest for two days at a time - i.e. for as long as they could remain without charging their batteries - and passing to them by radio the positions of radar-located destroyers; but this information always failed to agree with the observations of the boats themselves, so that doubt arose as to the accuracy of our radar ranges. These boats kept guard from 8th July to 2nd August without a single success.

The deterrent effect on the enemy of even minor counteraction was demonstrated by two *Luftwaffe* attacks on enemy formations off Brest, on 20th and 21st July, in which one destroyer was sunk and a cruiser damaged;[56] whereafter the enemy behaved more cautiously for a few days and kept well clear of the coast. But a little later, when it became clear to him that these *Luftwaffe* attacks had been only a flash in the pan, he resumed his inshore operations, with the result that we had to abandon our entire patrol system and to confine our swept channels to within the 200-metre line.

AUGUST-SEPTEMBER 1944
EVACUATION OF THE ATLANTIC BASES

449. Evacuation of Brest, Lorient and St Nazaire

The American breakthrough at Avranches on 4th August threatened the three northern Biscay bases with encirclement, and steps had therefore to be taken to evacuate the U-boats in good time. The primary requirement was to complete those boats currently fitting out with schnorkel at Brest, Lorient and St Nazaire, while those for whom there was no gear available in these bases were made ready for sea and sailed for La Pallice or Bordeaux, the opportunity being taken also to transfer experienced dockyard and specialist personnel, together with essential material such as schnorkel components, T5 torpedo testing gear and non-ferrous metals. The U-boat personnel

---

56 The cruiser HMS *Frobisher* was slightly damaged by a/c bomb on 18th July and the frigate HMCS *Mantane* on 20th July.

remained in the three northen bases, above all those whose boats were undergoing extensive refits and could not complete in the near future, were, as far as the land battle permitted, returned to Germany.

Subsequent to the enemy breakout, the situation deteriorated rapidly and our scanty forces in Brittany, retreating before the advancing enemy spearheads and the *Maquis*, hastily withdrew into the coastal fortresses. This influx of troops, many of whom, demoralised and undisciplined, sought shelter from enemy bombing in the U-boat bunkers, caused such disruption to work on the boats at Brest and Lorient that the latter's completion became doubtful. Furthermore, the army's erroneous and pessimistic evaluation of the general situation gave the impression that Lorient could not be held for long, whereupon the Senior Officer of the local flotilla, on his own initiative, sent several U-boats to sea; and only through the intervention of the Supreme Command was some semblance of order restored, allowing work on the U-boats to proceed.

On 6th August enemy spearheads had penetrated to within 20 miles of Angers, the headquarters of SO U-boats West, who was thus forced to evacuate to La Rochelle. Until the evacuation was completed on 8th, U-boat Command temporarily assumed control of operations in the Channel. This move had its compensations in that SO U-boats West was thereafter in close contact with his forces, allowing him, in the event of precipitate action by the military authorities, to take such measures on behalf of the U-boat arm as he thought fit.

450. Transfer to bases at La Pallice and Bordeaux

The transfer of U-boats from the three northern bases to La Pallice and Bordeaux proved to be a most hazardous undertaking. The enemy had apparently been warned of our intention and, quite understandably, used every means to destroy the boats during their passage, which, having no torpedoes, were unable to strike back. With enemy air and surface forces ever present, navigational accuracy was bound to suffer, and Commanding Officers were frequently unable immediately to find the escort that should have been awaiting them off their port of destina- tion; consequently, and in view of the fact that escorts dallied at the rendezvous for only a short while before returning to harbour, the boats had generally either to ensure an early arrival, so that the approach of the escort might be picked up by hydrophone, or to proceed into port unescorted. A few of them chose to withdraw to seaward for the time being, thereby re-entering the sphere of the hunter groups.

The danger experienced from aircraft and mines, even in the near approach channels, is well illustrated by the following extract from the log of U.309:

"… 12.8.44. 0345. Approaching escort rendezvous off La Pallice in company with U.981.

0415. U.981 mined. I send the following signal: 'U.981 mined. Incapable of diving. Everything out of action. Request escort at rendezvous forthwith. U.309'.

0620. Lying stopped with U.981, whose engines are still out of action. Halifax aircraft approaches, passing over us three times and dropping flares. U.981 now able to proceed on electric motors. We proceed at slow speed, steering 090 degrees, parallel with the line of buoys.

0624. Bomb attack on U.981… A further attack from the Halifax. The AA fire of both boats lies well on the target. A second mine detonates alongside U.981, which is again bombed by a twin-engined aircraft. U.981's diesels suddenly spring to life and she sheers off course.

0643. U.981 is clearing away rubber dinghies. She starts to sink. Her crew are jumping over- board. I close her and pick up 40 survivors…"

The transfer of U-boats to the southern ports was completed by 21st August. Of a total of 16 boats which left Brest, Lorient and St Nazaire, seven (two schnorkel and five non-schnorkel), or about 50 per cent, failed to arrive; and these heavy losses were all the more painful when it was dis- covered that most of them could have been avoided. In the event, once the enemy had broken out of the beachhead and had started to advance rapidly into Brittany, the German High Command expected that he would drive for the ports, which were urgently needed for the unloading of immense quantities of supplies; however, available Allied forces were apparently considered inadequate to this task and, with the exception of Brest, the U-boats could have remained in their bases to complete repairs, before being sailed direct to Norway.

451. Effect of bombs on U-boat bunkers

The ultimate concentration of U-boats in the bunkers at La Pallice, Brest and Bordeaux evoked heavy bombing by strong enemy formations between 9th and 13th August. The bunker at Bordeaux received 26 direct hits from 11,000-lb bombs, but only superficial damage was caused to the roof, which consisted of two thicknesses of reinforced concrete, one of 6.2 metres beneath a "burster course" of 3.5 metres. At Brest, the 5.6-metre roof of the bunker, which then had no "burster course", was partially penetrated in three places by extremely heavy bombs - estimated at six tons - one of these breaches being 10 metres in diameter and the others, situated over the dividing walls, small. The U-boats in the bunker were unaffected and only slight damage was sustained by bunker equipment. Specialists from the Todt organisation, who afterwards inspected the bunker at Brest, considered that, given a 3.5-metre "burster course", the roof would have withstood the heaviest bombs then known to exist. This inspection yielded valuable information, which was at once applied to the design of U-boat and dockyard bunkers currently under construction in Germany.

The last air attacks on the Biscay U-boat bases, in which all unprotected dockyard equipment was completely destroyed, provided conclusive proof of the vitally important role played by the U-boat bunkers since 1941. We wondered, indeed, why in 1941 and 1942 the RAF had not attempted to disrupt their construction, for at that time neither our AA defences nor our fighter force could have offered effective resistance to concentrated attacks. Continuous raids on the then unprotected bases would have so impeded U-boat repair work that, by the end of 1942, the U-boat campaign would have been rendered ineffective.[57]

452. Recall of the U-boats from the Channel

By 11th August two more boats had returned from the Seine area, where they claimed to have sunk six ships and damaged two; British records show, however, that only one LST was sunk and two ships totalling 17,180 tons damaged. According to these commanders, both the traffic situation and opportunities for attack were still as good as ever; but enemy activity had intensified. This latter assessment was reinforced by the experience of U.309, which, her batteries run down and her crew exhausted, had had to return after only six days in the operational area, and by that of U.275, which was forced to put into Boulogne, badly damaged. That enemy opposition had indeed increased seemed all the more likely since several other boats were overdue.

All in all the situation was far from satisfactory, and by 20th August we were beginning to wonder if there were, in fact, any boats left in the operational area, for there had been no recent intercepts of enemy sightings of, or attacks on, U-boats, while British broadcasts had announced the sinking of three, including one destroyed in an alleged attempt to break through the Straits of Dover from west to east.

Eight schnorkel boats were approaching readiness in western France; but in the existing circumstances, instead of sending them as reinforcements to the Seine area, we allocated these boats to the Bristol and North Channels, assuming that opposition there would be weaker. In occupying the Bristol Channel we were influenced by a radio report made on 22nd August by the returning U.667, which had been operating off the north Cornish coast since the end of July, claiming to have sunk a destroyer and 15,000 tons of shipping.[58] Unfortunately, we received no intelligence on the A/S situation in

57 A highly contentious view, which both greatly over-estimates the capability of the RAF at that time and underrates the efficacy of the German defences.

58 British records show one corvette, one LCI(L) and one steamship of 7,176 tons sunk and one LST damaged.

that area, as U.667 was destroyed by a mine on 25th while entering La Pallice.

As a final step, between 24th and 26th August we ordered the seven boats estimated to be still in the Channel to return to Norway and, to our great relief, five of them reported themselves subsequently. They claimed good results, aggregating one destroyer and five ships of 22,800 tons sunk and another ship damaged, while British records show that five ships totalling 17,635 tons and the minesweeper *Loyalty* were sunk, and two ships totalling 12,821 tons damaged.

453. Good results from *Alberich*

Of the last six boats to operate in the Channel, U.480 distinguished herself by sinking a minesweeper - HMS *Loyalty* - and about 14,000 tons of shipping. She was the second Atlantic U-boat to be treated with *Alberich* - a coating of rubber designed as a protection against asdic location - and the following extracts from her log give an excellent idea of the conditions in the Channel at that time:

"... 18.8.44. 0257. North of Seine Bay. My intention is to make for the buoyed route with the westerly current; there to lie on the bottom until 1630 - the time at which the previous observation has shown traffic to be at a maximum - when I shall rise to periscope depth, heading the current and using my motors as necessary to remain hove to in sight of the chosen buoy. I shall attack only largeish ships...

0653. Bottomed one mile south-west of buoy situated 34 miles north-west of Cape Barfleur ...

1500. North-bound convoy suddenly passes overhead... To explain the situation in the operational area, let it be said once more that barely five minutes pass without the sound of depth-charge detonations. Asdic impulses are constantly audible on all bearings. The noises made by 'circular saws' and sonic buoys[59] complicate our hydrophone listening, so that it is often impossible to use the hydrophone tactically. Machine-gun and pom-pom fire is frequently audible, apparently fired by patrol vessels. Landing-craft are to be

---

59 By "circular saws" he probably alludes to Foxer. Reference to sonic buoys is not understood.

encountered everywhere, not only on the defined routes, so that by day it is almost impossible to identify a convoy by hydrophone…

1530. Left bottom. Hove to at periscope depth…

2050. Since my expectation of an evening convoy is unfulfilled, I head away to the eastward, with the current, to schnorkel. In future I shall carry out the same procedure every afternoon, since I regard this as the only way of coping with these difficult tidal conditions…"

U.480 sank the ss St Enogat on 19th August and HMS *Loyalty* on 22nd. She was passed over by convoy FTM 74 on 25th, from which she sank a straggler - ss *Orminster* - with a T5 torpedo, and was then hunted for seven hours.

"… 25.8.44. 1508. Am being pursued by four A/S vessels, two of which are operating asdics; the third, which apparently acts as depth-charge dropper, approaches at intervals of from five to ten minutes and drops charges; the fourth can be heard to be running her engines at very low speed. Listening conditions are particularly good.

2140. Beginning of dusk. Pursuit lasts until 2200, during which time we have covered five miles over the ground. I have stopped the gyro and refrain from using the hydrophones. I maintain my depth by shifting the crew. One of the A/S vessels frequently lies directly above us with her engines just ticking over, when the least sound aboard her is clearly audible and asdic impulses are extremely loud. In these circumstances, any boat with a mechanical fault which causes the smallest noise must, at all costs, locate and rectify it. The depth-charge dropper, which has lately been lying stopped, approaches and drops five or six depth-charges, at intervals. These cause such trivial damage that I am convinced that the enemy is unable to locate us by asdic and so is without an accurate range. He has merely a hydrophone contact which, because of the absence of noise in the boat, is bound to be vague. I attribute the enemy's failure to locate me, mainly to the protection afforded by *Alberich*…"

454. Losses in the Channel justified by results

Our final assessment of the U-boat effort in the Channel and off the Cornish coast showed that in the period 6th June to the end of

August, a total of 30 schnorkel boats took part in 45 sorties, their achievements in both areas amounting to:

	As Estimated By U-boat Command	As Shown By British Records

Sunk	12 escort vessels
	20 ships including landing-craft
	    totalling 112,800 tons
		5 escort vessels
		4 landing-craft
		    totalling 8,404 tons
		12 ships
		    totalling 56,845 tons

Damaged	1 escort vessel
	7 ships
	    totalling 44,100 tons
		1 escort vessel
		1 landing-craft
		5 ships
		    totalling 36,000 tons

These U-boats also carried out three minelaying missions which, according to the Britis' records, resulted in the sinking of one and damage to two ships. Twenty U-boats were destroyed Related to the number of sorties, these losses amounted to 45 per cent, to the number of boat employed, 66 per cent. This high percentage was not, however, so serious in itself, since the 20 boat concerned were, after all, obsolete by this time. The loss of 1,000 men, of whom 238 - or about 2 per cent - were picked up by the enemy, was also not too high a price to pay for the results actuall achieved.

Having regard to the fact that nearly all the ships sunk were carrying war supplies, the validit of the following contemporary appreciation by FO U-boats cannot be denied, even in retrospect

"... 15.9.44. Our U-boat effort in the Channel is thereby terminated, and the old fighting spirit of the U-boat arm has again magnificently stood the test. A comprehensive survey of operation shows that, contrary to our initial misgivings and the doubts that assailed us during the course c the operations, we were right in employing the U-boats. Considering the extremely difficult operating conditions, the results achieved were good and losses tolerable, though heavy. Despite the fact that our blow at the enemy's supplies was indecisive, it was certainly severe and helped to relieve pressure on our troops ashore. Besides achieving tangible results, we also gained experience and knowledge of continuously submerged U-boat warfare which will be of great value, particularly for the new-type boats. We also tied down considerable sea and air escort forces, which would otherwise have been available for purposes such as the disruption of our supply traffic off the Dutch and Norwegian coasts, as well as for intensive air attacks on our lines of communication on the Western Front. Results would have been better and losses certainly lighter, had the boats been possessed of higher submerged speed and a greater endurance; the fact that these very qualities have been highly developed in the new-type boat gives us good hope for the future. The schnorkel was, in effect, decisive, and operations in these areas would have been out of the question without it. No one would have believed a few month ago that a U-boat could proceed submerged for 42 days without surfacing. It is the schnorkel alone, which now enables us again to operate close in to the British coast, and to continue using the older boats until the new-type are ready..."

455. The withdrawal to Norway

Several boats were still under repair in western France and, until such time as they were completed, the flotilla staffs and dockyard personnel had to remain behind; eager to return to Germany, the dockyard workers finished most of this work well ahead of the estimated date. Other boats, which had been paid off at Lorient and St Nazaire, were remanned and, after being temporarily; patched up, were sailed for Norway, some of them leaving with schnorkel masts fixed in the vertical position or with torpedo tubes blanked off. A few serviceable schnorkel boats also left for Norway there being no reliefs for their sick commanders. The only boats which, through lack of batteries could not be made ready for sea - U.123 and U. 129 at Lorient and U.178 and U. 188 at Bordeaux-were paid off and later scuttled.

After the last U-boat had left Bordeaux on 25th August, there was no further need to defend that harbour, and the base personnel were dispersed. Part went to reinforce the garrison at La Rochelle and the remainder, made up of some 20,000 naval and dockyard hands, formed a battalion which was detailed to return overland to Germany; but only a small proportion of the latter managed to fight their way through to the German lines, the majority falling prey to Allied troops or the *Maquis*.

The SO U-boats West, whose ultimate duties were limited to getting the boats to sea, was flown back to Germany and, after a brief period at U-boat Headquarters, he and his staff transferred to Norway to take over the administration of the operational Atlantic boats and to assume responsibility for base, dockyard and convoy matters.

From the middle of August a total of eighteen U-boats left the Biscay bases for Norway, the last to leave being U.267, which sailed from St Nazaire on 23rd September. The only boat to be lost was U.445, presumed sunk early on in her passage through the Bay. The general success of the operation was taken to indicate that the enemy had by then tightened up his blockade of the western Channel at the expense of his watch in the Bay itself. Quite a number of dockyard technicians and specialist naval officers took passage in the departing U-boats, while the U-boat personnel who remained behind were absorbed into the land defences, where they distinguished themselves by their toughness and courage.

OTHER AREAS

456. Schnorkel boats in British coastal waters

There were no U-boats in the North Atlantic from July to September 1944, apart from a few engaged on meteorological duties, the main reason being a lack of schnorkel equipment, coupled with the decision of 1st June not to send further non-schnorkel boats to that area.

Of eight schnorkel boats which sailed from Norway in June, four went to the Channel and the rest - U.423, U.478, U.715 and U.1225 - were all lost *en route* to the Atlantic. Certainly the waters through which these boats had to pass were heavily patrolled, but the schnorkel should have taken care of that problem. We were therefore forced to assume that, with crews only imperfectly trained, the boats in question had occasionally found it necessary to surface, an assumption supported by comparison of their plotted positions with those contained in intercepted British radio messages. A typical example lending weight to this theory was provided by U.865, which, between June and August, had been forced on four occasions to break off her passage owing to schnorkel defects, and in September, after further schnorkel training, met her fate on her fifth attempt to gain the Atlantic. As far as can be judged from the position of her sinking - learnt since the war - she had still been unable to manage her schnorkel and had been bombed and sunk while heading for base.

All non-schnorkel boats, as they became operational, continued to be sent as reinforcements to group *Mitte* in the Norwegian ports. Because of continuous daylight at this time of year and the consequent added danger from air attack, the six boats hitherto keeping watch off the coast were withdrawn on 16th July when it was revealed that U.319 was missing and that three other boats had suffered bomb damage. After the withdrawal of the anti-invasion guard, group *Mitte* remained distributed among Norwegian ports, its strength being maintained for a while at 22 boats; but, from the end of July, 14 of these were transferred, at intervals, to Libau and Revel for operations against Russian naval forces in the Gulf of Finland, their place being taken by six schnorkel boats.

The few Type IXC boats to become operational just sufficed to maintain about three on meteorological duty between Greenland and the Azores. The only Type VIIC boat to come into service in July was U.300 which, after a brief spell in the Minch, had to return owing to bomb damage, and it was not until mid-August that a number of medium boats were available for operations. Of these, two were disposed in attack areas off Reykjavik, two north of the Minch, one in the Moray Firth and three in the North Channel, the commencement of their activity being confirmed by several intercepted signals from enemy patrol forces.

The first report received from this batch of U-boats came in on 30th September and was very satisfactory. It originated from U.482, which had operated in the North Channel from 30th August to 10th September and claimed to have sunk one destroyer and four ships totalling 23,000 tons from an ingoing convoy. British records show that she sank the corvette HMS *Hurst Castle* and four ships aggregating 31,611 tons. On the strength of this report, two more boats from Norway, and five schnorkel boats on their way back from France, were sent to the area, where they were allocated prescribed attack sectors. At the same time, realising that continuous schnorkelling in the face of heavy enemy opposition imposed great strain on the crews - particularly the newcomers - we permitted those Commanding Officers working in inshore waters to decide for themselves whether to withdraw to the westward, or, in case of excessive strain, return to base before expending all their torpedoes.

Subsequent to U.482's successful sortie, the enemy appeared to cut down on traffic in the North Channel and succeeding boats, which remained there for only a few days, achieved nothing. The same conditions were experienced by U.262, U.714 and U.758, during a brief spell in the Bristol and St George's Channels, where they surprisingly reported very little traffic; what traffic there was consisted exclusively of convoys and, with slow-moving schnorkel boats operating in tidal waters, much skill was needed to make contact. Nevertheless, losses being slight - one boat west of the North Channel and another west of the Hebrides - we were encouraged to continue with this type of operation and to send schnorkel boats into all British coastal waters.

457. Remote areas, except the US coast

Five days after the commencement of the Normandy invasion, the few boats still operating in remote areas - two south of Nova Scotia, two in the Caribbean and two in the Gulf of Guinea - were instructed to start for home with sufficient fuel to take them, if necessary, to

Norway. As it happened, by the time that U.516 and U.539, returning from the Caribbean, had reached Cape Ortegal - in mid-August - the threat from the Allied Biscay blockade had become so serious that they were perforce ordered to proceed to Norway. U.539 needing additional fuel for the trip had subsequently to be supplied by U.858 - a meteorological boat - some 400 miles south-west of Iceland.

U.530 spent a considerable time close to Trinidad, but the routes of the convoys entering and leaving here were so widely dispersed that she failed to get in a single attack. Operations off the Brazilian coast finally ceased when U.861 left the area in July. The African coast north of Dakar was evacuated for good on the return of U.546 in August, and the return of U.170, late in September, marked the end of operations off Freetown. Two of the last Type IXC schnorkel boats to sail from the Biscay bases went to the St Lawrence, in which area, patrolled mainly by aircraft, the Commanding Officers felt confident of success; but neither of them had the good fortune to discover a convoy and they achieved nothing. Operations in the Indian Ocean, however, continued satisfactorily, using about three Penang-based boats at a time, and in August, U.198, U.859 and U.862 encountered considerable traffic around the Mozambique Channel and to the north of Madagascar, where they sank eight ships.

During the period under review, few of the Type IXD boats sent from Germany to the Indian Ocean reached Penang, U.860 being lost in the South Atlantic in June, U.198 to the north of Madagascar in August and U.871 and U.863 in the North and South Atlantic, respectively, in September. U.859 was torpedoed and sunk by an Allied submarine while entering Penang after an operational cruise lasting nearly six months, and at about the same time the torpedo-transport U-boat, U.1062, returning to Germany from Penang with a cargo of vital war materials, was sunk just north of the Equator.

The further loss at the end of May of the Penang-bound U.450 - the last available U-tanker - and of the Type IXC boats U.505 and U.549, was attributed to enemy carrier groups patrolling from the west of the Azores to the Equator. However, we never knew that

U.549, before her destruction, had sunk the (to us) notorious American aircraft carrier *Block Island* and damaged a destroyer. Neither did we know of the capture of U.505, owing to the excellence of Allied security and to the strict isolation of her crew by the Americans. It was not until the end of 1944, or the beginning of 1945, that a U-boat officer held in a Canadian prisoner-of-war camp managed to pass us a message warning of the probable capture of a U-boat, intact and complete with signal publications.[60] We were thus provided with a possible explanation of many curious incidents which had occurred in the Atlantic since the summer of 1944, when enemy forces had contrived to turn up at our prearranged rendezvous with the same punctuality as the U-boats themselves.

---

60 U.505 was captured on 4th June 1944 by USS *Guadalcanal*, USS *Chatelain*, USS *Pillsbury* and USS *Jenks*, and successfully brought into Bermuda. Many valuable documents were taken intact.

- C H A P T E R   1 1   -

OCTOBER 1944 - MAY 1945

THE NEW U-BOAT ARM TAKES SHAPE

458. Effect of the loss of the Atlantic bases

"… 15.9.44. Now that the French Atlantic ports are no longer in our possession, U-boat operations will be continued from Norway. A few Home ports will also be used, since the Norwegian bases have insufficient accommodation, and operational possibilities will thus be limited. The Type IXC boats will no longer be able to operate either in the Caribbean or on the Gold Coast without refuelling, and will therefore be obliged to concentrate mainly on the US coast, the Newfoundland area and also the St Lawrence, which is again accessible to schnorkel boats. As a rule we shall be unable to use the Type VIIC boats in the Channel, since the passage takes so long that they would be unlikely to arrive in a fit state to operate under such difficult conditions; the only other areas remaining to them are the Moray Firth, the Minch and the North Channel in British coastal waters, and Reykjavik.

"It must be assumed that the enemy will concentrate his A/S forces off Norway, and in the Atlantic passage, North Sea and Baltic approaches. Theoretically, he can build up such heavy concentration in these regions that the old-type boats, which need to schnorkel fairly often, are bound to be located sooner or later and subjected to a concerted attack. Hence, if it were necessary to continue the campaign with these old types, the loss of the Atlantic bases would prove to be grave and decisive; but the new Type XXI boats, by virtue of their very great endurance, high submerged speed and deep diving capability, should be able to thrust their way through the enemy A/S concentrations to operate successfully both in the North Atlantic and in remote areas…" (389).

This brief statement outlined the U-boat situation as FO U-boats saw it at the beginning of October 1944, irrespective of the general course of the war; and in order to understand his apparent confidence in the future success of the new-type boats, it would be well at this point, to examine the provisions of the 1943 Fleet Building Programme, in so far as they affected the U-boat (390).

459. The Central Shipbuilding Committee and the new building programme

In their original building proposals of July 1943, the German Naval Command envisaged the completion of the first two Type XXI U-boats in November and December 1944, with trials in the spring of 1945, after which serial delivery would gradually accelerate to 30 boats a month by the autumn. This programme presupposed that the Armaments Ministry was prepared to provide all the requisite building facilities and that work would proceed undisturbed by air raids and free of bottlenecks. Dönitz, who regarded it as completely inadequate, asked Speer to submit counterproposals; in reply, Speer promised to have the first boat completed in April 1944 and then to start serial production without trials, provided that the Type XXI programme was accorded priority over all other naval construction and that it proved possible to build the boats on prefabricated and mass-production principles. The eminent U-boat constructor Schürer saw no fundamental objection to this last proviso and Dönitz, in view of the immense amount of time that would so be saved, accepted Speer's proposal.

The task of winding up the previous naval construction programme and of implementing the new was taken over, in the summer of 1943, by the so-called Central Shipbuilding Committee, composed of representatives from both the Naval Command and the Armaments Ministry and on whose instructions planning of the new boats commenced at the Glückauf Construction Office, Blankenburg. In the Autumn of 1943 the first orders were placed with German firms for U-boat batteries, pressure-hull sections etc., on 8th December of that year the constructional drawings were completed, and on 1st

January 1944 the new naval building programme was first submitted for approval. The U-boat programme provided for the completion of the first Type XXI boat in April 1944 - as had been agreed with Speer in the summer of 1943 - and the remainder of the series of 30 boats by July. The first Type XXIII boat was to be completed in February 1944, with serial delivery of another 19 commencing in April (391).

460. The U-boat building programme taxes German productive capacity

A major barrier to successful implementation of the overall U-boat building programme lay in a dual requirement for both rapid achievement of mass production of the new boats and maintenance of the rate of delivery of the older types, which necessitated provision of double the quantity of materials and manufacturing capacity over a transition period of from six to eight months. One of the prime essentials was to step up the production of U-boat batteries, and to achieve this in the short time available before the new boats began to arrive from the builders was the Armaments Ministry's most difficult task; no plant for the manufacture of batteries existed in Germany itself, so it was necessary to produce the requisite machinery and equipment for this at the expense of current contracts, except those concerned with aircraft production, which had absolute priority. An additional problem, which at first appeared insoluble, was posed by the sheer quantity of lead and rubber needed for the batteries; but this difficulty was later overcome.

The new boats had also to be equipped with very powerful electric motors and a large number of other electrical fittings, such as cruising motors, trimming and bilge pumps, echo-ranging gear, underwater listening apparatus, radio and radar sets and radar search receivers, production of which engaged a considerable part of the whole German electrical industry and was only made possible by severe curtailment of such essential work as power-station and locomotive construction.

The provision of high-grade steel plate for the pressure hulls posed another difficult problem, for this commodity constituted the worst bottleneck in the whole of the steel industry and, since the old-type boats had still to be built and the new types required even more, demand for steel plate from the autumn of 1943 was three and a half times as great as the allocation hitherto. Furthermore, because of a heavy requirement for the repair of bomb damage to warships and local installations, the dockyards, already burdened with the expanded naval building programme, were now unable to cope with the shaping of pressure-hull sections, which had therefore to be delivered ready rolled.

The Chairman of the Central Shipbuilding Committee, Herr Merker, had taken on a difficult task. Considerable risk was involved in mass-producing a fundamentally new type of U-boat without trials, for if the boat proved to be a failure, the prodigious efforts of German industry would have been in vain and material allocated for the construction of 180 to 200 U-boats would have become so much scrap. Just as great a risk was involved in the introduction of prefabrication and mass-production methods into general shipbuilding; both methods were being applied for the first time to craft of considerable size under severe wartime conditions and against the advice of many experts, while those responsible were beset by the worry of completing the task at the earliest possible date. Nevertheless, contracts were placed with German yards for 360 Type XXI and 118 Type XXIII, and in the Mediterranean ports for 90 Type XXIII U-boats.

461. Prefabrication and mass production
The hull of the Type XXI U-boat was made up of eight separate sections - one section to a compartment - and these sections were constructed in 13 different yards, which allowed duplication and ensured that if a number of sections were destroyed in one yard a corresponding number of U-boats would not be lost. Nevertheless, the safety of the section-building and U-boat assembly yards was a matter of much concern, and in 1944 efforts were made to provide them all with bunker protection, a step already in hand at Hamburg-Finkenwerder and Bremen-Farge, with a few others being improvised

elsewhere. The situation would have been less critical if section building could have been moved inland; but this was impossible as, owing to their size, the sections could only be transported to the assembly yards by water.

The actual building process was roughly as follows. A section-building yard was supplied first with, say, 40 similar part-sections of section 1 - the stern section of the boat - and delivery of the remaining part-sections was then timed to ensure the completion of the sections in sequence; thus, at any given time there would be 40 sections in progressive stages of assembly. The larger part-sections were machined and prepared for assembly on the actual site, while the smaller ones passed through the machine shops on the conveyor-belt principle. As soon as the first section had been assembled it was fitted with the appropriate machinery, electrical equipment, messing accommodation etc., the same operation on each section being performed by the same workmen for the sake of speed.

The delivery of the completed sections to the U-boat assembly yards at Bremen (Deschimag), Hamburg (Blohm & Voss) and Danzig (Schichau), and the process of final assembly and launching, all had to follow a strict time-table, and it is not surprising that difficulties arose in the early stages of the programme. The section-building yards were at first unable to keep to the schedule, partly owing to delayed delivery from subcontractors of certain important fittings and partly to the first part-sections having been badly rolled and exceeding the specified tolerances, which necessitated additional work. As a consequence, the supposedly complete sections for the first boats arrived at the assembly yards late and in an unfinished state, which in their turn meant additional work in the time allotted for U-boat assembly. The Central Shipbuilding Committee, however, would permit no postponement of U-boat completion dates and ruthlessly insisted on strict observance of the timetable. The first boats to be launched, therefore, had much work outstanding - and a lot that was, perforce, skimped - so that they had later to spend long periods in dockyard hands. Indeed, so many imperfections showed up in the first seven boats that they could be used only for training and experimental purposes.

All these difficulties, together with prevailing differences of opinion, caused tension and antagonism between the Central Shipbuilding Committee, the Naval Command and the dockyard authorities. This unfortunate atmosphere prevailed until the summer of 1944, when there was a noticeable improvement, due in part to the influence of the Shipbuilding Commission, which under Admiral Topp had been created at the beginning of that year, and which thereafter acted as mediator between the Naval Command and the Armaments Ministry on behalf of the Shipbuilding Committee.

462. U-boat building under the administration of the Armaments Minister

There is no need here to go into details of how the great new building programme was implemented, or to discuss the differences which arose between the Naval Command, the Central Shipbuilding Committee and the dockyard authorities; but even if everything had proceeded smoothly and without interruption we would still have been hard put to it to meet the great demands for material and manpower needed in the section and assembly yards and other areas. Only those who had attended the conferences between the Naval Command and the Shipbuilding Committee in 1944 could form any opinion of the difficulties involved in implementing the programme under prevailing conditions. The country was strained to the utmost in coping with the overall demand for armaments while our industrial centres and dockyards were being blasted by bombs, and carefully timed schedules had continually to be retarded because of bomb damage to works and plant and frequent traffic disruption. At almost every conference some calamity was reported, for instance, the flight of dockyard workmen from the bombed cities, particularly Hamburg, the withdrawal of workmen from the Schichau yard, Danzig, for defence in the East and the destruction of pontoons and cranes used for the transport of U-boat sections. Supply arrangements had continually to be altered and work transferred to other factories in an effort to achieve continuity in production, and it was now manifest that the Commander-in-Chief Navy had been right in May 1943 when he turned over responsibility for shipbuilding to the Armaments Minister. None but the Minister himself could have risked taking on such a vast building programme and only he, with the entire German armaments industry at his command, was in a position to provide alternative production capacity after bombing attacks.

The following figures illustrate the tremendous scale of naval construction achieved from 1943 onwards. Despite great difficulties caused by Allied bombing and an increase in the production of surface craft, 234 U-boats totalling 220,000 tons came from the builders in 1944, against 238 in 1942 when German industry was unaffected by bombing. The highest ever monthly production of U-boats was achieved in December 1944, with 31 - including 22 Type XXI - totalling 38,100 tons; as compared with 24 totalling 20,881 tons in October 1941, 23 totalling 18,929 tons in November 1942, and 28 totalling 22,000 tons in December 1943. The average monthly rate of production in the first quarter of 1945 was still as high as 28,632 tons. These figures, coupled with the fact that completion time was cut down overall by eight to twelve months, show clearly that any disadvantages accruing from the transfer of responsibility for naval construction from the Naval Command to an independent Minister were far outweighed by the advantage of having unrestricted call on the whole armaments industry.

463. Delays in completion and training

Owing to the circumstances already mentioned, the whole U-boat building programme gradually dropped about five months behind schedule and, although the first Type XXI boat was launched as planned in April 1944, she was not commissioned until June. By the end of October, 32 Type XXI and 18 Type XXIII had been commissioned, while those under construction in the assembly yards were so far advanced that, even allowing for considerable destruction through bombing, a monthly delivery rate of 15 to 20 Type XXI and six to ten Type XXIII could be expected in the immediate future.

German records do not show the exact number of new-type boats completed; but from the record of those commissioned, shown in the table below, it can be seen that the expected rate was generally achieved.

As was mentioned in Section 461, the unorthodox methods used in the construction of these boats was responsible for an inordinate number of defects in the first to commission, and frequent interruptions for repair and modification combined to lengthen the crew training period from the usual three months to nearly six. However, by dint of close co-operation between the Construction Office at Blankenburg, the U-boat Acceptance Staff and the Admiral in Charge of U-boat Training, the fundamental defects were eliminated within a few months and, from the autumn onwards, the necessary modifications were incorporated into all U-boats delivered from the builders.

Numbers of New-Type U-boats Commissioned[61]

Year	Month	Type XXI	Type XXIII
1944	June	1	1
	July	3	3
	August	7	4
	September	8	6
	October	13	4
	November	13	7
	December	22	6
1945	January	17	11
	Februatry	17	7
	March	16	6
	April	3	5
	May	-	1
	Total	120	61

A nucleus of experienced U-boat commanders and petty officers formed the backbone of the new crews, who buckled down to their training with great enthusiasm. Meanwhile, the U-boat Command, which had previously studied the question of tactical employment

---

61 These figures are more accurate than those given in Appendix II to Volume I of this work, and are the result of further research carried out since the publication of the earlier volume. It is estimated that about 30 more of each type were completed by the end of the war, but not commissioned.

of the new-type boats, had passed on their findings to the training, experimental and trials staffs and to the U-boat commanders (392). It was thus possible to put the new theories quickly to the test and to incorporate suggested improvements, which thereby hastened the process of establishing a firm basis for both crew training and operational use of the boats. The final "Battle Instructions for Type XXI and XXIII U-boats" were compiled from the evaluation of extensive sea trials carried out in one boat of each type, commanded by two well-trained officers, *Korvettenkapitän* Topp and *Kapitänleutnant* Emmermann.

464. Outstanding fighting qualities of the new boats

During the first Type XXI trials run over the measured mile at Hela, it was at once evident that the designed submerged full speed of 18 knots for one hour 40 minutes would not be realised, the maximum submerged speed attained varying between 16J and \7\ knots for from 60 to 80 minutes. However, at medium speeds of from 8 to 14 knots the disparity between design and performance was not so great, and the cruising motors came up to expectations with a speed of 5 to 5 J knots.

A boat proceeding on cruising motors had to schnorkel for three hours daily to keep her batteries fully charged, and at a submerged cruising speed of five knots she could thus traverse the danger area between the Norwegian coast and the south of Iceland in about five days, raising her schnorkel on only five occasions. The schnorkel head was fitted with a *Tunis* aerial and coated with sorbo rubber as a protection against radar, so the boats were less vulnerable to location and attack from the air than hitherto. Even if the schnorkel were to be located by radar - which by virtue of its absorbent coating was only possible at short range - a boat would be in no great danger, since a sharp alteration of course coupled with a large increase in speed would quickly take her clear of the area and out of range of the aircraft's sonobuoys; she could then continue for as long as necessary at the silent running speed of five knots, at which it was possible to cover more than 300 miles, or at two to three knots, a speed which she could maintain for 80 to 100 hours without having to schnorkel. The new boats had, therefore, a much better chance than the old type of reaching the Atlantic unobserved.

The silent submerged cruising speed of 5 to 51 knots was also an excellent attack speed and, in the event that this proved too slow, a convoy attack could always be pressed home by using high speed. This capability and the newly introduced echo-ranging gear and plotting-table, specially designed for use in such attacks, gave the Type XXI a decisive advantage over the old schnorkel boats. Furthermore, the Torpedo Trials Staff had developed a special instrument for so-called "programmed firing" in convoy attacks: as soon as a U-boat had succeeded in getting beneath a convoy, data collected by echo-ranging was converted and automatically set on the *Lut* torpedoes, which were then fired in spreads of six, at five- and fifteen-second intervals. The torpedoes opened out fanwise until their spread covered the extent of the convoy, when they began running in loops across its mean course, making good a slightly greater or lower speed, and in so doing covered the whole convoy. In theory these torpedoes were certain of hitting every ship of from 60 to 100 metres in length; and the theoretical possibility of 95 to 99 per cent hits in an average convoy was, in fact, achieved on firing trails.

In addition to the *Lut*, an improved torpedo was now available[62] which was capable of homing onto propeller noises and virtually immune to Foxer.

Even if she did not entirely fulfil our expectations, the Type XXI U-boat was an excellent weapon when assessed against the A/S capability prevailing in 1944. She had overcome her worst teething troubles; and it was our intention to use a few of these boats within the next four months to resume the battle both in the Atlantic and in remote areas, later disposing an increasing number to the west of the British Isles. By virtue of its great endurance, the Type XXI could reach any part of the Atlantic and remain there for three to six weeks;

---

62 The T 11 acoustic homing torpedo.

it could, in fact, have just made the passage to Cape Town and back without refuelling.

It was decided that any attempt at submerged pack tactics, with the support of air reconnaissance, should be delayed until sufficient boats became available; but communication requirements for co-operation between Type XXI U-boats and aircraft had been dealt with and the procedures exercised. For reconnaissance west of the British Isles, the *Luftwaffe* intended to provide Do 335 aircraft, which by reason of their high speed of 430 to 470 mph could fly direct across the United Kingdom at night (393). FO U-boats did not believe that sufficient aircraft would be made available for proper support in such operations, despite the *Luftwaffe's* assurances; however, he was convinced that good results could be obtained without them, since the Type XXI required only one encounter with a convoy - particularly in a remote area - to fire all its torpedoes, with great prospects of attaining a number of hits.

465. Successful development of the Walter U-boat

Despite the tremendous effort devoted to the production of the Types XXI and XXIII, development of the Walter boat continued in 1943. In addition to two large experimental Type XVIII Atlantic boats - U.796 and U.797 - four small Type XVII were under construction, of which U.792 and U.794 were commissioned in November 1943 and U.793 and U.795 in February 1944. Trials with U.793 and U.795 were speedily and successfully concluded, and in March 1944, U.793 reached a submerged speed of 22 knots with the C-in-C Navy on board, eliciting the comment that "with more courage and confidence at the Naval Command we should have had this a year or two ago". In June 1944, U.792 covered the measured mile, submerged, at 25 knots, a speed never quite achieved by any other boat; but she was shortly afterwards damaged in a collision and was still under repair when the war ended. Work on the construction of U.794 and U.795 was unfortunately skimped, owing to a shortage of labour in the Germania yard at Kiel, and these two boats suffered from defects to such an extent that they were never used for other than experimental purposes. U.793, on the other hand, was very soon ready for service and was used for sea training of the future Walter boat crews, which had been on course at Hela since March 1944. The author actually went to sea in U.793 during October 1944 and was able to satisfy himself that she really could do 23 knots submerged, besides being remarkably easy to handle at high speed.

It was never intended that the U.792 to U.795 series boats should be used in operations; the operational Walter boat being the Type XVI IB, 24 of which were to have been built at Blohm & Voss, Hamburg. However, this order was unfortunately placed, for Blohm & Voss were already hard put to it to cope with their share of the Type XXI programme; thus the project was sadly neglected and the order cut, first to 12 and later to six boats. Furthermore; as labour was constantly removed for work elsewhere, completion of the first boat - U.1405 - was delayed six months to December 1944 and that of U.1406 and U.1407 to February and March 1945 respectively.

On conclusion of trials with the Type XVII in the spring of 1944, work on the two Type XVIIIs had been discontinued, and on 26th May contracts were placed for 100 large Atlantic Walter boats Type XXVIW, displacing 852 tons, the first two to be ready in March 1945 and the whole series completed by October of that year. These boats were designed for a maximum speed of 25 knots over a period of 10 to 12 hours and a performance on electric motors equal to that of the Type VIIC; and since the Walter propulsion unit had to be housed in a gas-tight compartment aft, the arrangement of the torpedo tubes was unorthodox, with four mounted in the bows and a further three on each side of the boat, pointing astern. The original plan had allowed for 250 Type XXVIW boats to replace the Type XXI in service during the summer of 1945; but an apparent shortage of both lead and rubber - later found to be fallacious - soon resulted in revision of this figure to a maximum of 100. Another factor affecting this reduction in the original total was the difficulty seen in producing sufficient Aurol - hydrogen peroxide fuel - for use in the turbines of the Type XXVIWs, as this fuel was also needed for the *Luftwaffe's*

V2 weapons and the Navy's allocation sufficed for only 70 boats at most. The building of new factories for the production of Aurol was out of the question, since the cost would have been prohibitive; but the figure of 100 Type XXVIWs was still allowed to stand, although it became clear in September 1944 that this requirement could never be met (394).

For the rest, plans were prepared for an even more advanced type of U-boat, embodying the high qualities of both the Type XXVIW and the Type XXI and equipped with either a closed-cycle diesel, or a Walter turbine adapted to use oxygen fuel. All these plans advanced to a stage where it could be seen that we were on the road to success, but none reached fruition.

OCTOBER 1944-JANUARY 1945
THE SCHNORKEL PROVES ITS WORTH

466. Disadvantages accruing from the loss of the Biscay bases
In an endeavour to keep the refit periods of the Biscay-based operational U-boats as short as possible, we had, since 1941, accorded priority to French west-coast ports as regards the provision of dockyard personnel, machinery and other equipment, at the expense of the U-boat repair yards at home and in Norway.

As a consequence of this policy, the repair facilities at Bergen and Trondheim had been devised to meet the requirements of only about 30 medium U-boats engaged on operations in Northern Waters and, even with an immediate increase of dockyard personnel, could not cope with more than one-third of the Atlantic boats now bereft of their French bases; the remainder had, therefore, to seek repair in German shipyards. In the event, all the large Atlantic boats were allocated to the 33rd Flotilla at Flensburg, which had been formed in the summer of 1944 and used for the reception and disposal of crews recalled from sea to man the new-type boats, and were then, together with the remaining Type VIIs, distributed amongst the Baltic and North Sea yards. This sudden rush of additional repair work imposed a heavy burden on these German dockyards, which were already functioning under difficult conditions, and although the repair of training boats was deferred and additional labour drafted in - mostly from the U-boat building yards - operational boats had still to wait a long time before being taken in hand for protracted periods. Their time spent non-operational was further, and indeed considerably, extended by the necessity of making the passage between Norway and Germany in company with routine supply convoys; the trip from Kristiansand to Kiel often taking from six to eight days, owing to fouling of the route by mines and casualties amongst the escort vessels.

For these reasons the operational boats were inactive for more than twice the time it had previously taken to refit them in western France; and the loss of the Biscay bases thus resulted not only in lengthening the passage to the operational area by 600 to 1,000 miles but also in a considerable reduction in the number of serviceable U-boats. On top of all this, the enemy sought to frustrate our operations from Norway by heavy air attacks on the yards at Bergen, Kiel and Hamburg, by increased minelaying in the Sound and Belts and by air attacks on our convoys. In one air attack on Bergen, on 4th October, two operational boats - U.228 and U.993 - and the crane installation were destroyed, while U.92 and U.437 were so severely damaged that they had to be paid off. Another attack, on 29th of the same month, completely destroyed all those dockyard installations not protected by bunkers and reduced the yard's repair capacity to about six boats; the bunkers themselves were also hit by bombs ranging from 1,100 to 2,200 lb, but the boats and equipment within escaped damage. On 28th December 1944 the harbour at Horten, where the U-boat crews received their initial schnorkel training, was attacked by 200 aircraft; and although six of the eight boats there managed to clear the harbour in time, of the remaining two, U.73S was sunk and U.682 sustained heavy damage.

Besides these RAF raids, attacks were also made by carrier-borne aircraft against our convoys off the coast and in the Inner Leads, the torpedo-transport U-boat U.1060 being destroyed in one such attack on 27th October 1944. Other U-boats were damaged in the course of these attacks, and those in transit between Norway and Germany, had subsequently to proceed on schnorkel when outside the Leads, which caused further extension of passage times.

SO U-boats West, Kapitan zur See Rosing, who became responsible for the allocation of repair berths and the control of U-boat convoys on 12th October 1944, took immediate steps to increase the capacity of the bases and dockyards in Norway. He also set about devising measures to simplify the U-boats' task in making rendezvous with their escorts on return from the Atlantic, which was an urgent matter, for there was such a concentration of enemy aircraft off the Norwegian coast that the U-boats could not take the risk of surfacing to fix their position; moreover, it was very difficult to identify the rugged coastline quickly through a periscope, and any prolonged search along the coast for a recognised landmark courted danger from our own protective minefields. Work was therefore put in hand to install new and more powerful radio beacons at prominent positions on the coast.

467. Further operations in the Channel

The selection of attack areas for the Norway-based boats presented somewhat of a problem from October 1944- onwards. Only limited enemy movement had been observed in the North Channel during September and, judging by the weight of A/S countermeasures encountered, returning commanders doubted if many convoys still traversed that area. Our radio intelligence gave similar indications. Since 15th September 1944, radio messages from the FOIC Liverpool to Atlantic convoys had also been transmitted by Land's End radio station. Furthermore, on 20th September an undecrypted message from the C-in-C Plymouth to convoy HX 307 was seen to be addressed, for information, to the naval authorities at Newhaven and Dover, while on 11th October the destinations of four ships from HX 310 were amended to Southampton and Southend. A September plot of D/F bearings of British forces at sea showed only a few centred off the North Channel and a broad concentration to the south-west of Ireland and in the Bristol Channel, with the old great-circle route between the North Channel and Newfoundland, which had formerly been so well defined, no longer apparent. Finally, convoys had been reported as sighted by three different U-boats, on 13th and 16th September and 4th October, 400 to 700 miles west-south-west of Land's End. There was, therefore, every indication that the enemy had virtually abandoned the North Channel and was now routing his convoys south of Ireland; certainly, he would only profit from his strenuous efforts to reopen the captured Channel ports if traffic from America were sent direct to France, and it was apparent that the Channel would see the bulk of this in the future.

By the middle of September we were still of the opinion that it would be a mistake to send U-boats from Norway to operate in the Channel; but favourable reports from the last five commanders to return from that area, together with an impression, gained from a study of all the U-boat logs, that the crews had now mastered the schnorkel, caused us to change our minds. We therefore determined to make another assault on the Channel, allowing considerable freedom of action to individual commanding officers. However, their final approach to this difficult area was to be sanctioned only after receipt of a report from each boat, transmitted from a position west of Ireland, confirming that the health of the crew and the state of machinery warranted entry into the Channel for a period of two to three weeks.

468. Operations in the Channel and British coastal waters

There were 36 U-boats at sea on 1st October 1944, with 28 homeward-bound and two outward-bound, and only six in the operational areas - four south of Nova Scotia, one off the North Channel and one north of the Minch - of which four would be returning in mid-month. It was three years since so few boats had operated and, as it was essential to restore pressure in the Atlantic as quickly as possible, six schnorkel boats from group *Mitte*, at readiness in Norway, were ordered to prepare at once for the Atlantic.

"… By withdrawing six schnorkel boats for the Atlantic we are taking a risk, for in the event of an attack on Norway or Jutland it will not be possible quickly to replace them. However, as it is now late in the year for a large-scale landing, the risk must be taken in the interest of the Atlantic campaign…" (395).

Of the first three boats destined for the Channel, U.1006 was presumably lost before reaching the Atlantic and U.246 had to return because of severe depth-charge damage received in an encounter with destroyers to the south-west of Ireland. The Commanding Officer of U.978, however, got through unmolested and decided to enter the Channel, operating there for three weeks and reporting that he had sunk three ships[63] in conditions which favoured continuance of such operations. Accordingly, without waiting for reports from the next two boats - U.991 and U.1200 - -we despatched others to the Cherbourg area, and in the latter half of December there were three or four boats there. That they were meeting with success was clear from numerous intercepted enemy signals; and this trend was confirmed by reports from our local people in Guernsey, who, besides hearing frequent heavy detonations and seeing the glow of burning ships by night, found the wreckage of ships and their boats on the foreshore. As enemy A/S vessels were often observed carrying out sweeps in the near vicinity, the Commandant of the Channel Islands Sea Defences was given permission to engage them with radar-controlled gunfire, irrespective of the presence of U-boats.

On 6th January 1945 excellent results were reported by U.486, which claimed to have sunk one steamship, three escort vessels and a corvette, and to have damaged a liner.[64] Three other boats which spent some time in the Channel - U.680, U.485 and U.325 - failed to get to grips with the enemy; and further confirmed successes of four ships aggregating 21,053 tons sunk and one of 7,176 tons damaged can only be attributed to U.772, which was subsequently sunk by

63 British records show one ship of 7,170 tons sunk and one of 7,176 tons damaged.
64 British records show that she actually sank two ships totalling 17,651 tons, the frigate *Capel* and the LSI(L) *Empire Javelin*, and damaged the frigate *Affleck*.

aircraft. A third boat was lost by the end of January, when U.1209 ran aground on the Wolf Rock.

Operations were also extended into the Irish Sea, following the same pattern as that laid down for the Channel; and when the first boat to arrive in the area - U.1202 - reported that she had sunk three ships[65] we sent a further six boats there in December and by January had achieved quite a heavy concentration. The subsequent loss of six more ships totalling 27,820 tons and damage to another of 2,198 tons, although accompanied by the sinking of three U-boats, caused the enemy to reroute his independent vessels up and down the centre of the Irish Sea instead of along the British coast; but this new route was decrypted on 12th January and passed to the boats, which were thereby able to sink two or three more ships.

In other areas - the North Channel, the north coast of Scotland and Reykjavik - which were patrolled by one or two boats, little was achieved.

469. U-boats demanded for extraneous tasks

Ever since the beginning of the invasion, increasing pressure on German-occupied territory had led to a spate of demands for the use of U-boats on transport and other extraneous tasks. To quote only a few examples: Naval Group West required provisions for the 80,000 men manning the coastal fortresses; ammunition was urgently needed at Dunkirk; and Army Group North was short of both ammunition and M/T fuel.

Each such demand received careful consideration, but almost all had to be rejected. Even the Type XIV supply U-boats, which carried 100 to 200 tons of cargo, would have been quite unable to satisfy the combined requirements of Group West and of Army Group North; but, as it was, only operational-type boats were available, capable of stowing 30 to 40 tons of cargo when eight of their torpedoes had been removed. Supplying the western fortresses, alone, would have monopolised all Type VIICs, bringing Atlantic operations to a halt for several months. In the case of Dunkirk, the transport of ammunition

---

65 British records give only one.

proved impossible in face of the mine threat and general navigational difficulties, but a single concession was made to the Commandant Sea Defences Loire when U.773 and U.722 were sent to St Nazaire with anti-tank weapons, ammunition and medical stores, returning to Norway in December with cargoes of non-ferrous metals.

A request from Naval Command, Norway, for the despatch of U-boats to seek out the enemy aircraft carriers operating off the Norwegian coast, had also to be turned down. Not even in the "good old days" had we succeeded in locating specific enemy formations by systematic search of the open sea, any such success being purely fortuitous, and now that it was necessary to operate U-boats continuously submerged the prospects for the older boats were nil. However, as incessant carrier-borne attacks on our convoys in Norwegian waters were threatening to paralyse the whole supply system, C-in-C Navy ordered that an attempt be made to attack the carriers as they entered and left Scapa Flow. Accordingly, at the beginning of December, U.297 was stationed south of Hoy and U.1020 south-east of Ronaldshay, with targets restricted to troop transports and above so long as they themselves remained undetected. These two boats were reinforced during the month by schnorkel boats from Northern Waters. U.274 and U.1020 never returned; the former was destroyed by aircraft to the south-west of Hoy, after sinking the frigate Bullen, and the latter was lost through cause unknown. Another boat - U.312 - carried away her rudder on the rocks while attempting, on her own initiative, to enter Hoxa Sound, but managed to escape and eventually reached Trondheim. The watch on Scapa Flow was finally abandoned on 14th January, after four fruitless weeks, when the two boats still on patrol were given freedom to operate southwards along the Scottish coast, which they did without success.

From November 1944, in another effort to waylay the enemy forces operating off the southwest coast of Norway, convoys were frequently escorted by a U-boat, stationed on the seaward quarter and ready to counter-attack. On 11th January 1945 one of these escorting U-boats - U.427 - claimed to have observed a hit by one of two T5 torpedoes fired at an attacking force of three British cruisers or destroyers. This hit was confirmed by hydrophone from another boat, and an aircraft, which was in radar contact with the retiring enemy, later established the presence of only two ships; we thus considered that one vessel had definitely been sunk and announced this in an official report, but British records make no mention of any such loss. At various times in February and March 1945, more than ten U-boats were employed on these escort duties.

470. Successes off Halifax and Gibraltar: Return of the U-boats from the Indian Ocean

From October 1944 onwards an average of two large U-boats patrolled the North American coast from the Gulf of St Lawrence to the Gulf of Maine, where, by the end of December, two ships totalling 12,677 tons had been sunk and another of 7,134 damaged.[66] In addition, U.1228 sank the Canadian corvette Shawinigan and U.1230 the Canadian minesweeper Clayoquot, while U.1223 damaged the Canadian frigate Magog. During two convoy attacks, on 4th and 14th January 1945, U.1232 sank four ships totalling 24,531 tons and damaged another of 2,373 tons. In a clandestine operation on 30th November 1944, U.1230 landed two agents near Boston without being observed, but according to press reports the agents were arrested a few days later. The German Secret Service was consistently unfortunate in its landing of agents on the coast of the United States; either the coast was too closely watched or the agents themselves were inadequately trained, for it was never long before they were apprehended. However, at this stage of the war it is not inconceivable that agents preferred to give themselves up.

U.1227 arrived off Gibraltar in mid-October 1944 and remained there for four weeks; but, apart from torpedoing the Canadian frigate Cheboque on the outward passage, she failed to get in an attack. Nevertheless, she reported such favourable operational conditions in

---

66 Latest research shows one ship of 5,458 tons sunk and three of 15,723 tons damaged during this period.

that area that we sent U.870 to follow her. While outward bound and 400 miles north-west of the Azores, U.870 chanced to be overrun by a convoy on 20th December, from which she torpedoed LST 359 and the US destroyer escort Fogg. She maintained patrol west of Gibraltar for three weeks, and between 3rd and 10th January 1945 attacked several east- and west-bound convoys, from which she sank one ship of 4,634 tons and damaged one of 7,207 tons.

As none of the Indian Ocean boats was equipped with schnorkel, they were all ordered to leave the area by mid-January 1945, at the latest, so as to clear the danger zone, which stretched from the south of Ireland to the Norwegian coast, while the nights were still long. Each carried a cargo of vital raw materials. The first boat to leave - U.168 - which sailed from Jakarta at the beginning of October, was sunk off the Javanese coast by an Allied submarine, and so became the second boat to be lost in this way within a fortnight; and although the remaining commanders were warned to take every precaution when traversing the Allied submarine zones off Penang and Jakarta, the next two boats - U.537 and U.196 - were both lost in the same way.[67] Of the rest, U.181 succeeded in reaching the Cape, where she developed bearing trouble, was forced to return to Jakarta and was subsequently turned over to the Japanese, U.510, U.532 and U.861 sailed in mid-January, their fortunes having already been recounted in Section 431, and U.862, whose commander was a former merchant service officer well acquainted with Australian waters, was given permission to visit the west coast of that country before returning to Germany. She put to sea in mid-November 1944, without divulging her intention, and on 24th December sank an American Liberty ship to the south of Sydney. Another ship was sunk 700 miles west of Perth on 6th February, while U.862 was on her return passage; but we never discovered why no other targets were encountered in the busy area south of Sydney.

67 U.168 was sunk by the Netherlands submarine *Zwaardvish* and U.537 by the US submarine *Flounder*. U.196 was lost through unknown cause.

471. Surprisingly good results in the period October 1944 to January 1945

In the spring of 1944, during the transition to containing operations in the Atlantic, Dönitz was firmly convinced that it would no longer be possible to use the old-type U-boats offensively. Certainly he expected the introduction of schnorkel to ease the situation, and this had been confirmed to his satisfaction during the anti-invasion operations in the Channel; but, as these boats were forced to operate in the face of the strongest opposition from both air and sea without having had time properly to test or practice with the new equipment, he was unable to form a positive opinion as to its true merit. Moreover, it was impossible to assess what percentage of our heavy losses sustained in June and July had been due to schnorkel failure as opposed to mistakes in drill.

From October 1944, however, all outward-bound U-boats were equipped with an improved type of schnorkel and had undergone special training in its use at Horten, or in some other fjord. They were, of course, now working in areas where the degree of enemy opposition varied considerably; nevertheless, to our surprise, a survey of operations up to the end of January 1945 showed, not only that these old-type boats were again capable of achieving results, but that losses had sharply decreased at the same time. Their effectiveness while actually in the operational area and measured in tonnage sunk per boat per day was exactly equal to the figure for August 1942. However, in those early days the operational area had been entered on crossing the line joining Iceland and Scotland. Now it lay right under the enemy coast. As a consequence of this much longer passage at a slow schnorkelling speed, but also owing to a disproportionate time spent in harbour, the boats were not fully utilised. Whereas in August 1942, out of 100 days the average U-boat spent 40 in harbour and 60 at sea, of which 40 were spent in the operational area, in December 1944 she spent 63 in harbour and 37 at sea, only nine of which were in the operational area. The number of effective boats was therefore much smaller, with total sinkings proportionately reduced (396). The most surprising revelation of the whole survey was to be found in the fact that our losses, amounting to 18 boats in four months, at something over 10 per cent of the boats at sea, were little higher than those recorded from the latter half of 1942. Thus it was no longer correct to talk of containing operations; on the contrary, in seeking out the enemy in his own coastal waters the U-boats were, in every respect, operating offensively.

"… It might have been expected that, with large numbers of schnorkel boats working in difficult areas, losses would increase; but this has not been the case. On the contrary, losses are down to the 1942-1943 level, which fact provides fresh and, perhaps, the most striking proof of the inestimable worth of the schnorkel…

"This changed situation in the latter part of 1944 has not only given the crews of old-type boats new faith in their weapons, but has also shown the new-type boats, with their high submerged speed and endurance, to have been rightly conceived and promising of great achievements…" (397).

472. Shallow water as the best protection against location

The remarkable drop in U-boat losses was attributable to two factors: the schnorkel, and the conditions prevailing in coastal waters, where the U-boats were almost exclusively employed.

After several unsuccessful attempts, our constructors had at last devised a satisfactory method of fixing the *Wanze* and *Naxos* aerials to the schnorkel head, which at normal height have a radar echo only one-quarter to one-eighth the strength of that from a surfaced U-boat and could thus be located from the air only at short range, when the aircraft's radar would also be apparent on the search receiver. Moreover, the schnorkel was very difficult to identify in a seaway. Thus, with the aid of her search receiver and periscope (the latter had to be manned while schnorkelling) a U-boat was reasonably certain of observing an attacking aircraft, by day or night, in time to reach depth before bomb release. Even in a smooth sea the trace left by a diving schnorkel provided a poor point of aim and bombing in surprise attacks had generally proved inaccurate.

Since U-boats in the open sea, particularly in rough water, were now less frequently located from the air, the enemy A/S forces had fewer opportunities for attack and relied more on their hydrophones for the long-range detection of schnorkelling U-boats. This constituted a serious danger, since the noise of the U-boat's diesels effectively drowned that of an approaching vessel. To minimise this danger, schnorkelling was interrupted every 20 minutes for an all-round hydrophone search, during which the boats usually went to 20 metres. But despite this added precaution, boats were sometimes taken by surprise and, like U.246, received damage from the first depth-charge attack. The threat was particularly acute if enemy vessels in the U-boat transit areas - between the Shetlands and Faroes, south-west of Ireland and west of the English Channel - lay with engines stopped and could not, therefore, be detected by hydrophone sweep. However, it was undesirable to interrupt schnorkelling more often for listening purposes, since, even with three periods an hour as the standard, only 10 to 12 minutes in every 20 remained available for battery-charging. Any shortening of this time would have entailed schnorkelling for half the night in order to ensure a capacity charge. The new Type XXI boats would be in no danger of a surprise surface attack while schnorkelling, for they were to be equipped with supersonic echo-ranging gear (S-Gerdt) capable of locating other vessels within a radius of 4,000 to 7,000 metres.

During the first Channel operations, boats actually in the area had frequently found insufficient time for schnorkelling, but four months' experience now showed that no great difficulty was to be expected in recharging when operating in coastal waters where enemy opposition was of normal proportions. Moreover, the enemy shore radar stations could locate a schnorkel only at very short range; at all events, while protected against air- and sea-borne radar by the coastal formation, rocks, buoys, fishing vessels and the like, individual U-boats had schnorkelled offshore undisturbed, with land-based radar audible up to strength 4 to 5. On detection by surface A/S forces, the U-boat certainly stood a better chance of evasion by heading into shallow water rather than into the open sea, as rocks and wrecks both produced false asdic echoes, while tide-rips and density layers deflected the asdic beam and restricted hydrophone performance. Furthermore, if a boat were damaged, she could bottom and effect repairs as soon as her pursuers were out of range.

FO U-boats continually impressed upon his commanders that, when pursued, they should act contrary to enemy expectations. For instance, after attacking a coastal convoy they should make for shallow water rather than deep water, a procedure which had often proved successful in the North Channel and the English Channel and in the Irish Sea. There were also instances when U-boats, after making a night attack with acoustic torpedoes, had raised their schnorkels and eluded their pursuers by retiring at the maximum permitted speed.

Neither in 1939 and 1940 nor during the US coastal battle of 1942 was the excellent protection of the coast, combined with the effects of tidal streams, so manifest as it was now.

473. Difficulty of finding targets
Although poor hydrophone listening conditions afforded considerable protection to the U-boats, they also had their disadvantages. On several occasions U-boats lying bottomed, or proceeding at depths of 30 to 40 metres, had been run over by ships and convoys whose propeller noises remained unheard until right overhead. In these circumstances there was rarely time to carry out an attack, although a few commanders were quick-witted enough to get off a stern shot with a *Lut* or T5 torpedo, which, to their surprise, sometimes hit the then distant target after a five- to ten-minute run. As a result of this experience, on 14th December 1944 U-boats operating in coastal waters were ordered to remain at periscope depth during the day, and to refrain from going deeper unless they found a water layer in which hydrophone range was likely to exceed optical visibility.

In these coastal waters targets could not generally be sighted by periscope, or located by hydrophone, at more than 6,000 to

8,000 metres, which was a short range for normal reconnaissance purposes, but regarded as long by boats operating in such areas as the North Channel, the Minch and the Bristol and St George's Channels. Furthermore, it occasionally happened that, when two U-boats were patrolling the same area, one would be able to make several attacks, while the other, not being exactly on the traffic route, met no targets at all. It was therefore more than ever necessary that the Command should produce a precise and detailed evaluation of all radio intelligence, together with information concerning the enemy's coastal routes and the times at which traffic passed given points, and that the boats should be kept constantly in the picture. If, despite receipt of this information, a boat still found no traffic:

"… the commander was at liberty to carry out his search for targets beyond the limits of his allotted area and into bays and inlets, without informing the Command…" (398).

There was another reason why U-boats should be free to leave their prescribed attack areas in search of traffic. The enemy, aware that the old-type boats were unable to use their Fat and *Lut* torpedoes in the dark, so timed most of his convoys that they traversed the more dangerous areas - prominent headlands and areas in which the depth of water ranged between 60 and 120 metres - at night, thereby repeatedly outmanoeuvring the U-boats and saving many of his ships from destruction. Thus, if a U-boat found that propeller noises were audible in her patrol area only at night, she had, perforce, to proceed along the coast until she reached that part of the route traversed in daylight.

474. Intelligence difficulties caused by reduced radio traffic

The restriction of U-boat operations to coastal waters caused the enemy to cut down on his air and surface A/S forces in the Atlantic and to concentrate them in Home Waters. U-boats on passage, while west of 15 degrees West, could, therefore, have surfaced to recharge their batteries at night, or could even have made this part of the passage on the surface. But although commanders made every endeavour to hasten their transit time, they seldom availed themselves of this possibility, the reason for which is well illustrated by the following extract from the log of U.480.

"… 12th September 1944. 0511. 300 miles west of Ireland. Surfaced for the first time in 40 days. The boat stinks. Everything is covered with phosphorescent particles. One's footmarks on the bridge show up fluorescently. One's hands leave a luminous trace on the weather cloth. Schnorkel fittings and flooding slots also glow brightly in the darkness. Because of a high stern sea the bridge is constantly awash and the men cannot stand up on the slippery wooden deck; it is therefore impossible either to change or to dismantle the AA guns. The shields of the twin AA guns cannot be opened; the hinges appear to have rusted up and cannot be attended to in the dark. The 3 -7-cm gun is out of action; so shall first transmit my situation report and then proceed on schnorkel until the state of the sea permits me either to change the AA guns, or dismantle them for overhaul below. In view of the strong phosphorescence, however, I shall first surface at daylight to ascertain the outboard state of the boat…"

"… 2nd October 1944.1710. Off the west coast of Norway. Surfaced. The whole flak armament is unserviceable. The gun shields have been torn away from their mountings and are fouling the guns. Everything, including the 3-7-cm gun, is corroded and covered with growth…"

"… 1720. Dived. I do not want to remain on the surface in this state, unless I am compelled to…"

In such conditions commanders preferred to remain submerged, and to surface only to rectify some serious outboard defect - such as a sticky schnorkel valve - or to transmit the required W/T reports on entering the Atlantic and leaving patrol.

At this stage of the war the transmission of a radio message was an event in itself. The loss of France and Belgium, Allied bombing and other causes had deprived us of a number of good radio receiving stations and, moreover, the boats' radio operators were less efficient and experienced than previously; consequently, messages often failed to reach the home receiving stations, or were received incomplete. The U-boat commanders were generally averse - and rightly so - to using their radio and were apt to give up after one or two abortive attempts to pass a message; in fact, the more cautious of them made no attempt at all. The result was that nearly 50 per cent of the boats maintained radio silence during the whole of their patrol, except to report their arrival at the escort rendezvous position the day before entering a Norwegian base. Indeed, many commanders failed even to do this and merely waited off the coast until they could join up with the escort detailed for another boat.

In former times, if nothing was heard from a U-boat for a fortnight, at most, we could consider her to have been lost; now, however, it took seven to nine weeks - the average duration of a patrol - to establish this fact. Furthermore, since we had now to rely mainly on verbal reports from the commanders, the assessment of the current situation in an operational area was even more difficult than it had been in the Channel during the invasion. There was thus a danger that we should be unable to detect a sudden deterioration in time to take the necessary counteraction.

FEBRUARY-MAY 1945
THE FINAL PHASE

475. The war situation calls for the intensification of the U-boat campaign

The period from autumn 1944 to the end of January 1945 saw a marked deterioration in the over-all war situation. In December our Ardennes offensive had proved a failure; while the great

Russian offensive, which opened on 12th January, achieved a decisive breakthrough at Baranow and brought about a complete collapse on the Eastern Front. In a swift, almost unopposed advance, the Russian spearheads penetrated deep into the industrial area of Upper Silesia, and as far as Kustrin on the Middle Oder, and

Frankfurt. On 28th January they established a bridgehead on the left bank of the Oder at Wriezen, only 30 km from Camp Koralle, the U-boat and Naval Staff Headquarters. No forces were available to defend the headquarters against a possible armoured thrust from this bridgehead; the Naval Staff was therefore dissolved, the U-boat Staff and those members of the Naval Staff considered indispensable to the future conduct of the war moving to Sengwarden, Wilhelmshaven, where they remained until the end of April. Dönitz, with a skeleton staff, stayed on in Berlin, thus severing his connection with the U-boat Command and relinquishing personal control of Atlantic U-boat operations for the first time since the beginning of the war (399).

The gravity of the situation did not affect our plans to continue the U-boat campaign, except in so far as operations had to be intensified for the relief of enemy pressure against our coastal communications. In fact, it was preoccupation with the U-boat offensive in British coastal waters that prevented the Allies from taking more effective action against our shipping on the Norwegian coast, in the Skagerrak and in the North Sea, which was important, for, ever since the end of November 1944, a continuous stream of transports had been plying between Norway, Denmark and Germany, carrying reinforcements for the Western Front (400). Besides these nearly 400,000 tons of service stores, ore and pyrites awaited shipment to the Fatherland, and any dislocation of this traffic would have proved a serious handicap.

The U-boats were also committed to an attack on the Allied supply routes to France and the Scheldt, where every ton of war materials sunk in transit would help to delay the Allied build-up for their offensive in the west, a view echoed in a Supreme Command memorandum to the Naval Staff dated 31st December 1944, which pointed out that American stockpiles in Europe could now be regarded as expended and that, hereafter, they would have to rely solely upon sea supplies, which made the role of the U-boat decisive (401).

476. Allied bombing and minelaying delay completion of the new-type boats

Really effective offensive U-boat action was only possible by use of the new-type boats, which should have been ready for operations in November and December 1944, but they were not completed on time. Dönitz, when reporting to Hitler on 12th October, had, in fact, estimated that the first of the Type XXIII and 40 Type XXI U-boats would be operating in the Atlantic in January and February 1945, respectively (402).

From a variety of reports emerging at the end of 1944, it was clear that the enemy possessed precise information on the fighting qualities of the new boats. Allied political and military leaders and the foreign press all warned of the imminent revival of the U-boat campaign, stating that, since withdrawing from the Atlantic, the German U-boat fleet had been reinforced by new boats carrying novel devices for countering Allied A/S weapons and boasting a submerged speed of 15 knots, which would enable them to pursue and attack a convoy even by day. These statements, which revealed an extensive knowledge of the specifications of the new types, also showed that it was almost impossible to keep such information secret over a long period of time (403). By degrees the British people were being prepared for a resurgence of the U-boat war, and at the same time Allied A/S vessels were warned to be ready for encounters with the new type boats. For instance, our Radio Intelligence Service intercepted a voice message from the SO of an Allied task force announcing special measures to be taken during the winter against an expected intensification of U-boat operations.

The German Naval Staff, indeed, expected that the Allies would be ready with counter-measures when the time came:

"… 3rd December 1944. C-in-C Navy has no qualms as to the outcome of operations by the new-type U-boats, with their much improved underwater fighting qualities. In his opinion the greatest problem arising from a resumption of operations will be for the Homeland and the dockyards, for, as soon as we start to sink his ships, the enemy will bring his whole strength to bear against our U-boat transit routes, building and repair yards and bases. Whereas other industries can be moved to areas less threatened, shipbuilding has to remain on the coast and in the large ports, and allows of no substitution..." (404).

Despite an urgent need to protect the new boats against this anticipated enemy reaction, the building of bunkers for the U-boat section and assembly yards lagged behind requirement; furthermore, the hope that by the beginning of 1945 an expanded fighter-aircraft programme, together with production of the new jet fighters, would provide "a roof over Germany" remained unfulfilled. As a consequence the enemy air offensive, which had continued unabated since the end of 1944, succeeded in delaying U-boat production to a much greater extent that had been foreseen by the Naval Staff. These delays were due less to the actual destruction of U-boats - the raid on Hamburg on 31st December 1944 destroyed only one Type XXI and damaged three - than to a retardation in the rate of construction. The 30 to 50 Type XXIs already in commission were principally affected, often having to wait for several weeks for repairs which, in normal conditions and with spares readily available, would have taken only a few days. Frequent fouling of the Baltic routes and of the exercise areas by mines also served to protract the U-boat training programme, so that by the end of January 1945 it was apparent that only one or two Type XXIs - instead of 40 - would become operational during the following month and that no increase could be expected until April. The first of the Type XXIII boats, however, commenced operations in February, as planned.

477. Expectation of increased enemy opposition and minelaying in British coastal waters

As the Type XXI boats were not yet ready, we had to carry on with the old types, but it was doubtful if the battle would continue on such a favourable note as in the previous months, since the enemy was bound to reinforce his A/S defences around the British Isles in an attempt to drive the U-boats from the coast. Dönitz raised this subject on several occasions when in conference with Hitler (405).

"... 1st March 1945. The confining of U-boat operations exclusively to British home waters is undesirable, since it enables the enemy to concentrate his A/S forces in a small area. But, as the slow submerged speed of the old-type boats (VIIC) precludes their employment in any other region, the extension of operations to areas further afield, which might split the enemy defence forces, will only be possible when the Type XXI U-boats become operational. If we still held the Biscay coast, the Type VIIs could, of course, still operate in remoter areas such as the American coast. We do not think that the enemy has yet devised any fundamentally new methods of locating and attacking a submerged U-boat. Nevertheless, we must be prepared for increasing losses in British waters, where the enemy will apply his whole resources to mastering the U-boat menace. And in time he will meet with increasing success by virtue of the strength of his forces..." (406).

The increased use by the enemy of anti-U-boat mines was a danger of unknown quantity and difficult to assess. The German Naval Staff was acquainted with the positions of the two deep mine barrages, laid earlier, in the Rosengarten (between the Faroes and Orkneys) and across the St George's Channel, but it was not known whether these fields had been supplemented, or if the mines were still active. However, a first indication of the recent laying of anti-U-boat mines came in an agent's report, received on 15th November 1944, stating that U.1006 had been sunk by a mine in October, to the south of Ireland. The same agent reported, on 24th November, that new minefields were being laid here and there in the North Channel, in small groups close to the sea bed, as a counter to the new, permanently submerged U-boats. He went on to say that these deep mines were being laid outside the declared mine zones and in mine-free passages as a trap for U-boats pursuing convoys, that over 2,000 mines had been laid by the minelayers Plover and Apollo in September and that similar fields were to be laid to the south of Ireland. This information was allegedly obtained from a member of the ship's company of one of the minelayers (407), but we placed little credence upon it as it seemed improbable that 2,000 mines had been laid in the North Channel on the first appearance of U-boats in that area, where mines were very likely to break adrift in the prevalent heavy ground swell and thereby endanger British shipping. The reported fate of U.1006 was also doubted since, we estimated, correctly, she had been lost between the Faroes and Orkneys.[68] Incidentally, none of the intelligence supplied by this agent, who had been in England for over three years, was ever substantiated, so he may possibly also have been working for the enemy, and in this case transmitted an Admiralty-inspired report designed to discourage the U-boats from frequenting coastal waters.

The possibility of an increased use of anti-U-boat mines had, however, been taken into account; indeed, since November 1944 all U-boats proceeding to the Irish Sea had been directed either to transit the St George's Channel surfaced and close to the Irish Coast or to cross the danger area on a known shipping route and at a maximum depth of 30 metres, above which depth moored mines were unlikely to be found because of the danger to Allied shipping.

478. Climax of operations round the British Isles

In February 1945 a good 50 old-type boats became ready for sea. The provision of fuel for these boats presented a problem, as the navy was then receiving only part of its allocation owing to the widespread destruction of transport and other facilities. This difficulty was, however, overcome by taking oil from the Scheer, the *Lutz*ow and other laid-up units. Thirty-six boats sailed from Norway in February, 38 in March and 40 in April and, with the exception of those destined for the British East Coast, all were sent first to a waiting position to the west of Ireland. Their attack areas were then allocated at the last possible moment, based upon the most up-to-date reports of boats returning from operations, the intention being to occupy as many as

---

68 U.1006 was sunk off the Faroes on 16th October 1944 by HMCS *Annan*.

possible of those coastal areas in which the boats had some prospect of success.

"... The enemy is thereby compelled to provide escorts everywhere, thus dispersing his forces and weakening him in individual areas. There is little point in sending more boats to these confined waters than is commensurate with the volume of traffic, for any considerable success is likely to evoke strong countermeasures, which would temporarily eliminate not only one but probably several boats simultaneously. The occupation of several areas at a time has a further advantage in that it will provide us with greater details of enemy countermeasures and methods of defence and a better idea of how the enemy situation is developing..." (408).

In February and at the beginning of March, reports from the boats operating in the English Channel were most satisfactory. Traffic between Portsmouth and Cherbourg was still plentiful, although it was becoming increasingly confined to the hours of darkness; good opportunities for attacks were also offered between Land's End and Start Point, where, in addition to routine coastal convoys, parts of incoming HX convoys passed in daylight, and it was here that the Channel boats had found their targets. The A/S situation also appeared generally favourable, our survey to the end of February showing that enemy action had accounted for the loss of only one U-boat (U.772) out of five operating in the area in December, and one out of three in January. U.650 was presumed to have been sunk before reaching the Channel.

On the strength of this appreciation, we sent nearly a dozen more U-boats to the Channel during the first half of March, disposing them off Cherbourg, south of Portsmouth, north of Ushant and off the south-west coast of Britain, but, as the outward and return passages occupied nearly six weeks, there were never more than five boats in the operational area at any one time. In addition, as a result of favourable reports from commanders returning from the Irish Sea, we followed up in February and March with another seven boats, disposing them north of the Isle of Man, off Liverpool and

Holyhead, and in the St George's and Bristol Channels. Four boats then operating off the North Channel were given freedom to extend their activity to the Irish Sea or the Clyde, while four others were sent to the Scottish coast, between the North Minch and the Pentland Firth, and a further three to the Moray Firth and Firth of Forth.

In February a carefully planned operation - code-named Brutus - was carried out against the Thames-Scheldt traffic by U.245, under the command of *Korvettenkapitän* Schuman Hindenburg, a highly efficient officer especially selected for the task. Sailing from Kiel, via Heligoland, she proceeded first to the north-west and then south-westward to the Dogger Bank, whence she made due south into the operational area. Her commander was in possession of precise details concerning the convoy time-table, including the times of passing the various buoys marking the route. On 6th February he sank the Henry P. Plant (7,240 tons), some 10 miles east of the North Foreland, and on 15th he torpedoed a small Dutch tanker in the same area. U.245 then returned to Heligoland, which had not been used as a U-boat base for two and a half years.

Most of the large U-boats were sent to the American and Canadian coasts, but U.868 and U.878 were used to transport essential stores and ammunition to St Nazaire, where they turned over some of their fuel to U.255. U.255 had been paid off in August after being severely damaged, but, on the initiative of the SO of the flotilla, she had been repaired meanwhile and manned by base personnel, the SO himself taking command and training the crew. In April she was used to lay mines at Les Sables. U.869 and a Type VIIC boat - U.300 - were sent to the Gibraltar area, the latter at her commander's request.

Of the Indian Ocean boats, U.862 - the last to operate - returned to Jakarta from Australia on 15th February, while the four on their way back to Germany entered the South Atlantic in February and later sank three independent vessels, a sign that, in face of a diminished threat, the Allies were once more sailing their ships independently.

479. Withdrawal from the British coast

During February and March, only one in four outgoing boats reported their arrival in the Atlantic; in fact, of 114 which sailed in the period February to April only 30 did so, while few of them made a situation report during the return passage. At no other period of the war had we felt our appreciation of the situation to be so unreliable, or an error in that appreciation to be so dangerous for the boats.

Although returning commanders still reported having encountered surprisingly little opposition, the few scraps of information that our greatly reduced Radio Intelligence Service was still able to obtain led us to believe that, from mid-February onwards, the enemy was concentrating his A/S forces in British coastal waters, which the volume of enemy radio traffic evoked by each U-boat contact certainly seemed to confirm, since this traffic appeared to have become greater and to be addressed to a larger number of units than before, particularly in the Plymouth and Lyme Bay areas and in the North Channel.

During March, concern was felt for some of the boats which had been sailed in January and were now approaching the limit of their 70 days at sea, and also for a few others that had sailed later. According to our reckoning they should already have been in their operational areas for two or three weeks, but enemy radio activity had given no indication of their presence so far, and we therefore feared that they might have fallen victim to hunter groups patrolling off the Norwegian coast or between the Orkneys and Shetlands. Our apprehension of mounting danger was further increased by the first confirmation of the laying of new enemy minefields. This came from U.260, which on 13th March, while proceeding submerged at 80 metres and about 20 metres from the bottom approximately 15 miles south of Cape Clear, was severely damaged by a contact or antenna mine. She fortunately managed to surface and make a radio contact and, after getting her engines restarted, landed her crew on the Irish coast.[69]

When, at the end of March, it became clear that our losses in the English and North Channels had mounted considerably since the

---

69 U.260 was scuttled by order of U-boat Command, her whole crew escaping by dinghy and landing in the vicinity of Galley Head.

beginning of February, FO U-boats took the only course open to him and withdrew the boats to seaward from the coastal areas, additionally giving them the option of returning to base if the opposition proved too strong. On 30th March and 10th April, in pursuance of this policy, seven boats bound for the English Channel were diverted to new attack areas, 200 and 300 miles west of the Channel entrance, while on 15th April, six more, destined for the North Channel, were given attack areas 30 to 100 miles north of Donegal Bay and three, *en route* to the Irish Sea, were allowed operational freedom. A number of minelays were also planned, which was always the case when final evacuation of an area was contemplated.

In an attempt to tie down enemy forces in the Atlantic, six boats bound for the American coast were formed into group Seewolf on 14th April, for a westward sweep along the great-circle convoy routes. It was thought that Atlantic convoys were probably less strongly protected at this time and that a surprise success against one of them might induce the enemy to transfer some of his hunter groups from British coastal waters into the open ocean, thereby weakening, to some extent, his A/S concentration in the former area.

480. Losses in the last three months

We heard practically nothing of the course of operations subsequent to March 1945, until the capitulation. However, what information we had showed that U.315 torpedoed three ships south of the Lizard, U.1107 sank two ships of a convoy at the western entrance to the Channel, while U.1022 off Reykjavik and U.245 on a second operation off the Thames had each two ships to their credit. Only two of the planned minelaying operations were carried out, as shown in the following table.

Date (1945)	Position	No. of Mines	Type of Mine	U-boat	Remarks
18.4	Clyde	13	SMA	U.218	-
18.4	Les Sables	8	TMC	U.255	-
-	Dundee	-	-	U.1065	Sunk on outward passage, 9th April
-	Cherbourg	-	-	U.1055	Sunk at entrance to Channel, 30th April
-	Hartlepool	-	-	U.975	Cancelled owing to surrender
-	Portland Bill	-	-	U.963	Cancelled owing to surrender

When, after the capitulation, the Allies ordered all boats to report their positions, many failed to respond, and it was only then that the magnitude of our losses in the last months of the war became apparent. There had been a particularly steep rise since the beginning of the year, with seven boats lost in January, 13 in February, 16 in March and 29 in April, this last figure representing about 54 per cent of the boats at sea and being the highest of the whole campaign. In retrospect, and taking into account the location of U-boat sinkings, it is evident that nearly all those boats proceeding to or from various parts of the Channel had tried their luck in the coastal area between the Lizard and Hartland Point - described by their predecessors as favourable - and had fallen victim to the numerous A/S vessels awaiting them there. Whether our losses, generally, resulted from a concentration of the enemy's A/S forces or from improved underwater location and new A/S weapons, we were no longer able to judge, but the fact that we lost no fewer than 10 out of 16 boats which had sailed for the American and Canadian coasts, an area containing no great number of A/S vessels, seemed to subscribe to the latter possibility. The real situation, as now revealed, was infinitely worse than we had feared and, had the war not terminated on 9th May, we should without doubt have been compelled to withdraw all the remaining old-type boats from the Atlantic. Such severe losses might not have seriously affected the morale of the crews of the new-type boats, but the U-boat arm could not have endured them for another month.

481. The Type XXI U-boats approach operational readiness

From February 1945 onwards, we began to feel the effect of the gradual severance of Northern Germany from the industrial interior. Oil and coal, the most important of all the commodities required by the navy, dockyards and other supporting services, no longer arrived; and stocks remaining in the ports were only just sufficient to satisfy our extensive transport commitments, together with repairs to transports and U-boats. Owing to the Russian threat, U-boat building stopped at the Schichau and Danzig yards in February, and thereafter gradually came to a standstill in the remaining Baltic and North German ports, where work was undertaken only on those Type XXI boats that had already completed their training.

Although it became increasingly clear that the war was approaching its end, officers and men of the U-boat arm redoubled their efforts to get the first Type XXIs to sea, for they wanted, at least, to assure themselves that their labours had not been wasted, but they were to fail in this. The Allies were determined to delay the new U-boat offensive sufficiently for it to be overtaken by complete victory on land, and, as such a decision was taking longer than expected, they had recently intensified their air bombardment of U-boat bases and dockyards. In contrast to the results obtained in 1944, U-boats were frequently destroyed in these latest attacks, Bremen alone losing five Type XXIs between 17th February and 25th March, while another nine were destroyed in Bremen, Hamburg and Kiel between 30th March and 10th April. Four of these boats had already completed their training and were to have become operational in April (409).

The first Type XXI U-boat to be ready - U.2511 - sailed for Norway on 18th March, commanded by *Korvettenkapitän* Schnee, but on arrival she had to remedy certain mechanical defects and make good some slight damage sustained during her deep diving trials, so that it was 30th April before she was ready to sail on her first operational cruise. A further five boats, which had by then reached Norway, were carrying out schnorkel trials and generally equipping for sea, and should have been ready to commence operations by mid-May at the latest, while another 30 to 50 had finished their training and were mostly completing outstanding items of work prior to sailing operations.

On 4th May all boats at sea were ordered to cease hostilities and to return to base (Section 486). A few hours after receiving this message, U.2511, then to the north of the Faroes, sighted a British cruiser and her destroyer escort at long range. Closing at high speed and then reducing to silent-running speed, the U-boat attained an attacking position inside the screen, from which she carried out a dummy attack, albeit with six tubes at the ready. After a final look at the target, which was too close to miss, U.2511 went deep. This was the only attack of any sort carried out by a Type XXI U-boat under action conditions.

482. Operations by Type XXIII U-boats

Operations carried out by Type XXIII U-boats up to the end of the war provided limited, though convincing proof, of the fighting qualities of these boats. The first two - U.2324 and U.2322 - sailed from Kristiansand on 31st January and 6th February 1945, respectively, to operate off the British coast between Aberdeen and Newcastle, their main activity being centred off the Firth of Forth. As their commanders needed some time to familiarise themselves with newly installed schnorkels and with the general features of the operational area, it was not until 18th February that a first contact was made with the enemy. Then, U.2324 encountered a convoy in bad visibility 15 miles east of the Coquet light and fired two torpedoes at a range of about 400 metres, both of which missed, owing to a gyro-angling failure. Later, on 25th February, U.2322 sank a freighter of 1,317 tons eight miles south-east of St Abb's Head.

Type XXIII boats made a further six sorties before the war ended, U.2321, U.2326 and U.2336 patrolling in the same area as the first two, and U.2322 - also presumably U.2324 and U.2329 - between Lowestoft and the Thames. Unfortunately, the German naval archives in possession of the Allies contain no further reference to these operations, so that the table opposite has, perforce, been constructed partly from memory, or from verbal accounts of the officers concerned, and cannot be regarded as strictly accurate.

The commanding officers were unanimous in their opinion of the new boats, finding them fast, handy and easy to control, while their small silhouette reduced the chances of detection and counterattack; in fact they were ideal boats for short operations in coastal waters, their only defect being an inadequacy of radio transmitting and receiving equipment. Using the full submerged speed of 13 knots, the commanders were always able to reach a close attacking position and to attack two targets in quick succession; however, in four cases lack of experience caused them to underestimate their .own speed, with the result that in the second attack the torpedo was fired inside its safety range and so failed to arm. The only boat to hit in both attacks was U.2336, which on 7th May sank two ships close south-east of May Island in the Firth of Forth. Her Commanding Officer - a former U-boat staff officer - had been one of those responsible for developing the tactics of the new-type boats and anxious to prove his theory, carried out his attacks in truly academic style. Incidentally, this attack served to underline the inadequacy of the radio receiver fitted in Type XXIIIs, for U.2336 received no radio messages subsequent to her sailing and therefore missed the signal of 4th May ordering all boats to cease operations and return to base. Only on their return passage did she pick up fragments of a plain-language version of the surrender order, but the situation then appeared so uncertain to the Commanding Officer that he returned to Kiel.

In their eight sorties the Type XXIII boats entirely fulfilled our expectations. Although they had operated in difficult waters, not one was lost, while only two failed to achieve any results, both through torpedo failure. They exceeded our expectations in one respect, by remaining at sea for four to five weeks instead of two or three as we had estimated. U.2321's patrol lasted for 33 days.

Operations By Type XXIII U-boats

U-boat	Operational Area	Duration Of Operation (1945)	Results Claimed	Results By Records	Remarks
U.2324	Newcastle to St Abb's Head	30.1 to 24.2	-	-	2 torpedo failures
U.2322	Ditto	6.2 to 3.3	1 freighter	One of 1,317 tons	-
U.2321	Ditto	12.2 to 14.4	1 freighter	One of 1,406 tons	-
U.2322	Lowestoft to Thames	5.4 to 5.5	1 ship	One of 7,029 tons	-
U.2324	Ditto	3.4 to 26.4	1 ship of 5,000 tons	One of 4,856 tons	It is not clear which of these boats sank this ship
U.2329	Ditto	12.4 to 27.4	1 ship of 5,000 tons		
U.2326	Newcastle to St Abb's Head	19.4 to 28.4	-	-	2 torpedo failures
U.2326	Ditto	1.5 to 14.5	2 ships	Two totalling 4,669 tons	-

THE END

483. Transport of refugees from the Eastern Baltic

The loss of Upper Silesia marked our military defeat. The enemy's insistence on unconditional surrender, however, and his own intention to split Germany into separate zones, decided us to fight on and hold out at all costs. A chart captured from the enemy and held at Hitler's headquarters for some months past, showed that the country was to be divided at the Oder-Neisse line (410), and the fearful certainty that unconditional surrender would therefore entail abandoning to the Bolsheviks the whole area east of that line, together with our fighting men on the Eastern Front and millions of women and children, was the main reason why Dönitz, himself, also considered it necessary to continue to fight. The German Navy's prime task, as he saw it, was to rescue from the Russians in the short time available as many of our people as possible. Thus, from February onwards, firstly merchant vessels and then by degrees all serviceable warships were used to transport troops and wounded from Lithuania and East Prussia, while later they were devoted mainly to the rescue of refugees from East Prussia and Pomerania. At the same time our heavy warships bombarded the coast, in support of the land battle for the Baltic ports.

Some idea of the immensity of this task can be gained from a summary of the numbers transported, compiled on 9th May 1945 by Naval Group East (411). According to this summary, between 21st January and 8th May more than a million soldiers and refugees were brought back from East Prussian ports, while a further million were rescued from the East Prussian and Pomeranian coast, making a total of 2,022,000. But this summary is by no means complete and the ultimate total must have been much higher.

As far as the U-boats were concerned, Memel, Pillau, Danzig and Gotenhafen had all to be abandoned as bases, and the use of U-boats for transport purposes on their passage to the west enabled officers and men to witness at first hand the indescribable misery of the refugees.

484. Dönitz nominated as Hitler's successor
The great Russian offensive on the Oder front, which opened on 16th April, achieved a decisive breakthrough three days later and the final battle for Berlin then began. On 24th April, on Hitler's orders, the C-in-C Navy and the rest of his staff moved from Berlin to Plön, in Schleswig-Holstein, to. make immediate preparations for the defence of the northern area, should it be cut off (412).

Since mid-April, refugees and columns of base and garrison personnel had been streaming into Schleswig-Holstein from the east. Furthermore, all those warships and merchant vessels which had managed to leave Eastern Baltic and North Sea ports ahead of the Allied advance, and were not engaged on transport duty, had now assembled in the Western Baltic, while, by the end of April, nearly 200 U-boats had arrived at Kiel, Flensburg, Eckernförde and Travemunde, and in the Strander and Geltinger Buchten. Communication between these U-boats and their administrative Admiral had practically ceased owing to loss of radio stations.

The enemy's advance to the line Lubeck-Hamburg caused the staff of U-boat Command to be moved to Flensburg on 30th April, while the C-in-C Navy remained at Plön. Dönitz was determined to surrender the German Navy on his own responsibility and to expiate this act by seeking death in battle (413), but on the evening of 30th, to his great surprise, he received a radio message from the Chancellery in Berlin appointing him as Hitler's successor. Thus he was saddled with the bitter and thankless task of signing the capitulation, a political act that was to lead to his final humiliation. Yet, putting his scruples on one side, Dönitz assumed his new office, conscious that an orderly capitulation was essential if further bloodshed was to be avoided; he also still intended to save as many of our people as possible from Russian captivity, and attempted to gain time for the further transfer of troops and refugees from the Eastern Zone by negotiating with the Western Allies for a separate surrender.

485. Heavy U-boat losses *en route* to Norway

On 30th April, instructions were issued for the scuttling of the fleet (414). The executive for this operation was the codeword *Regenbogen*, upon receipt of which all warships, excluding those craft which would be required later for fishing, transport and mine clearance, were to be sunk or destroyed.

On 2nd May, at Flensburg, U-boat staff officers handed out these instructions to the 30th U-boat Flotilla, and to about 80 U-boat commanders assembled there from other U-boats lying either in that port or at Kiel, Eckernförde and in the Strander and Geltinger Buchten. At the same time all U-boats capable of diving were ordered to move to Norway, away from the threat of attack from low-flying aircraft and to a position where it was thought that their presence, in large numbers, might strengthen the hand of the German representatives in their negotiations with Field-Marshal Montgomery. Similar orders were passed, visually, to unrepresented boats in the Flensburg and Geltinger Buchten, and, against a possible future requirement for the conduct of U-boat operations from Norway, the Chief of the U-boat staff - Konteradmtral Godt - and the Author, then Staff Officer Operations, were flown forthwith to the headquarters of SO U-boats West, at Bergen.

Since the beginning of April, enemy aircraft had been operating over the Western Baltic and Kattegat in daylight, unchallenged, and had accounted for no less than five U-boats on passage through the Kattegat. The sudden exodus to Norway, swollen by the unauthorised presence of a great many boats that were unable to dive, was therefore quickly spotted, and the enemy, seizing this opportunity of dealing a last-minute blow to the U-boat arm, concentrated large numbers of aircraft of all types in the area. In the absence of any German fighter opposition, these aircraft were able to pursue their hunt over the whole of the Kattegat Sound and Belts and even into bays and harbours, destroying in a last bloody massacre between 2nd and 6th May, twenty-one U-boats, the majority of which were unable to dive. A proportion of the crews were rescued by other U-boats and by German and Danish coastal vessels.

486. Operation *Regenbogen*

Dönitz's intentions were made known to the military commanders on the various fronts by radio, teleprinter and courier; and, in so far as they were still in a position to do so, they conformed to his orders, for those were consistent with their own desires.

On 3rd May General-Admiral von Friedeburg proceeded to Field-Marshal Montgomery's headquarters to negotiate a separate surrender on Dönitz's behalf. Montgomery agreed to accept the surrender of the North German area on condition that Holland, Denmark and the German fleet were included and that no weapons or ships be destroyed before the surrender, which was to take effect from 0800 on 5th May. This meant handing over every available unit of the Navy, a heavy blow to Dönitz, since any such action violated tradition and every concept of military honour. While high-ranking officers at Supreme Headquarters regarded this condition as incapable of fulfilment, the Grand Admiral on the other hand decided, with heavy heart, to accept it, in order not to prejudice the chances of escape of a great part of our eastern armies and many refugees.

In accordance with Dönitz's decision, on 4th May all U-boats at sea were ordered to cease hostilities and to return to base forthwith, marking the end of the U-boat campaign and leaving U-boat Command with the melancholy task of carrying out all future Allied orders. The message was transmitted continuously on all wavelengths; but it was only to be expected that a few boats would fail to receive it in time to prevent them from carrying further attacks. In fact there were two such cases - U.853 sank the ss *Black Point* on 5th, off Long Island, USA, and U.2336 two ships in the Firth of Forth on 7th.

Details of the surrender terms were transmitted to all German forces late on 4th May. However, the commanders of U-boats in the Western Baltic, who had already prepared their boats for scuttling in accordance with the orders for *Regenbogen* and were of the opinion that the order forbidding the sinking of their ships was contrary to Dönitz's intention and given under duress - -which was, of course the ultimate truth - scuttled their boats that night. Altogether, a total of 218 boats - including 82 Type XXIs and 29 Type XXIIIs - went to the bottom just before the armistice. These scuttlings came as a surprise to Dönitz, but there were no repercussions since, presumably, they suited the purpose of the Allies.

487. The surrender of the U-boats from sea

After signing the armistice with Montgomery, von Friedeburg proceeded to General Eisenhower's headquarters in the hope of negotiating a separate surrender to the Americans and so gaining a further few days in which to withdraw our still embattled eastern armies to the Anglo-American front line. Here he met with failure; Eisenhower categorically demanding unconditional capitulation in both the East and West and threatening severe penalties unless the

Germans signed at once. Our delegates - von Friedeburg and Jodl - nevertheless managed to secure a period of 48 hours in which to transmit the surrender orders to our far-flung army units; and the German Navy worked feverishly until the last minute to evacuate the maximum number of troops and refugees from the Eastern Baltic. These delaying tactics, in the nine days between Dönitz's accession and the final ending of hostilities, enabled us to save two and a half to three million compatriots from the Russians.

The general surrender came into force at 0001 on 9th May, the Allied demand for the German fleet to be handed over intact having been passed to the U-boats on the previous day. In a personal message to the U-boat arm, Dönitz, while recognising that he was demanding great forbearance from them, pointed out that he expected absolute obedience to his order, since failure to comply with Allied demands would inevitably bring serious consequences and further suffering to the German people. His U-boat commanders understood him and told him so in a large number of radio messages, but they made no secret of the fact that it went much against the grain to surrender their boats, and that it was only their loyalty to Dönitz, personally, which prevented them from disobeying this order.

In compliance with the Allied order, the U-boats duly surfaced and, flying the black flag, proceeded to their allotted surrender ports. Of 43 boats at sea on 8th May, 23 surrendered in English ports, three in Canada and four in the United States, while seven returned either to Kiel or Norway. Additionally, U.1277 and U.963 scuttled themselves off the Portuguese coast, U.979 grounded at Amrun, U.287 struck a mine and sank as she was entering the Elbe and U.530 with U.977 went to the Argentine. These last two and all the operational boats in Norway and Germany were taken over by the Allies, 154 boats all told.

488. In retrospect

Germany started the war with 57 U-boats. In the course of the war, 908 Types II to XVII, 181 Types XXI and XXIII and seven Walter boats were built and commissioned, making a total of 1,153 U-boats of all types. Contracts were placed for another 1,394, more than half of which were cancelled before being laid down and a proportion shortly after the laying of their keels. Of the boats commissioned, 830 took part in 3,000 operations in all theatres and claimed to have sunk over 3,500 ships totalling 18·3 million tons. British records place the figures at 2,603 ships aggregating 13·5 million tons, of which 2,452 ships totalling 12·8 million tons were sunk in the Atlantic. In addition, U-boats sank 175 Allied warships and auxiliaries, comprising two battleships, three aircraft carriers, three escort carriers, six light or minelaying cruisers, four depot ships, 48 destroyers, 37 large escort vessels (frigates, sloops, corvettes and the like), 33 smaller vessels (trawlers, minesweepers, gunboats and patrol boats), and five submarines and seven landing craft totalling about 21,000 tons. There were also 10 auxiliary cruisers and 18 other ships operating under Allied control, totalling 242,996 tons, which have not been included in the above total of merchant shipping sunk..

The U-boats fought a hard battle in which they suffered heavily. From the very beginning they had to contend with well trained A/S forces possessing the most up-to-date weapons and equipment. After the entry of America into the war, the Allies so increased the strength of these forces that each U-boat at sea eventually found itself up against vastly superior numbers of air and surface A/S craft. Six hundred and thirty-six U-boats were destroyed by enemy guns, torpedoes, depth-charges, mines and bombs and 63 by air attack on U-boat bases and yards. Eighty-five were lost through collision, internal explosion, mining in Home Waters and other causes; 154 surrendered after the capitulation and 218 were scuttled by their crews on the eve of the surrender.

The U-boat arm fought bravely and fairly, preserving their discipline, morale and spirit of ready service to the end, capitulating only after a battle of unparalleled heroism. Out of 40,000 officers and men 28,000 laid down their lives for their country.

- A P P E N D I X 1 -

LIST OF SOURCES

243

- A P P E N D I X   2 -

SHORT TITLES OF CONVOYS

GUS   US "Torch" convoys, west-bound, slow

HG   Gibraltar to UK

HX   Halifax (later New York) to UK 9 knots

KMS   UK to North Africa (Oct–Nov 1942). Continued to Mediterranean (Gibraltar to Alexandria – first arrived 26 May 1943)

MKS   Mediterranean to UK slow. (Later Port Said – Alexandria – North Africa – UK slow)

OB   Liverpool to Western Approaches (Outward Atlantic). Superseded 15 July 1941 by ON

OG   UK to Gibraltar (including sections for South Atlantic ports). $7\frac{1}{2}$ knots. Deleted 8 Aug 1941

ON   UK to North America (Outward north-bound). 9 knots. Superseded OB

ONS   As above. $7\frac{1}{2}$ knots

OS   UK to West Africa (Outward south-bound). Including sessions for West Indies and South Atlantic ports

PG   Panama to Guantanamo (Cuba)

RB1   River steamers from New York via Baltimore to UK (Special 1942). see Section 225

RS   Gibraltar – Sierra Leone (Freetown)

SC   Sydney (Cape Breton) or Halifax or New York to UK (slow)

SG   Sydney (Cape Breton) to Greenland

SL   Sierra Leone (Freetown) to UK

TAG   Trinidad – Aruba – Guantanamo

TAW   Trinidad – Curacao – Key West

TM   Trinidad to Gibraltar (tanker convoy). Amendment was Trinidad to Mediterranean

UC   UK to New York (special). See Section 292

UG   USA to North Africa (later to Mediterranean)

UGS   US "Torch" convoys east-bound, slow

US   Australia and New Zealand to UK

WAT   Key West – Curacao – Trinidad (amended to Key West – Aruba – Trinidad)

WS   UK to Middle East and India via Cape (troops and motor transport) "Winston's Specials"

XK   Gibraltar to UK (special)

Note: This list is far from exhaustive and some designations were reallocated. Those listed here relate to the relevant periods in the text.

DATES ON WHICH U-BOATS SAILED AND RETURNED TO BASE, AND THE BASES USED

(May 1943 to the end of the war)

(H = Base in Germany; F = Base in Western France; N = Base in Norway;
Hel = Heligoland; P = Penang; J = Jakarta; S = Surabaya)

U-BOAT	SAILED	RETURNED
U.43	F 13. 7.43	sunk 30. 7.43
U.66	F 16. 1.44	sunk 6. 5.44
U.68	F 12. 6.43	F 16. 6.43
	F 8. 9.43	F 23.12.43
	F 27. 3.44	sunk 10. 4.44
U.84	F 10. 6.43	sunk 24. 8.43
U.86	F 8. 7.43	F 11. 9.43
	F 11.11.43	sunk 29.11.43
U.91	F 21. 9.43	F 22.11.43
	F 25. 1.44	sunk 25. 2.44
U.92	F 12. 4.43	F 26. 6.43
	F 25. 9.43	F 7.10.43
	F 21.11.43	F 18. 1.44
	F 5. 3.44	F 10. 5.44
	F 16. 8.44	N 29. 9.44
U.103	F 23. 9.43	N 1. 1.44
U.105	N 16. 3.43	sunk 2. 6.43
U.106	F 28. 7.43	sunk 2. 8.43
U.107	F 28. 7.43	F 3.10.43
	F 16.11.43	F 8. 1.44
	F 10. 5.44	F 22. 7.44
	F 16. 8.44	sunk 18. 8.44
U.117	F 22. 7.43	sunk 7. 8.43
U.118	F 25. 5.43	sunk 12. 6.43
U.123	F 16. 8.43	F 7.11.43
	F 9. 1.44	F 24. 4.44
U.129	F 27. 7.43	F 5. 9.43
	F 12.10.43	F 31. 1.44
	F 22. 3.44	F 18. 7.44
U.134	F 10. 6.43	sunk 24. 8.43
U.135	F 7. 6.43	sunk 15. 7.43
U.154	F 2.10.43	F 20.12.43
	F 31. 1.44	F 28. 4.44
	F 20. 6.44	sunk 3. 7.44
U.155	F 12. 6.43	F 16. 6.43
	F 30. 6.43	F 11. 8.43
	F 21. 9.43	F 1. 1.44
	F 11. 3.44	F 23. 6.44
	F 9. 9.44	N 17.10.44
U.159	F 12. 6.43	sunk 15. 7.43
U.160	F 28. 6.43	sunk 14. 7.43
U.161	F 8. 8.43	sunk 27. 9.43
U.168	F 3. 7.43	P 11.11.43
	P 7. 2.44	J 24. 3.44
	J 3.10.44	sunk 5.10.44
U.170	H 27. 5.43	F 9. 7.43
	F 29. 8.43	F 23.12.43
	F 9. 2.44	F 27. 5.44
	F 4. 8.44	N 30.11.44
U.172	F 29. 5.43	F 7. 9.43
	F 22.11.43	sunk 12.12.43
U.177	F 1. 4.43	F 1.10.43
	F 2. 1.44	sunk 6. 2.44
U.178	P 27.11.43	F 24. 5.44
U.180	F 20. 8.44	sunk 22. 8.44
U.181	F 23. 3.43	F 14.10.43
	F 16. 3.44	P 8. 8.44
	P 19.10.44	J 5. 1.45
U.183	P 10. 2.44	P 21. 3.44
	P 17. 5.44	P 7. 7.44
	J 21. 4.45	sunk 23. 4.45
U.185	F 9. 6.43	sunk 24. 8.43
U.188	F 30. 6.43	P 31.10.43
	P 9. 1.44	F 19. 6.44
U.190	F 1. 5.43	F 19. 8.43
	F 17.10.43	F 15. 1.44
	F 16. 3.44	F 20. 6.44
	F 22. 8.44	N 1.10.44
	N 22. 2.45	surrendered in Canada
U.193	F 12.10.43	Ferrol 10. 2.44
	Ferrol 19. 2.44	F 25. 2.44
	F 23. 4.44	sunk 28. 4.44
U.194	H 12. 6.43	sunk 24. 6.43
U.195	F 20. 8.44	J 28.12.44
	J 26. 1.45	J 4. 3.45
U.196	F 16. 3.44	P 10. 8.44
	P 30.11.44	sunk 30.11.44
U.198	H 9. 3.43	F 25. 9.43
	F 20. 4.44	sunk 12. 8.44
U.199	H 13. 5.43	sunk 31. 7.43
U.200	H 12. 6.43	sunk 24. 6.43
U.211	F 14.10.43	sunk 19.11.43
U.212	N 11.10.43	F 2.12.43
	F 13. 1.44	F 12. 3.44
	F 6. 6.44	F 8. 6.44
	F 12. 6.44	F 16. 6.44
	F 22. 6.44	F 24. 6.44
	F 28. 6.44	F 4. 7.44
	F 5. 7.44	sunk 21. 7.44

U-BOAT	SAILED		RETURNED
U.214	F	22. 8.43	F 30.11.43
	F	19. 2.44	F 29. 4.44
	F	11. 6.44	F 14. 6.44
	F	16. 6.44	F 1. 7.44
	F	22. 7.44	sunk 26. 7.44
U.218	F	29. 7.43	F 6. 8.43
	F	19. 9.43	F 8.12.43
	F	12. 2.44	F 7. 5.44
	F	13. 6.44	F 9. 7.44
	F	10. 8.44	N 23. 9.44
	N	23. 3.45	N -. 5.45
U.219	H	5.10.43	N 9.10.43
	N	22.10.43	F 1. 1.44
	F	23. 8.44	J 11.12.44
U.220	N	8. 9.43	sunk 28.10.43
U.221	F	20. 9.43	sunk 27. 9.43
U.226	F	5.10.43	sunk 6.11.43
U.228	F	25.10.43	F 20.12.43
	F	9. 3.44	F 26. 3.44
	F	6. 6.44	F 15. 6.44
	F	12. 8.44	N 20. 9.44
U.229	F	31. 8.43	sunk 22. 9.43
U.230	F	5. 7.43	F 8. 9.43
	F	22.11.43	Mediterranean
U.231	F	27. 9.43	F 22.11.43
	F	26.12.43	sunk 13. 1.44
U.232	H	8. 5.43	sunk 8. 7.43
U.233	H	27. 5.44	sunk 5. 7.44
U.234	N	17. 4.45	surrendered in USA 16.5.45
U.238	N	5. 9.43	F 8.10.43
	F	11.11.43	F 12.12.43
	F	27. 1.44	sunk 9. 2.44
U.240	H	14. 5.44	sunk 16. 5.44
U.241	N	13. 5.44	sunk 18. 5.44
U.242	N	8. 6.44	N 26. 6.44
	N	4. 3.45	sunk 30. 4.45
U.243	N	8. 6.44	N 11. 6.44
	N	15. 6.44	sunk 8. 7.44
U.244	N	23. 8.44	N 10.10.44
	N	9. 1.45	N 13. 3.45
	N	15. 4.45	surrendered in England
U.245	N	14. 8.44	N 24.10.44
	H	-. 1.45	Hel 19. 2.45
	Hel	9. 4.45	N 10. 5.45
U.246	N	7.10.44	N 11.11.44
	N	22. 2.45	sunk 29. 3.45
U.247	N	31. 5.44	F 27. 7.44
	F	26. 8.44	sunk 1. 9.44
U.248	N	17. 8.44	N 14.10.44
	N	3.12.44	sunk 16. 1.45
U.249	N	22. 3.45	N 25. 3.45
	N	4. 4.45	surrendered in England
U.251	H	17. 4.45	sunk 19. 4.45

U-BOAT	SAILED		RETURNED
U.255	N	26. 2.44	F 11. 4.44
	F	6. 6.44	F 15. 6.44
	F	1. 5.45	surrendered in England
U.256	F	4.10.43	F 17.11.43
	F	25. 1.44	F 22. 3.44
	F	6. 6.44	F 7. 6.44
	F	3. 9.44	N 17.10.44
U.257	F	12. 6.43	F 14. 9.43
	F	2. 1.44	sunk 24. 2.44
U.260	F	25. 8.43	F 17.10.43
	F	18.12.43	F 27. 2.44
	F	6. 6.44	F 16. 6.44
	F	7. 8.44	F 13. 8.44
	F	3. 9.44	N 17.10.44
	N	21. 2.45	sunk 12. 3.45
U.262	F	24. 7.43	F 2. 9.43
	F	20.10.43	F 7.12.43
	F	14. 2.44	F 29. 4.44
	F	6. 6.44	F 15. 6.44
	F	23. 8.44	N 1.11.44
U.263	F	19. 1.44	sunk 20. 1.44
U.264	F	22. 9.43	F 15.10.43
	F	5. 2.44	sunk 19. 2.44
U.267	F	4. 7.43	F 13. 7.43
	F	3.10.43	F 26.11.43
	F	26. 2.44	F 20. 5.44
	F	23. 9.44	N 29.10.44
U.269	N	4.11.43	F 15.12.43
	F	23. 5.44	F 27. 5.44
	F	6. 6.44	sunk 25. 6.44
U.270	F	26. 6.43	F 2. 7.43
	F	7. 9.43	F 6.10.43
	F	8.12.43	F 17. 1.44
	F	6. 6.44	F 17. 6.44
	F	10. 8.44	sunk 12. 8.44
U.271	H	29. 5.43	F 16. 7.43
	F	2.10.43	F 3.11.43
	F	12. 1.44	sunk 28. 1.44
U.273	H	8. 5.43	sunk 19. 5.43
U.274	N	1. 9.43	N 13. 9.43
	N	13.10.43	sunk 23.10.43
U.275	N	9. 9.43	F 10.10.43
	F	8.12.43	F 11. 1.44
	F	6. 6.44	F 24. 6.44
	F	16. 7.44	F 1. 8.44
	F	2. 9.44	N 18. 9.44
	N	13. 1.45	F 10. 2.45
	F	25. 2.45	sunk 10. 3.45
U.276	N	10. 6.44	N 29. 6.44
U.278	N	24.12.44	N 11. 2.45
U.279	H	4. 9.43	sunk 4.10.43
U.280	H	12.10.43	sunk 16.11.43
U.281	N	6.10.43	F 26.11.43
	F	5. 1.44	F 5. 3.44
	F	6. 6.44	F 15. 6.44
	F	9. 8.44	F 14. 8.44
	F	4. 9.44	N 28.10.44
U.282	H	11. 9.43	sunk 29.10.43
U.283	H	13. 1.44	sunk 11. 2.44

U-BOAT	SAILED		RETURNED		U-BOAT	SAILED		RETURNED	
U.284	H	23.11.43	sunk 21.12.43		U.327	N	30. 1.45	sunk 27. 2.45	
U.285	N	24. 8.44	N	18. 9.44	U.328	H	25. 4.45	surrendered in	
	N	20.12.44	N	31. 1.45				England	
	N	26. 3.45	sunk 15. 4.45		U.332	F	26. 4.43	sunk 2. 5.43	
U.287	N	29. 4.45	sunk 16. 5.45*		U.333	F	2. 6.43	F	31. 8.43
U.288	H	23. 3.44	sunk 3. 4.44			F	20.10.43	F	1.12.43
U.289	H	7. 5.44	sunk 30. 5.44			F	14. 2.44	F	20. 4.44
U.290	N	1. 6.44	N	16. 6.44		F	6. 6.44	F	12. 6.44
U.292	N	24. 5.44	sunk 27. 5.44			F	23. 7.44	sunk 31. 7.44	
U.294	N	31. 5.44	N	21. 6.44	U.334	N	5. 6.43	sunk 14. 6.43	
U.295	N	13. 7.44	N	17. 7.44	U.338	F	15. 6.43	F	21. 6.43
U.296	N	16. 8.44	N	29. 9.44		F	25. 8.43	sunk 20. 9.43	
	N	4.11.44	N	25.12.44	U.340	F	6. 7.43	F	2. 9.43
	N	28. 2.45	sunk 22. 3.45			F	17.10.43	sunk 1.11.43	
U.297	N	26.11.44	sunk 6.12.44		U.341	H	25. 5.43	F	10. 7.43
U.299	N	5. 7.44	N	17. 7.44		F	31. 8.43	sunk 19. 9.43	
U.300	H	13. 7.44	N	17. 8.44	U.342	N	3. 4.44	sunk 17. 4.44	
	N	4.10.44	N	2.12.44	U.343	H	14.10.43	F	26.11.43
	N	21. 1.45	sunk 22. 2.45			F	26.12.43	Mediterranean	
U.302	N	6.12.43	F	30. 1.44	U.358	F	10. 6.43	F	1. 9.43
	F	11. 3.44	sunk 6. 4.44			F	25.10.43	F	15.12.43
U.304	H	27. 4.43	sunk 28. 5.43			F	14. 2.44	sunk 1. 3.44	
U.305	F	23. 8.43	F	16.10.43	U.359	F	29. 6.43	sunk 28. 7.43	
	F	8.12.43	sunk 17. 1.44		U.364	H	23.11.43	sunk 30. 1.44	
U.306	F	10. 6.43	F	11. 8.43	U.373	F	7. 7.43	F	16. 8.43
	F	14.10.43	sunk 31.10.43			F	6.10.43	F	26.11.43
U.308	H	29. 5.43	sunk 4. 6.43			F	7. 6.44	sunk 8. 6.44	
U.309	N	25. 9.43	F	7.11.43	U.377	F	9. 9.43	F	10.10.43
	F	19.12.43	F	14. 2.44		F	15.12.43	sunk –. 1.44	
	F	21. 6.44	F	25. 6.44	U.378	F	6. 9.43	sunk 20.10.43	
	F	29. 6.44	F	6. 7.44	U.382	F	19. 6.43	F	7. 9.43
	F	13. 7.44	F	2. 8.44		F	11.12.43	F	26. 1.44
	F	7. 8.44	F	12. 8.44		F	6. 6.44	F	13. 6.44
	F	29. 8.44	N	9.10.44		F	10. 9.44	N	19.10.44
	N	8. 2.45	sunk 16. 2.45		U.383	F	29. 7.43	sunk 1. 8.43	
U.311	H	25.11.43	F	26. 1.44	U.385	N	5. 4.44	F	4. 6.44
	F	9. 3.44	sunk 24. 4.44			F	9. 8.44	sunk 11. 8.44	
U.312	N	13.12.44	N	3. 1.45	U.386	F	29. 6.43	F	8. 7.43
U.313	N	23.12.44	N	15. 2.45		F	29. 8.43	F	8.10.43
U.315	N	25.12.44	N	6. 1.45		F	29.12.43	sunk 19. 2.44	
	N	15. 2.45	N	25. 4.45	U.388	H	8. 6.43	sunk 20. 6.43	
U.317	N	21. 6.44	sunk 26. 6.44		U.389	N	18. 9.43	sunk 5.10.43	
U.319	N	5. 7.44	sunk 15. 7.44		U.390	H	2.12.43	F	13. 2.44
U.320	H	5. 5.45	sunk 7. 5.45			F	21. 6.44	F	24. 6.44
U.321	N	17. 3.45	sunk 2. 4.45			F	27. 6.44	sunk 5. 7.44	
U.322	N	16.11.44	sunk 25.11.44		U.392	H	2.12.43	F	20. 1.44
U.325	N	11.12.44	N	14. 2.45		F	29. 2.44	sunk 16. 3.44	
	N	22. 3.45	sunk 30. 4.45		U.396	H	20. 6.44	N	3. 7.44
U.326	N	28. 3.45	sunk –. 4.45			N	21.10.44	N	19.12.44
						N	13. 3.45	sunk 23. 4.45	
					U.397	N	8. 6.44	N	25. 6.44
					U.398	N	26. 8.44	N	14.10.44
						N	17. 4.45	sunk –. 5.45	

* Mined in the Elbe.

247

U-BOAT		SAILED		RETURNED
U.399	N	8. 2.45		sunk 26. 3.45
U.400	N	18.11.44		sunk 17.12.44
U.402	F	4. 9.43		sunk 13.10.43
U.403	F	13. 7.43		sunk 17. 8.43
U.404	F	24. 7.43		sunk 28. 7.43
U.405	F	10.10.43		sunk 1.11.43
U.406	F	26. 6.43	F	15. 9.43
	F	5. 1.44		sunk 18. 2.44
U.409	F	26. 5.43		Mediterranean
U.413	F	8. 9.43	F	18. 9.43
	F	2.10.43	F	21.11.43
	F	3. 2.44	F	27. 3.44
	F	6. 6.44	F	9. 6.44
	F	2. 8.44		sunk 20. 8.44
U.415	F	12. 6.43	F	8. 9.43
	F	21.11.43	F	6. 1.44
	F	2. 3.44	F	31. 3.44
	F	6. 6.44	F	7. 6.44
U.417	H	3. 6.43		sunk 11. 6.43
U.419	N	13. 9.43		sunk 8.10.43
U.420	H	12. 6.43	F	16. 7.43
	F	9.10.43		sunk 26.10.43
U.421	H	6.11.43	F	8. 1.44
	F	19. 2.44		Mediterranean
U.422	N	8. 9.43		sunk 4.10.43
U.423	H	9. 6.44		sunk 17. 6.44
U.424	H	2.10.43	F	15.12.43
	F	29. 1.44		sunk 11. 2.44
U.425	H	7. 2.45		sunk 17. 2.45
U.426	H	5.10.43	F	29.11.43
	F	3. 1.44		sunk 8. 1.44
U.437	F	26. 9.43	F	19.11.43
	F	2. 2.44	F	1. 4.44
	F	6. 6.44	F	15. 6.44
	F	9. 8.44	F	13. 8.44
	F	24. 8.44	N	22. 9.44
U.440	F	26. 5.43		sunk 31. 5.43
U.441	F	22. 5.43	F	26. 5.43
	F	8. 7.43	F	13. 7.43
	F	19.10.43	F	7.11.43
	F	20. 1.44	F	14. 3.44
	F	20. 5.44	F	27. 5.44
	F	6. 6.44		sunk 18. 6.44
U.445	F	10. 7.43	F	15. 9.43
	F	29.12.43	F	10. 1.44
	F	1. 2.44	F	27. 2.44
	F	6. 6.44	F	15. 6.44
	F	12. 8.44	F	17. 8.44
	F	22. 8.44		sunk 24. 8.44
U.448	F	6. 9.43	F	12. 9.43
	F	14. 9.43	F	3.11.43
	F	14. 2.44		sunk 14. 4.44
U.449	H	1. 6.43		sunk 24. 6.43
U.450	H	25. 5.43	F	22. 6.43
	F	17.10.43		Mediterranean

U-BOAT		SAILED		RETURNED
U.454	F	29. 7.43		sunk 1. 8.43
U.455	F	30. 5.43	F	31. 7.43
	F	20. 9.43	F	11.11.43
	F	6. 1.44		Mediterranean
U.459	F	22. 7.43		sunk 24. 7.43
U.460	F	30. 8.43		sunk 4.10.43
U.461	F	27. 7.43		sunk 30. 7.43
U.462	F	19. 6.43	F	23. 6.43
	F	28. 6.43	F	6. 7.43
	F	27. 7.43		sunk 30. 7.43
U.466	F	29. 6.43	F	16. 8.43
	F	20.10.43	F	19.11.43
	F	4. 3.44		Mediterranean
U.468	F	7. 7.43		sunk 11. 8.43
U.470	N	28. 9.43		sunk 16.10.43
U.471	H	27.11.43	F	29. 1.44
	F	16. 3.44		Mediterranean
U.473	N	19. 3.44	N	22. 3.44
	N	27. 3.44	F	18. 4.44
	F	24. 4.44		sunk 5. 5.44
U.476	N	20. 5.44		sunk 24. 5.44
U.477	N	28. 5.44		sunk 3. 6.44
U.478	H	20. 6.44		sunk 30. 6.44
U.480	N	10. 6.44	F	6. 7.44
	F	3. 8.44	N	4.10.44
	N	6. 1.45		sunk 24. 2.45
U.482	N	14. 8.44	N	26. 9.44
	N	18.11.44		sunk 16. 1.45
U.483	N	5.10.44	N	21.11.44
	N	7. 2.45	N	-. 3.45
U.484	N	14. 8.44		sunk 9. 9.44
U.485	N	29.11.44	N	2. 2.45
	N	24. 3.45	F	24. 4.45
	F	26. 4.45		surrendered at Gibraltar
U.486	N	28.11.44	N	15. 1.45
	N	7. 4.45		sunk 12. 4.45
U.487	F	15. 6.43		sunk 13. 7.43
U.488	F	7. 9.43	F	12.12.43
	F	22. 2.44		sunk 26. 4.44
U.489	H	22. 7.43		sunk 4. 8.43
U.490	N	6. 5.44		sunk 11. 6.44
U.504	F	27. 7.43		sunk 30. 7.43
U.505	F	3. 7.43	F	13. 7.43
	F	18. 9.43	F	30. 9.43
	F	9.10.43	F	7.11.43
	F	25.12.43	F	2. 1.44
	F	16. 3.44		captured 4. 6.44
U.506	F	6. 7.43		sunk 12. 7.43
U.508	F	7. 6.43	F	14. 9.43
	F	9.11.43		sunk 12.11.43
U.509	F	3. 7.43		sunk 15. 7.43

U-BOAT	SAILED		RETURNED	
U.510	F	3. 6.43	F	29. 8.43
	F	3.11.43	P	5. 4.44
	J	26.11.44	J	3.12.44
	J	11. 1.45	F	24. 4.45
U.514	F	3. 7.43	sunk 8. 7.43	
U.515	F	29. 8.43	F	12. 9.43
	F	9.11.43	F	14. 1.44
	F	30. 3.44	sunk 9. 4.44	
U.516	F	8. 7.43	F	23. 8.43
	F	4.10.43	F	26. 2.44
	F	7. 5.44	N	1.10.44
	N	6. 4.45	surrendered in UK	
U.518	F	18. 8.43	F	1.12.43
	F	23. 1.44	F	7. 5.44
	F	15. 7.44	N	22.10.44
	H	13. 3.45	sunk 22. 4.45	
U.523	F	22. 5.43	F	26. 5.43
	F	16. 8.43	sunk 25. 8.43	
U.525	F	27. 7.43	sunk 11. 8.43	
U.530	F	29. 5.43	F	2. 7.43
	F	16.10.43	F	22. 2.44
	F	22. 5.44	N	1.10.44
	H	20. 2.45	N	3. 3.45
	N	4. 3.45	arrived in the Argentine on 11. 7.45	
U.532	F	3. 7.43	P	31.10.43
	P	4. 1.44	P	19. 4.44
	J	13. 1.45	surrendered in England	
U.533	F	6. 7.43	sunk 16.10.43	
U.534	N	8. 5.44	F	13. 8.44
	F	25. 8.44	N	24.10.44
	N	3. 5.45	sunk 5. 5.45	
U.535	H	25. 5.43	sunk 5. 7.43	
U.536	H	1. 6.43	F	9. 7.43
	F	29. 8.43	sunk 20.11.43	
U.537	N	30. 9.43	F	8.12.43
	F	25. 3.44	J	2. 8.44
	S	9.11.44	sunk 9.11.44	
U.539	F	3. 1.44	F	21. 3.44
	F	1. 5.44	N	17. 9.44
U.540	N	4.10.43	sunk 17.10.43	
U.541	H	4.11.43	F	9. 1.44
	F	29. 2.44	F	22. 6.44
	F	6. 8.44	N	6.11.44
	N	11. 4.45	surrendered at Gibraltar	
U.543	H	9.11.43	F	24. 1.44
	F	28. 3.44	sunk 2. 7.44	
U.544	H	9.11.43	sunk 16. 1.44	
U.545	H	9.12.43	sunk 10. 2.44	
U.546	H	23. 1.44	F	23. 4.44
	F	15. 6.44	F	22. 6.44
	F	25. 6.44	N	6.11.44
	N	22. 3.45	sunk 24. 4.45	
U.547	N	28.12.43	F	23. 2.44
	F	30. 4.44	F	11. 8.44
	F	24. 8.44	N	27. 9.44

U-BOAT	SAILED		RETURNED	
U.548	H	21. 3.44	F	24. 6.44
	F	11. 8.44	N	25. 9.44
	N	7. 3.45	sunk 30. 4.45	
U.549	H	11. 1.44	F	26. 3.44
	F	14. 5.44	sunk 29. 5.44	
U.550	H	6. 2.44	sunk 16. 4.44	
U.552	F	3.10.43	F	30.11.43
	F	16. 2.44	N	22. 4.44
U.563	F	29. 5.43	sunk 31. 5.43	
U.564	F	9. 6.43	sunk 14. 6.43	
U.566	F	5. 7.43	F	1. 9.43
	F	18.10.43	sunk 24.10.43	
U.571	F	8. 6.43	F	1. 9.43
	F	8. 1.44	sunk 28. 1.44	
U.572	F	2. 6.43	sunk 3. 8.43	
U.575	F	6.10.43	F	28.11.43
	F	29. 2.44	sunk 13. 3.44	
U.584	F	2. 9.43	sunk 21.10.43	
U.586	F	16.10.43	F	3.12.43
	F	1. 2.44	Mediterranean	
U.590	F	8. 6.43	sunk 9. 7.43	
U.591	F	26. 6.43	sunk 30. 7.43	
U.592	F	29. 5.43	F	14. 7.43
	F	5.10.43	F	25.11.43
	F	10. 1.44	sunk 31. 1.44	
U.594	F	23. 5.43	sunk 4. 6.43	
U.598	F	26. 6.43	sunk 23. 7.43	
U.600	F	12. 6.43	F	9. 9.43
	F	7.11.43	sunk 25.11.43	
U.603	F	9. 9.43	F	3.11.43
	F	5. 2.44	sunk 1. 3.44	
U.604	F	24. 6.43	sunk 3. 8.43	
U.607	F	10. 7.43	sunk 13. 7.43	
U.608	F	2.10.43	F	28.11.43
	F	19. 1.44	F	3. 4.44
	F	6. 6.44	F	14. 6.44
	F	22. 7.44	F	23. 7.44
	F	7. 8.44	sunk 10. 8.44	
U.610	F	12. 9.43	sunk 8.10.43	
U.613	F	10. 7.43	sunk 23. 7.43	
U.614	F	25. 7.43	sunk 29. 7.43	
U.615	F	12. 6.43	sunk 6. 8.43	
U.618	F	8. 6.43	F	5. 9.43
	F	11.11.43	F	4. 1.44
	F	23. 2.44	F	8. 4.44
	F	2. 8.44	F	4. 8.44
	F	11. 8.44	sunk 14. 8.44	
U.621	F	22. 8.43	F	28. 9.43
	F	6. 1.44	F	23. 1.44
	F	21. 2.44	F	19. 4.44
	F	6. 6.44	F	23. 6.44
	F	15. 7.44	F	11. 8.44
	F	13. 8.44	sunk 18. 8.44	

249

U-BOAT		SAILED	RETURNED	U-BOAT		SAILED	RETURNED
U.625	N	15.11.43	F 6. 1.44	U.709	F	5. 7.43	F 10. 7.43
	F	29. 2.44	sunk 10. 3.44		F	6.10.43	F 28.11.43
U.628	F	1. 7.43	sunk 3. 7.43		F	25. 1.44	sunk 1. 3.44
U.629	N	22.11.43	F 5. 1.44	U.714	N	13.10.43	F 2.12.43
	F	9. 3.44	F 15. 3.44		F	20. 1.44	F 25. 2.44
	F	6. 6.44	sunk 8. 6.44		F	6. 4.44	F 15. 6.44
U.631	F	18. 9.43	sunk 17.10.43		F	27. 8.44	N 24.10.44
					N	4. 3.45	sunk 14. 3.45
U.634	F	12. 6.43	sunk 30. 8.43	U.715	N	8. 6.44	sunk 13. 6.44
U.637	H	7. 6.44	H 21. 7.44	U.719	N	22. 5.44	sunk 26. 6.44
	N	23. 4.45	N 28. 4.45	U.722	N	16.10.44	F 20.11.44
U.641	F	5. 9.43	F ?.10.43		F	7.12.44	N 29.12.44
	F	11.12.43	sunk 19. 1.44		N	21. 2.45	sunk 27. 3.45
U.642	F	16.10.43	Mediterranean	U.731	F	29. 8.43	F 1.11.43
					F	19.12.43	F 18. 2.44
U.643	N	14. 9.43	sunk 8.10.43		F	18. 4.44	sunk 15. 5.44
U.645	F	23. 8.43	F 22.10.43	U.732	F	10. 6.43	F 31. 8.43
	F	2.12.43	sunk 24.12.43		F	16.10.43	sunk 31.10.43
U.648	F	1. 7.43	F 10. 8.43	U.734	H	6.11.43	F 25.12.43
	F	9.10.43	sunk 23.11.43		F	21. 1.44	sunk 9. 2.44
U.650	F	1. 1.44	F 2. 3.44	U.736	N	1. 4.44	F 26. 5.44
	F	6. 6.44	F 15. 6.44		F	5. 8.44	sunk 6. 8.44
	F	12. 8.44	F 17. 8.44	U.739	H	1. 4.45	H 4. 5.45
	F	22. 8.44	N 22. 9.44				
	N	9.12.44	sunk –. 1.45	U.740	N	27. 3.44	F 21. 4.44
					F	6. 6.44	sunk 9. 6.44
U.653	F	10. 6.43	F 11. 9.43	U.741	H	25.11.43	F 27. 1.44
	F	21.11.43	F 13. 1.44		F	29. 2.44	F 3. 5.44
	F	2. 3.44	sunk 15. 3.44		F	20. 6.44	F 28. 6.44
U.662	F	26. 6.43	sunk 21. 7.43		F	5. 7.44	F 15. 7.44
U.664	F	21. 7.43	sunk 9. 8.43		F	3. 8.44	sunk 15. 8.44
U.666	F	6. 9.43	F 16.10.43	U.743	N	21. 8.44	sunk 9. 9.44
	F	25.12.43	sunk 10. 2.44	U.744	H	2.12.43	F 15. 1.44
U.667	F	18. 9.43	F 11.10.43		F	24. 2.44	sunk 6. 3.44
	F	18.11.43	F 6. 1.44				
	F	8. 3.44	F 19. 5.44	U.745	H	24. 5.44	N 7. 7.44
	F	22. 7.44	sunk 25. 8.44		N	23.12.44	sunk 4. 2.45
U.669	H	27. 5.43	F 14. 7.43	U.752	F	22. 4.43	sunk 23. 5.43
	F	29. 8.43	sunk 7. 9.43	U.753	F	5. 5.43	sunk 15. 5.43
U.671	N	28. 5.44	F 5. 7.44	U.757	F	7. 7.43	F 4. 8.43
	F	26. 7.44	sunk 4. 8.44		F	29.12.43	sunk 8. 1.44
U.672	H	13.11.43	F 15. 1.44	U.758	F	26. 5.43	F 25. 6.43
	F	24. 2.44	F 12. 5.44		F	1. 9.43	F –.10.43
	F	6. 7.44	sunk 18. 7.44		F	16.12.43	F 20. 1.44
U.673	N	4. 6.44	F 23. 7.44		F	6. 6.44	F 15. 6.44
	F	14. 9.44	N 19.10.44		F	23. 8.44	N 10.10.44
U.675	N	18. 5.44	sunk 24. 5.44	U.759	F	7. 6.43	sunk 26. 7.43
U.677	N	8. 6.44	N 29. 6.44	U.760	F	24. 7.43	Vigo 8. 9.43
U.678	N	8. 6.44	sunk 6. 7.44	U.761	N	17.11.43	F 26.12.43
					F	12. 2.44	sunk 24. 2.44
U.680	N	14. 8.44	N 8. 9.44	U.762	N	28. 9.43	F 15.11.43
	N	13.11.44	N 18. 1.44		F	28.12.43	sunk 8. 2.44
U.681	N	16. 2.45	sunk 11. 3.45	U.763	H	14.12.43	F 7. 2.44
U.683	N	6. 2.45	sunk 12. 3.45		F	19. 3.44	F 27. 3.44
					F	11. 6.44	F 18. 6.44
U.706	F	29. 7.43	sunk 2. 8.43		F	20. 6.44	F 14. 7.44
					F	9. 8.44	F 14. 8.44
U.707	F	16.10.43	sunk 9.11.43		F	23. 8.44	N 25. 9.44

U-BOAT	SAILED		RETURNED	
U.764	N	27.10.43	F	11.12.43
	F	7. 1.44	F	14. 3.44
	F	18. 5.44	F	27. 5.44
	F	6. 6.44	F	23. 6.44
	F	6. 8.44	N	19. 9.44
	N	26.12.44	N	10. 2.45
	N	1. 5.45	surrendered in UK	
U.765	N	3. 4.44	sunk 6. 5.44	
U.766	N	23. 3.44	F	16. 4.44
	F	6. 6.44	F	15. 6.44
	F	2. 8.44	F	6. 8.44
	F	8. 8.44	F	18. 8.44
U.767	N	22. 5.44	sunk 18. 6.44	
U.771	N	21. 6.44	N	15. 7.44
U.772	N	13. 8.44	N	6.10.44
	N	19.11.44	sunk 30.12.44	
U.773	N	15.10.44	F	18.11.44
	F	7.12.44	N	10. 1.45
	N	19. 2.45	N	15. 4.45
U.774	N	15. 3.45	sunk 8. 4.45	
U.775	N	18.11.44	N	22.12.44
	N	8. 2.45	N	19. 3.45
U.776	N	24. 3.45	surrendered in UK	
U.778	N	6. 3.45	N	7. 4.45
U.801	H	6.11.43	F	8. 1.44
	F	26. 2.44	sunk 16. 3.44	
U.802	H	29. 1.44	F	2. 5.44
	F	22. 6.44	F	8. 7.44
	F	16. 7.44	N	12.11.44
	H	9. 4.45	surrendered in UK	
U.804	H	12. 6.44	N	17. 6.44
	N	19. 6.44	N	7.10.44
	N	4. 4.45	sunk 9. 4.45	
U.805	H	4. 3.45	surrendered in Canada	
U.806	N	30.10.44	N	21. 2.45
U.821	N	19. 3.44	F	12. 4.44
	F	6. 6.44	sunk 10. 6.44	
U.825	N	29.12.44	N	18. 2.45
	N	3. 4.45	surrendered in UK	
U.826	N	11. 3.45	surrendered in UK	
U.841	N	4.10.43	sunk 17.10.43	
U.842	N	5.10.43	sunk 6.11.43	
U.843	H	7.10.43	F	15.12.43
	F	19. 2.44	J	11. 6.44
	J	10.12.44	sunk 9. 4.45	
U.844	N	6.10.43	sunk 16.10.43	
U.845	N	8. 1.44	sunk 10. 3.44	
U.846	H	1.12.43	F	3. 3.44
	F	29. 4.44	sunk 4. 5.44	

U-BOAT	SAILED		RETURNED	
U.847	H	6. 7.43	N	20. 7.43
	N	29. 7.43	sunk 27. 8.43	
U.848	H	18. 9.43	sunk 5.11.43	
U.849	H	2.10.43	sunk 25.11.43	
U.850	H	18.11.43	sunk 20.12.43	
U.851	H	26. 2.44	sunk –. 3.44	
U.852	H	18. 1.44	sunk 3. 4.44	
U.853	N	29. 4.44	F	3. 7.44
	F	27. 8.44	N	11.10.44
	N	23. 2.45	sunk 6. 5.45	
U.855	H	3. 7.44	sunk 24. 9.44	
U.856	H	24. 2.44	sunk 7. 4.44	
U.857	H	9. 5.44	F	13. 8.44
	F	25. 8.44	N	7.10.44
	N	8. 2.45	sunk 7. 4.45	
U.858	H	12. 6.44	N	27. 9.44
	H	2. 3.45	N	10. 3.45
	N	14. 3.45	surrendered in USA	
U.859	H	4. 4.44	sunk 23. 9.44	
U.860	H	11. 4.44	sunk 15. 6.44	
U.861	H	20. 4.44	P	22. 9.44
	J	14. 1.45	N	18. 4.45
U.862	N	3. 6.44	P	9. 9.44
	J	18.11.44	J	15. 2.45
U.863	N	26. 7.44	sunk 29. 9.44	
U.864	N	5. 2.45	sunk 9. 2.45	
U.865	H	20. 6.44	N	5. 7.44
	N	27. 7.44	N	28. 7.44
	N	1. 8.44	N	3. 8.44
	N	10. 8.44	N	13. 8.44
	N	8. 9.44	sunk 19. 9.44	
U.866	N	5. 2.45	sunk 18. 3.45	
U.867	N	12. 9.44	sunk 19. 9.44	
U.868	N	22. 1.45	F	18. 2.45
	F	19. 3.45	N	8. 4.45
U.869	N	8.12.44	sunk 28. 2.45	
U.870	H	31.10.44	N	3.11.44
	N	12.11.44	N	20. 2.45
U.871	N	31. 8.44	sunk 26. 9.44	
U.873	N	1. 4.45	surrendered in USA	
U.877	N	26.11.44	sunk 27.12.44	
U.878	N	12. 2.45	F	20. 3.45
	F	6. 4.45	sunk 10. 4.45	
U.879	N	11. 2.45	sunk 19. 4.45	
U.880	N	14. 3.45	sunk 16. 4.45	
U.881	N	7. 4.45	sunk 6. 5.45	
U.889	N	6. 4.45	surrendered in Canada	

U-BOAT	SAILED	RETURNED
U.901	N 5. 4.45	N 15. 5.45
U.905	N 11.12.44	N 1. 2.45
	N 13. 3.45	sunk 20. 3.45
U.907	N 4. 1.45	N 16. 3.45
U.925	N 24. 8.44	sunk 18. 9.44
U.927	N 31. 1.45	sunk 24. 2.45
U.951	H 13. 5.43	sunk 7. 7.43
U.952	F 6. 9.43	F 17.10.43
	F 16.12.43	Mediterranean
U.953	F 4.10.43	F 17.11.43
	F 26.12.43	F 20. 2.44
	F 22. 5.44	F 27. 5.44
	F 6. 6.44	F 18. 6.44
	F 24. 6.44	F 21. 7.44
	F 10. 8.44	F 18. 8.44
	F 31. 8.44	N 11.10.44
	N 21. 2.45	N 3. 4.45
U.954	H 8. 4.43	sunk 19. 5.43
U.955	H 15. 4.44	sunk 7. 6.44
U.956	H 3. 8.43	N 6. 8.43
	N 31. 3.45	surrendered in UK
U.958	N 25. 5.44	N 27. 5.44
	N 3. 6.44	N 23. 6.44
U.959	H 22. 4.44	sunk 2. 5.44
U.960	N 4.12.43	F 3. 2.44
	F 19. 3.44	F 27. 3.44
	F 27. 4.44	Mediterranean
U.961	N 25. 3.44	sunk 29. 3.44
U.962	N 3.11.43	F 28.12.43
	F 14. 2.44	sunk 8. 4.44
U.963	N 4. 9.43	N 17. 9.43
	N 5.10.43	F 3.12.43
	F 26. 1.44	F 27. 3.44
	F 6. 6.44	F 7. 6.44
	F 11. 7.44	F 12. 7.44
	F 13. 8.44	F 21. 8.44
	F 29. 8.44	N 7.10.44
	N 16. 1.45	N 4. 3.45
	N 23. 4.45	sunk 21. 5.45*
U.964	N 5.10.43	sunk 16.10.43
U.965	H 14.12.43	N 23.12.43
	N 15. 2.45	N 26. 2.45
	N 6. 3.45	sunk 27. 3.45
U.966	N 5.10.43	sunk 10.11.43
U.967	N 11.10.43	F 1.12.43
	F 20. 1.44	Mediterranean
U.969	N 5.10.43	F 6.12.43
	F 24. 1.44	Mediterranean
U.970	N 16. 3.44	F 22. 4.44
	F 6. 6.44	sunk 7. 6.44
U.971	N 8. 6.44	sunk 24. 6.44
U.972	H 30.11.43	sunk -. 1.44

U-BOAT	SAILED	RETURNED
U.973	N 4. 3.44	sunk 6. 3.44
U.974	H 23. 3.44	sunk 19. 4.44
U.975	N 8. 6.44	N 26. 6.44
U.976	H 25.11.43	F 29. 1.44
	F 20. 3.44	sunk 25. 3.44
U.977	H 14. 4.45	arrived in the Argentine in August 1945
U.978	N 9.10.44	N 16.12.44
	N 25. 2.45	N 18. 4.45
U.979	N 29. 8.44	N 10.10.44
	N 9.11.44	N 16. 1.45
	N 29. 3.45	sunk 25. 5.45†
U.980	N 3. 6.44	sunk 11. 6.44
U.981	H 27.11.43	F 30. 1.44
	F 6. 6.44	F 17. 6.44
	F 7. 8.44	sunk 12. 8.44
U.982	N 10. 6.44	N 29. 6.44
U.984	H 30.12.43	F 24. 2.44
	F 22. 5.44	F 27. 5.44
	F 6. 6.44	F 9. 6.44
	F 12. 6.44	F 4. 7.44
	F 26. 7.44	sunk 20. 8.44
U.985	N 19. 1.44	F 12. 3.44
	F 6. 6.44	F 15. 6.44
	F 30. 8.44	N 23.10.44
U.986	H 8. 2.44	sunk 17. 4.44
U.988	N 23. 5.44	sunk 29. 6.44
U.989	H 11. 1.44	F 4. 3.44
	F 6. 6.44	F 7. 6.44
	F 8. 7.44	F 9. 7.44
	F 9. 8.44	N 25. 9.44
	N 8. 2.45	sunk 14. 2.45
U.990	N 22. 5.44	sunk 25. 5.44
U.991	N 18.10.44	N 26.12.44
U.993	N 25. 3.44	F 22. 4.44
	F 6. 6.44	F 14. 6.44
	F 17. 8.44	N 18. 9.44
U.994	H 22. 6.44	N 19. 7.44
U.998	H 12. 6.44	N 17. 6.44
U.999	N 8. 6.44	N 27. 6.44
U.1000	N 4. 6.44	N 19. 6.44
U.1001	N 8. 6.44	N 5. 7.44
	N 12. 3.45	sunk 8. 4.45
U.1002	N 21. 2.45	N 10. 4.45
U.1003	N 11.10.44	N 16.12.44
	N 19. 2.45	Scuttled 20. 3.45
U.1004	H 22. 8.44	N 23.10.44
	N 28. 1.45	N 21. 3.45
U.1005	N 21. 2.45	N 21. 3.45

* Grounded and scuttled off the Portuguese coast. † Stranded at Amrum.

U-BOAT		SAILED		RETURNED	U-BOAT		SAILED		RETURNED
U.1006	N	9.10.44		sunk 16.10.44	U.1191	N	22. 5.44		sunk 25. 6.44
U.1007	N	10. 6.44	N	27. 6.44	U.1192	N	21. 6.44	N	27. 6.44
U.1009	N	11.12.44	N	8. 2.45	U.1195	N	24. 2.45		sunk 6. 4.45
	N	1. 4.45		surrendered in UK	U.1199	N	14. 9.44	N	5.11.44
U.1010	N	15. 4.45		surrendered in UK		N	1. 1.45		sunk 21. 1.45
					U.1200	N	19.10.44		sunk 11.11.44
U.1014	N	18. 1.45		sunk 4. 2.45	U.1202	N	30.10.44	N	1. 1.45
U.1017	N	29.12.44	N	28. 2.45		N	4. 3.45	N	27. 4.45
	N	14. 4.45		sunk 29. 4.45	U.1203	N	17. 1.45	N	31. 3.45
U.1018	N	21. 1.45		sunk 27. 2.45	U.1206	N	7. 4.45		sunk 14. 4.45
U.1019	N	10. 2.45	N	10. 4.45	U.1208	N	14. 1.45		sunk 20. 2.45
U.1020	N	24.11.44		sunk -. 1.45	U.1209	N	24.11.44		sunk 18.12.44
U.1021	N	20. 2.45		sunk 20. 3.45	U.1221	N	20. 8.44	N	26.11.44
U.1022	N	12. 2.45	N	2. 4.45	U.1222	H	13. 4.44		sunk 11. 7.44
U.1023	N	7. 3.45		surrendered in UK	U.1223	N	28. 8.44	N	14.12.44
U.1024	N	3. 3.45		sunk 12. 4.45	U.1225	H	17. 6.44		sunk 24. 6.44
U.1051	N	29.12.44		sunk 27. 1.45	U.1226	N	30. 9.44		sunk 28.10.44
U.1053	N	7.11.44	N	22. 1.45	U.1227	H	31. 8.44	N	26.12.44
U.1055	N	11.12.44	N	8. 2.45	U.1228	H	5. 9.44	N	20. 9.44
	N	5. 4.45		sunk 30. 4.45		N	12.10.44	N	28.12.44
U.1057	N	26. 4.45	N	9. 5.45		H	14. 4.45		surrendered in USA
U.1058	N	16. 1.45	N	18. 3.45	U.1229	H	13. 7.44	N	18. 7.44
	N	28. 4.45		surrendered in UK		N	26. 7.44		sunk 20. 8.44
					U.1230	N	8.10.44	N	-. 1.45
U.1059	N	12. 2.44		sunk 19. 3.44	U.1231	N	15.10.44	N	30. 1.45
U.1060	N	25.10.44		sunk 27.10.44		N	27. 4.45		surrendered in UK
U.1061	H	26.10.44	N	29.10.44					
U.1062	N	3. 1.44	P	19. 4.44	U.1232	N	12.11.44	N	14. 2.45
	P	19. 6.44	P	2. 7.44	U.1233	N	24.12.44	N	28. 3.45
	P	15. 7.44		sunk 30. 9.44	U.1235	N	20. 3.45		sunk 15. 4.45
U.1063	N	12. 3.45		sunk 15. 4.45	U.1274	N	5. 4.45		sunk 16. 4.45
U.1064	N	8. 2.45	N	10. 4.45	U.1276	N	27. 1.45		sunk 3. 4.45
U.1065	H	4. 4.45		sunk 9. 4.45	U.1277	H	15. 4.45		sunk -. 5.45*
U.1104	N	28. 1.45	N	22. 3.45	U.1278	N	11. 2.45		sunk 17. 2.45
U.1105	N	13. 4.45		surrendered in UK	U.1279	N	30. 1.45		sunk 3. 2.45
U.1106	N	23. 3.45		sunk 29. 3.45	U.1302	N	6. 2.45		sunk 7. 3.45
U.1107	N	30. 3.45		sunk 25. 4.45	U.1305	N	5. 4.45		surrendered in UK
U.1109	N	23. 3.45	N	6. 4.45					
	N	18. 4.45		surrendered in UK	U.2321	N	12. 3.45	N	13. 4.45
U.1163	N	13. 7.44	N	17. 7.44	U.2322	N	6. 2.45	N	3. 3.45
						N	5. 4.45	N	5. 5.45
U.1165	N	10. 6.44	N	5. 7.44	U.2324	H	29. 1.45	N	24. 2.45
U.1169	N	20. 2.45		sunk 5. 4.45		N	3. 4.45	N	25. 4.45
U.1172	N	23.12.44		sunk 25. 1.45	* Scuttled off the Portuguese coast.				

U-BOAT	SAILED		RETURNED	U-BOAT	SAILED		RETURNED
U.2326	N	19. 4.45	N 28. 4.45	UIT 22	F	−. 1.44	sunk 11. 3.44
	N	3. 5.45	surrendered at				
			Dundee	UIT 23	*	13. 2.44	sunk 14. 2.44
U.2329	N	12. 4.45	N 26. 4.45				
U.2336	N	1. 5.45	H 14. 5.45	UIT 24	F	8. 2.44	P 4. 4.44
U.2511	N	30. 4.45	N 6. 5.45	* Moving from Shonan to Penang.			

- A P P E N D I X 4 -

ALLIED WARSHIP AND AUXILIARY LOSSES
THROUGH GERMAN U-BOATS

1939–1945

Note: Auxiliaries listed are those that do not appear in B.R. 1337, *British and Foreign Merchant Vessels lost or damaged by Enemy Action during Second World War.*

BRITISH

TYPE	NAME		NUMBER
Battleships:	*Barham*		
	Royal Oak		2
Aircraft Carriers:	*Ark Royal*		
	Courageous		
	Eagle		3
Escort Carriers:	*Audacity*		
	Avenger		2
Cruisers:	*Dunedin*	*Welshman* (Minelayer)	
	Galatea		
	Hermione		
	Naiad		
	Penelope		6
Destroyers:	*Belmont*	*Isaac Sweers* (R. Neth. N.)*	
	Beverley	*Jaguar*	
	Broadwater	*Laforey*	
	Bath (R. Nor. N.)*	*Mahratta*	
	Blean	*Martin*	
	Cossack	*Matabele*	
	Daring	*Orkan* (Polish)*	
	Deiatelnyi (USSR)†	*Ottawa*	
	Exmouth	*Partridge*	
	Firedrake	*Porcupine*	
	Grafton	*Puckeridge*	
	Grove	*St Croix*	
	Gurkha	*Somali*	
	Hardy	*Stanley*	
	Harvester	*Tynedale*	
	Heythrop	*Veteran*	
	Holcombe	*Warwick*	
	Hurricane	*Whirlwind*	36
Frigates:	*Bickerton*	*Gould*	
	Blackwood	*Itchen*	
	Bullen	*Mourne*	
	Capel	*Tweed*	
	Goodall	*Valleyfield* (RCN)	10
Corvettes:	*Alysee*	*Montbretia* (R. Nor. N.)*	
	Arbutus	*Picotee*	
	Asphodel	*Polyanthus*	
	Bluebell	*Regina* (RCN)	
	Charlottetown (RCN)	*Salvia*	
	Denbigh Castle	*Shawinigan* (RCN)	
	Fleur de Lys	*Spikenard*	
	Gladiolus	*Trentonian*	
	Hurst Castle	*Vervain*	
	Levis (RCN)	*Zinnia*	
	Mimosa		21
Sloops:	*Dundee*	*Penzance*	
	Kite	*Paramatta*	
	Lapwing	*Woodpecker*	6

---

* Operating under British control.
† Late HMS *Churchill*, on loan to Soviet Navy.

TYPE	NAME		NUMBER
Trawlers:	Alouette Barbara Robertson Bedfordshire† Birdlip Bredon Ellesmere Eoor Wyke Ganilly	Hayburn Wyke Kingston Sapphire Laertes Lady Shirley Notts County Orfasy Rosemonde Tervani	16
Minesweepers:	Clayoquot (RCN) Esquimalt (RCN) Guysborough (RCN)	Hythe Leda Loyalty	6
Cutter:	Culver		1
Yacht:	Rosabelle		1
Whalers:	Cocker Maaløy	Southern Floe (SA)	3
Submarines:	Spearfish Thistle	P 615 Doris (French)*	4
Landing Ships:	LSI (L) Empire Javelin LSI Prince Leopold	LST 305 LST 362 LCI 99	5
Depot Ships:	Hecla	Medway	2
River Gunboat:	Gnat		1
Armed Merchant Cruisers:	Andania Carinthia Dunvegan Castle Forfar Laurentic	Patroclus Rajputana Salopian Scotstoun Transylvania	10
Ocean Boarding Vessels:	Camito Crispin	Lady Somers Manistee	4
Auxiliary Fighter Catapult Ship:	Springbank		1
Special Service Vessel:	Fidelity		1
Admiralty Tug:	St Issey		1
Salvage Vessel:	Salviking		1
Tankers:	Cairndale Darkdale Dinsdale	Montenol Slavol	5
Freighters:	Cape Howe	Williamette Valley	2

AMERICAN

TYPE	NAME		NUMBER
Escort Carrier:	Block Island		1
Seaplane Depot Ship:	Gannet	Joseph Herwes	2
Destroyers:	Borie Bristol Buck Fechteler Fiske Frederick C. Davis	Holder Jacob Jones Leary Leopold Reuben James Sturtevand‡	12

* Operating under British control.
† On loan to USN.
‡ Sunk on mine laid by U-boat.

TYPE	NAME		NUMBER
Minesweeper:	*Skill*		1
PC Boat:	*PC* 558		1
Gunboats:	*Alexander Hamilton* *Erie*	*Plymouth*	3
Landing Ships:	*LST* 348	*LST* 359	2
Transports:	*Edward Rutledge* *Hugh L Scott*	*T H Bliss*	3

MORE FROM THE SAME SERIES

Most books from the 'World War II from Original Sources' series are edited and endorsed by Emmy Award winning film maker and military historian Bob Carruthers, producer of Discovery Channel's Line of Fire and Weapons of War and BBC's Both Sides of the Line. Long experience and strong editorial control gives the military history enthusiast the ability to buy with confidence.

The series advisor is David McWhinnie, producer of the acclaimed Battlefield series for Discovery Channel. David and Bob have co-produced books and films with a wide variety of the UK's leading historians including Professor John Erickson and Dr David Chandler.

Where possible the books draw on rare primary sources to give the military enthusiast new insights into a fascinating subject.

For more information visit www.pen-and-sword.co.uk